EAST ASIAN WELFARE REGIMES IN TRANSITION

From Confucianism to globalisation

Edited by Alan Walker and Chack-kie Wong

To Carol and Peggy

First published in Great Britain in March 2005 by

The Policy Press
University of Bristol
Fourth Floor
Beacon House
Queen's Road
Bristol BS8 1QU
UK

Tel +44 (0)117 331 4054
Fax +44 (0)117 331 4093
e-mail tpp-info@bristol.ac.uk
www.policypress.org.uk

© Alan Walker and Chack-kie Wong 2005

British Library Cataloguing in Publication Data
A catalogue record for this book is available from the British Library.

Library of Congress Cataloging-in-Publication Data
A catalog record for this book has been requested.

ISBN 1 86134 552 6 paperback

A hardcover version of this book is also available

Alan Walker is Professor of Social Policy, Department of Sociological
Studies, University of Sheffield, UK.
Chack-kie Wong is Professor, Social Work Department, Chinese University
of Hong Kong.

Cover design by Qube Design Associates, Bristol.
Front cover: photograph supplied by kind permission of Arup.
Printed and bound in Great Britain by Hobbs the Printers, Southampton.

Contents

List of tables and figures

Tables

Preface

This book has been a long time in the making. Its origins lie in our first meeting in Sheffield in 1987, the day after the spectacular stock market crash. More recently our joint paper published in 1996 was an argument against the exclusion of East Asian welfare systems, especially China's, from the welfare state 'club' and the ethnocentrism of western social policy research. Eight years on, it is not possible to say that this exclusion and ethnocentrism have been overcome in the analysis of welfare systems, but there are certainly more publications on welfare in China and East Asia and signs of a growing interest in this topic. We hope that this book will fuel that interest. There are many excellent scholars in East Asian countries who would like to collaborate with their western counterparts.

We have accumulated many debts in the production of this book and our thanks go first to the authors, many of whom are good friends as well as colleagues. It has been a privilege to work with such a talented team. Sen Gong provided helpful advice. Thanks to Dawn Rushen, Natasha Ferguson, Laura Greaves and Rowena Mayhew at The Policy Press for their patience and support. Marg Walker, Alison Ball and Rachel Bunting prepared the manuscript for publication with great skill and perseverance. Finally, thanks go to our families, especially Carol and Peggy, who supported us while we completed this project, and during many others as well.

Alan Walker   *Chack-kie Wong*
University of Sheffield   *Chinese University of Hong Kong*
March 2004

List of acronyms

CCEJ   Citizens' Coalition for Economic Justice
CPF   Central Provident Fund
CSD   Census and Statistics Department
CSSA   Comprehensive Social Security Assistance
DIB   Daily Information Bulletin
DJP   Democratic Justice Party
DPP   Democratic Progressive Party
EANIC   East Asian newly industrialising country
EHI   Employee Health Insurance
EPA   Economic Planning Agency
EPP   Enhanced Productivity Programme
ERC   Economic Review Committee
FDI   Foreign direct investment
FER   Fundamental Efficiency Review
FHI   Farmers' Health Insurance
FKTU   Federation of Korean Trade Unions
GDP   Gross Domestic Product
GEI   Government Employee's Insurance
GNP   Gross National Product
HA   Housing Authority
HOS   Home Ownership Scheme
HPLS   Home Purchase Loan Scheme
HRN   Health Right Network
HS   Housing Society
HSLS   Home Starter Loan Scheme
IPE   International Political Economy
ISA   Internal Security Act
JNC   Japanese National Committee of International Council on Social Welfare
KCTU   Korean Confederation of Trade Unions
KMT   *Kuomintang*
KWS   Keynesian Welfare State
LI   Labour Insurance
MHLW   Ministry of Health, Labour and Welfare
MHW   Ministry of Health and Welfare
MPF   Mandatory Provident Fund
NGO   Non-governmental organisation
NHI   National Health Insurance

NSC	National Security Council
NWC	National Wages Council
PAP	People's Action Party
PLC	Provisional Legislative Council
PSPD	People's Solidarity for Participatory Democracy
SAR	Special Administrative Region
SCH	Sandwich Class Housing
SCHLS	Sandwich Class Housing Loan Scheme
SIR	Second Industrial Revolution
SSRS	Support for Self-Reliance Scheme
SWD	Social Welfare Department
SWS	Schumpeterian Workfare State

List of contributors

Sang-hoon Ahn, Assistant Professor, College of Social Sciences, Seoul National University, www.drahn.com; hoonco@snu.ac.kr

Chak Kwan Chan, Senior Lecturer in Social Policy, Division of Social Work, Social Policy and Human Services, Nottingham Trent University, chakkwan.chan@ntu.ac.uk

Ruby C.M. Chau, Lecturer in Applied Sociology, University of Sheffield, www.shef.ac.uk/socst/staff/r_chau.htm

Sammy Chiu, Head of Department and Associate Professor, Department of Social Work, Hong Kong Baptist University, www.hkbu.edu.hk/~sowk/

Michael Hill, Emeritus Professor of Social Policy, University of Newcastle upon Tyne, Michael_j_hill@msn.com

Yuan-shie Hwang, Professor, Department of Social Policy and Social Work, National Chi-nan University, Taiwan, yshwang@ncnu.edu.tw

Makoto Kono, Professor, Hyogo University, Department of Economics and Information Science, kono@hyogo-dai.ac.jp

So-chung Lee, Researcher, Institute of Social Welfare, Seoul National University snowvill@empal.com

Joe C.B. Leung, Head, Department of Social Work and Social Administration, University of Hong Kong, hrnwlcb@hkucc.hku.hk

Alan Walker, Professor of Social Policy, Department of Sociological Studies, University of Sheffield, www.shef.ac.uk/socst/staff/a_walker.htm

Vincent Wijeysingha, Local Government Policy Officer, London Borough of Enfield, vincent.wijeysingha@enfield.gov.uk

Chack-kie Wong, Professor, Social Work Department, Chinese University of Hong Kong, web.swk.cuhk.edu.hk/about_us/staff/staff_profile.php?id=1070

Victor Wong, Associate Professor, Department of Social Work, Hong Kong Baptist University, www.hkbu.edu.hk/sosc/sowk

Wai Kam Yu, Senior Lecturer, Division of Social Studies, City University of Hong Kong, www.cityu.edu.hk/cityu/dpt-academic/col-dss.htm

Part 1
Welfare in East Asia

ONE

Introduction: East Asian welfare regimes

Alan Walker and Chack-kie Wong

The aim of this book is to provide an up-to date, accessible and critical account of the welfare regimes of the main East Asian states and China. It puts the spotlight on the Chinese and East Asian welfare regimes – the so-called 'Confucian Welfare States' – in order to provide an assessment of their nature and development, their current dilemmas and their future prospects. It is also important that all the contributions to this book are either authored or co-authored by indigenous experts. Much has been speculated about the nature of the so-called 'East Asian Model of Welfare' by western scholars but, until recently, very little has been available in English by Asian researchers (Aspalter, 2001, 2002). As all students of comparative social policy know, it is a long and difficult task to become so immersed in the language and culture of a foreign country that you can claim expertise in aspects of its culture and development. By the same token, of course, it is sometimes equally difficult for indigenous scholars to gain sufficient perspective to enable critical analysis of their own societies. This may be especially problematic in cultures where critical scholarship is not common. Well, the proof of the pudding in this case lies in the following chapters: the authors have drawn on a variety of critical perspectives to analyse the past and future development of the welfare regime in their society.

Following two introductory chapters, the bulk of the book consists of case studies of six countries: China, Hong Kong, Japan, Taiwan, South Korea and Singapore. Our key themes are the factors that account for the development of welfare regimes, especially the influence of Confucianism, the current pressure points towards change, including globalisation and the East Asian financial crisis triggered by the devaluation of the Thai baht on 2 July 1997, and the likely future path of development. The chapters in this book provide the reader with an understanding of how Confucianism, an important internal component of the East Asian welfare regimes, is being analysed by local experts predominantly as a means for political legitimisation. So, our approach is not so much about what is Confucianism and how Confucian are East Asian welfare regimes, but about how Confucianism is used by the Chinese and East Asian states to justify restrictive social policies. Before introducing the case studies in more detail, we first of all explain the importance of a focus on non-western welfare systems in the study of social policy; then we assess the nature of the East Asian 'model' of welfare'; finally, we outline the important role of globalisation in this region.

The western construction of the welfare state

The origins of this book lie in a paper we published nearly a decade ago criticising the western bias in social policy (Walker and Wong, 1996). We were in tune with Jones Finer's persistent arguments against the neglect of Asian Pacific perspectives in comparative social policy (Jones, 1990, 1993; Jones Finer, 2001, 2003), even though we disagree with her label 'Confucian Welfare States' (to be discussed later). In western theory the welfare state is located at the interface of the two sets of rights, or 'rules of the game' (Gintis and Bowles, 1982, pp 341-5): citizen rights underlying the democratic institution of society, and property rights underlying the capitalist market system; these are in constant and persistent conflict with each other. Situated at the interface of these two contradictory sets of rights, the welfare state has been viewed by welfare theorists, especially neo-Marxists, as functional to the very existence of capitalism because it legitimises the accumulation function of capital (O'Connor, 1973; Gough, 1979; Offe, 1984). Unfortunately this western institutional analysis of the welfare state cannot accommodate the emergence of welfare systems in recently industrialised societies where democratic institutions, in the western sense, are either absent or rudimentary. This fact is particularly evident in the study of welfare systems in East Asian societies such as Singapore, Hong Kong and China. Because they contradict the western model, such systems are seldom classified as welfare states (Walker and Wong, 1996; Lin, 1999). This exclusion is legitimatised to some extent by the fact that the political leaders of these countries tend to take a negative view about the idea of the welfare state and have an aversion to public services (Esping-Andersen, 1996, 1999; Wong and Wong, 2001).

In fact, neither capitalism nor democracy are necessary conditions for constituting a welfare state or explaining its development. Non-capitalist and authoritarian states such as the former Soviet bloc countries and pre-reform Maoist China had established many essential social policies on a par with those in the West. For instance, they had full employment, free or cheap education and healthcare services, retirement insurance, and even heavily subsidised food and rent programmes (Deacon, 1992, p 2; Dixon and Macarov, 1992). In this light, welfare state programmes are not only driven by the economic and political 'rules of the game' underlying capitalism and democracy. The driving force of welfare development underlying non-democratic states or non-western capitalist societies is often their quest for political legitimacy for their authoritarian power over society. This is not to abandon the baby with the bath water – the functionalist analysis of the importance of the welfare state for capital accumulation or economic development is also a significant factor in welfare development, East and West. Welfare state programmes, such as education, health and housing, perform important economic functions (George and Wilding, 1984) as the case studies will demonstrate. However, a 'state-led' or 'top-down' theory seems more likely to explain welfare system development in those societies where capitalism or democracy is either absent or rudimentary.

The preceding analysis suggests that it is better to study the role of the state when examining welfare in East Asia, rather than focusing on the political process as in western research on welfare state development. On the basis of the case studies in this book, it is clear that, when it thinks of welfare programmes, the primary concern of the East Asian state is either political legitimisation or economic development.

Welfare state regime theory and East Asian welfare systems

The political and economic functions served by welfare states cannot explain the differences between societies in the nature and development of their welfare states. Esping-Andersen's (1990) seminal work on welfare state regime types filled this gap by suggesting that class coalitions of power resources explain different regime types in the form of social settlements among capital, labour and state actors. According to this theory, the stratification by class-based power also defines the different outcomes of decommodification among welfare state regimes (Esping-Andersen, 1990, p 52). Critics have suggested other sources of stratification such as religion, ethnicity and gender. The feminist critique, which focuses on gender relations, is directly relevant to the study of East Asian welfare systems because, in these societies, the central role of the family is evident. Other critiques of welfare regime theory look at alternatives to decommodification as outcome variables from regimes. For example, Room (2000) suggests a missing dimension from his reading of early Marx: human self-creation through work, or decommodification for self-development. Other alternative measures, such as human needs (Doyal and Gough, 1991) and social quality (Beck et al, 1997), are also promising. The interest in outcome variables indicates an important departure from the longstanding foci of welfare state research: the size of public expenditure, the state's role and functions, levels of state benefits or pensions and so on.

The contribution, role and functions of society to welfare, be it family or third (that is, voluntary) sector, and outcome measures especially in terms of developmental indicators, have begun to be emphasised by some welfare theorists (Gough, 1999, p 16; Room 2000). This indicates a greater willingness of western scholars to consider a more active role for society in welfare. This does not necessarily mean that society is the normatively *preferred* agent in welfare systems, but it reflects a broadening of social policy analysis to consider those societies, including developing ones, where non-state welfare is dominant. This change is also reflected in the use of the term 'welfare regime' rather than 'welfare state regime' in Esping-Andersen's (1999) later work signifying a downplaying of the role of the state (Gough, 1999). This new focus on a broad range of welfare inputs should also direct attention to the distribution of benefits and costs across different sections of the population. Western thinking about welfare states tends to regard the East Asian systems as reflecting inadequate decommodification for social consumption; thus, they have less social protection against poverty than in the West and lack measures to eliminate social inequalities. In contrast, the development dimension engendered by the involvement of non-state societal actors points to the addition of social capital through work, education and training. On this basis, East Asian welfare systems would receive a higher rating from the developmental perspective than they do under the western welfare regime analysis.

To emphasise the inadequacies of the western welfare state analyses and the need to reformulate regime theory to embrace East Asian countries, we have mainly employed the term 'welfare regime' throughout this book. We use this term in the sense coined by Esping-Andersen (1990, p 2) to denote the complex socio-political, legal and organisational features that are systematically interwoven in the relation between the state and the economy, although we include also the relation between the state and society. In the same mould, social policy is not limited to a written or verbal statement, or an institutional structure, but is the rationale underlying the wide variety of means by which groups, organisations and societies seek to achieve social ends (Walker, 1984).

Confucian welfare states?

Despite the appearance of a series of studies in the past decade or so, research on East Asian welfare remains relatively underdeveloped in comparison, for example, with the European welfare systems and there is a dearth of work on South East Asian social policy (a few exceptions are Chan et al, 2002; Tang and Wong, 2003; Ramesh, 2004, which are recent publications). Most of the literature on East Asian welfare suggests that there is something distinctive about it (Jones, 1990, 1993; Gould, 1993; Goodman and Peng, 1996) and, as Kwon (1998) has argued, there is a tendency to homogenise these regimes by terms such as 'Confucianism' and 'industrialisation'. The Confucian label is the most commonly used but, in what is only a small collection of studies, there are a large number of contending characterisations: 'Oikonomic welfare state' (Jones, 1990), 'Confucian welfare states' (Dixon, 1981; Jones, 1993; Goodman and Peng, 1996), 'liberal welfare regimes' in the Japanese case (Esping-Andersen, 1990) or later, 'conservative' because of familialism (Esping-Andersen, 1999), 'liberal welfare capitalism' (McLaughlin, 1993), 'East Asian welfare model' (Kwon, 1997) 'conservative welfare state systems' (Aspalter, 2001) and 'productivist welfare capitalism' (Holliday, 2000), to name a few. According to Jones (1993, p 214), the main elements of a 'Confucian welfare state' are:

> Conservative corporatism without (Western-style) worker participation; subsidiarity without the Church; solidarity without equality; laissez faire without libertarianism: an alternative expression for all this might be 'household economy'; welfare states – run in the style of a would-be traditional, Confucian, extended family.

This Confucian characterisation dominates discussion of welfare in East Asia and, as we show later, it has an important political dimension too. Jones (1993) has even suggested that Confucian welfare states could provide a model for Europe. So how accurate a label is this for East Asian welfare regimes?

At first glance, East Asian societies – China, Taiwan, Hong Kong, Singapore, Korea and Japan – are not all homogenous in terms of their political, social and economic systems, and states of economic

Table 1.1: Selected socioeconomic indicators for the six East Asian societies (2002)

	China	Hong Kong	Japan	Singapore	South Korea	Taiwan
Population (million)	1,294.9	7.0	127.5	4.2	47.4	22.6
Human development rank	94	23	9	25	28	–
GDP per capita (US$, Purchasing power parity)	4,580	26,910	26,940	24,040	16,950	23,400
Distribution of industries	Agriculture: 14.5 Industries: 51.7 Service: 33.8	Agriculture: 0.1 Industries: 12.9 Service: 87.1	Agriculture: 1.4 Industries: 30.9 Service: 67.7 (2001)	Agriculture: negligible Industries: 30.0 Service: 70.0 (2001)	Agriculture: 4.4 Industries: 37.6 Service: 58.0	Agriculture: 1.8 Industries: 30.4 Service: 67.8 (2003)
Percentage aged 65 and over	7.1	11.0	18.2	7.6	7.8	9.4 (2004 estimate)

Sources: United Nations Human Development Programme (2004); World Bank (2004); Central Intelligence Agency, US (2004)

and social development (Table 1.1). Nevertheless, they share a common cultural heritage in Confucianism. In Rozman's (1991) words:

> Confucian family solidarity and paternalistic groupism that made up Japan did not fit popular notions of capitalism; Confucian tradition of diligence, entrepreneurism, striving for education, and state co-ordination led South Korea, Taiwan, Hong Kong, and Singapore to achieve the 'economic miracle', and also, the deep-seated family- and community-orientations deviates the mainland China from other ex-socialist countries. These striking similarities indicated a 'Confucian region' in East Asia.

There are attempts to relate the region's massive economic achievements to the common cultural heritage of Confucian values (Clammer, 1985; Berger, 1987; Yamasuchi, 1991; Ornatorwski, 1996). Indeed, western value sets such as Victorian values, American values, the Protestant work ethic and even the 'Third Way' of the British New Labour Party also share similar moral tones. They all place a premium on the work ethic, virtues of self reliance, entrepreneurial spirit and the care role of the family (Digby, 1989, pp 9-12; Lipset, 1992; Giddens, 1998). In other words, Confucianism is not unique, in a comparative sense, because some similar values are espoused in the western world; and East Asian societies do not have common political, social and economic systems, and states of economic and social development.

Having said that, it does not mean that there are no common features in the East Asian approach to social policy, such as low social expenditures, low benefit levels, priority for spending on education and government as 'regulator' rather than 'provider' (Goodman and Peng, 1996, p 207; Jacobs, 1998, pp 90-8; White and Goodman, 1998, pp 17-19). When added to the shared cultural heritage, it is understandable that these welfare regimes have been classified as Confucian welfare states (Jones, 1993; Saunders, 1996) or as belonging to a Confucian welfare cluster (Lin, 1999, p 37). Nevertheless, on closer scrutiny, what we see is diversity rather than homogeneity. This diversity is shown in Table 1.1 with regard, for example, to Gross Domestic Product (GDP) per capita and industrial complexion, and in Table 1.2 with reference to social expenditure. It is also evident with regard to the different paths of development followed by the East Asian welfare regimes. For instance, China has embarked on the restructuring of its socialist *workfare* system to accommodate the new economic reforms (Chen, 1999; Wong, 1999). South Korea and Taiwan

Table 1.2: Public and social expenditure as a percentage of GDP in China, Japan, Korea, Hong Kong, Singapore and Taiwan (1980, 1990 and 2000)

	China[3]			Japan[4]			Korea[5]			Hong Kong			Singapore			Taiwan[6]		
	1980	1990	2000	1980	1990	2000	1980	1990	2000	1980	1990	2000	1980	1990	2000	1980	1990	2000
Public expenditure % of GDP[1]	26.8	15.3	17.8	17.8	15.7	16.3	17.4	16.2	24.5	15.6	16.3	20.6	20.0	21.4	18.9	14.2	21.4	32.9
Social expenditure % of GDP[2]	3.7	4.3	3.3	10.1	10.8	14.7	4.5	5.2	9.0	7.7	9.0	13.7	5.8	7.0	7.7	3.8	6.8	13.1

Notes:

[1] Public expenditure includes central government expenditure in areas of general public services, defence, education, health, social security and welfare, housing and community amenities, economic affairs and services, and other expenditures.

[2] Social expenditure: please refer to notes below.

[3] China, source UN, *Statistical Yearbook for Asia and the Pacific*. Social expenditure includes central government expenditure on education and social security and welfare for years 1980 and 1990. Public health expenditure is included in year 2000 in China.

[4] Japan, public expenditure, source UN; social expenditure, source OECD. The public social expenditure includes: old age cash benefits; disability cash benefits, occupational injury and disease, sickness benefit; services for the elderly and disabled people, survivors, family cash benefits, family services, active labour market programmes, unemployment, health, housing benefits and other contingencies.

[5] Korea, Hong Kong and Singapore, source UN. Social expenditure includes central government expenditure on education, health, social security and welfare, housing and community amenities.

[6] Taiwan, source Executive Yuan, *Statistical Yearbook of the Republic of China 2003*. Social expenditure includes central government expenditure on education and social security for the year 1980. Government final consumptions on housing and health are included in the years 1990 and 2000 in Taiwan.

Sources: United Nations, *Statistical Yearbook for Asia and the Pacific*, various years; World Bank, *World Development Indicator* (2002, CD-rom11.308338); OECD Social Expenditure Database (1980-1998, 2001 editions); Directorate General of Budget, Accounting and Statistics, Executive Yuan *Statistical Yearbook of the Republic of China 2003*.

followed Japan in adopting aspects of the Bismarckian model (Goodman and Peng, 1996; Hort and Kuhnule, 2000) and without excessive income inequalities (Jacobs, 1998, p 95), while Singapore and Hong Kong have the most market-oriented economic systems and their approach to social policy is residual, which allows substantial income inequalities (Liew, 1993; Walker and Wong, 1996). Thus, the Confucian welfare state label is not a very precise classification and, therefore, doubt must be cast on its scientific validity, an issue we return to in Chapter Ten.

Globalisation and East Asian welfare

The role and social policy impact of globalisation can be understood on the basis of welfare regime theory. Recent studies of globalisation indicate diverse patterns of responses according to the type of welfare regime (Esping-Andersen, 1999; Mishra, 1999). The globalised economy has weakened national power and posed serious challenges to wages, taxes and jobs because economic efficiency is its driving force. Despite the prevalence of the view that globalisation will create convergence, welfare regimes have responded differently to these challenges. For instance, instead of welfare retrenchment, the Nordic countries are still the most open economies among advanced industrial societies and retain the most generous social security systems in the world (Palme, 1999). They seem to have reconciled the trade off between social equity and economic efficiency and, therefore, contradict a common assumption about globalisation.

How has globalisation changed East Asian welfare regimes? The claim that the "spectre haunting South East Asia is no longer Communism. It is globalisation" (Hewison, 2002, p 241) is an overstatement, at least with regard to the northern part of the region. As noted earlier, these states had internationalised their economies at an early stage of development. Some policy makers in East Asia adopted neo-liberal economic policies before they became the orthodoxy of the international economic agencies and, since the dominant form of globalisation is neo-liberal economic globalisation, its prescriptions could not have been a surprise to them. In some cases the policy makers themselves were neo-liberal economists who believed in a growth/welfare trade off and aspired to a US style market society. Nonetheless, the impact of the financial crisis that began in 1997 was a shock because the long boom years of the 1980s and 1990s had not only legitimised the policies adopted by the political elites but had also made the East Asian states the economic envy of the world. The financial crisis has challenged neo-liberal economic orthodoxy and weakened confidence because of the flight of capital and the protectionist responses of the EU and US (Hewison, 2002).

The chapters in Part Two provide evidence of the impact of globalisation on each of the welfare regimes and we summarise this in Chapter Ten.

Plan of the book

The contributors to this book, in their different ways, highlight the diversity of the nature, development and dilemmas of the Confucian welfare regimes. Indeed, none of the contributors argues that any of the East Asian welfare regimes is 'Confucian' – they see Confucianism as being utilised chiefly for purposes of political legitimisation. Moreover, they stress that, just like their western counterparts, the East Asian welfare regimes have not been static in the past but have undergone periodic and in some cases continuous reform and change. The present theoretical and policy shift to embrace a more active role of society in welfare arrangements is likely to face the problems and dilemmas that are identified by the various contributors in this book. Following this introduction, there is another general chapter and then the second part of the book consists of six case studies, starting with the largest and most populous country, China. Then come two chapters on Hong Kong. The inclusion of two chapters on this city state is justified by its importance as a bridge between China and the West, the long history of welfare development, the regional importance of Hong Kong in financial terms, the recent transition from British to Chinese rule and, pragmatically, its relative wealth of literature and social policy research. Finally, there is a short concluding chapter.

In Chapter Two Ruby Chau and Wai Kam Yu tackle a question that lies at the heart of the debate about welfare in East Asian countries: is social welfare unAsian? With reference to both the Hong Kong Special Administrative Region (SAR) and the rest of China, they first of all, show the connection between anti-welfarism and market ideologies. Second, they carefully demolish the three core assumptions that underpin the claim that welfare is unAsian: social welfare is underdeveloped in Asia, this underdevelopment is a key factor in the economic success of Asian countries and 'Asian' values are antithetical to social welfare. Third, they provide a critical assessment of why the two governments have become so strongly associated with market ideologies in spite of their proven deficiencies – Hong Kong historically and China much more recently. Finally, they show how the commitment to capitalism of both the Hong Kong SAR and Chinese government is reinforced by globalisation and the Asian economic crisis.

Chapter Three focuses on social welfare reform in China. Joe Leung traces in detail the progress of social welfare reform in the wake of the market-oriented economic reforms that began in 1978 and marked a distinct break with the egalitarian/needs-based social policy of the previous Maoist era. He catalogues first of all the remarkable progress made by China under Mao in terms of public health, education and social welfare, which gave the country a much higher human development index ranking than many more economically prosperous countries. He outlines the pragmatic reform strategy and describes its impact on the work-based welfare system established by Mao. In essence, the government is reducing its interventions and regulation of the people, and trying to share responsibility with the family, individuals, neighbourhoods, charities and private enterprises. Thus there is increasing reliance on state-led private charities and philanthropy, non-governmental organisations (NGOs) and self-help initiatives; in short, a more mixed or pluralistic system. In social insurance Leung highlights the reforms of the pension, unemployment and health care systems. He shows how social welfare provision, for example for mental health service users and people with disabilities, has been shifted from work units to local government and neighbourhoods. In terms of poverty relief, the government has tried to unify the system but the assistance benefit line is a minimum subsistence one, which varies from city to city (it is only paid in urban areas) and is subject to a stigmatising public monitoring that is intended to deter all but the most needy. Like the previous chapter, this one emphasises the way that traditional Confucian precepts are being used by the government to minimise demands for social welfare and enable the creation and maintenance of a residual system of social welfare.

Chapter Four is the first of the two covering Hong Kong. Sammy Chiu and Victor Wong concentrate on the ways in which the new Hong Kong SAR government has been appealing to traditional Confucian values to emphasise nationhood and reinforce and legitimise the maintenance of a residual form of social welfare provision. They show how the Chinese government of the SAR is actually building on the twin pillars of the colonial legacy in social policy: positive non-intervention and familistic residualism. Policies towards younger and older people are used to illustrate the heavy political emphasis on Confucian values in the new Hong Kong.

In Chapter Five Chak Kwan Chan continues the analysis of social policy in the Hong Kong SAR. His focus is on the mode of welfare management: the essential nature of state intervention in welfare, especially housing, for the success of a 'free' market, the heavy impact of the Asian economic crisis on the main finance capital of the region and the consequences for social welfare provision. The chapter details the recent cuts in public expenditure and contracting out of core welfare services that have been implemented in response to the economic crisis. As well as the importance of the free market and Chinese familism, Chan emphasises the essential role of the undemocratic polity of Hong Kong and the privileged position of the business community within the governing elite. Having shown how the economic success of Hong Kong was founded partly on the incorporation of the middle class, Chan questions whether this is sustainable in view of the undermining of the security of middle-class welfare professionals, for example in health and higher education.

In Chapter Six Makoto Kono analyses Japan's welfare system. He charts the emergence of the 'Japanese Type Welfare Society' and illustrates the twin key characteristics of family-based informal welfare and enterprise welfare. As in the other country case studies, the Japanese state uses traditional family solidarity to legitimate residual welfare provision as in the example of care for older people. Unusually, though, enterprise welfare has played a critical role, though not in the same form as work unit welfare under China's socialist regime, which encompassed all aspects of the lives of workers and their families (Chapter Two). Nonetheless, Japanese enterprise welfare is significant but, of course, varies between enterprises and status levels. It too has been used by the Japanese state to legitimate residual public provision. Kono criticises the industrialisation thesis and argues that insufficient attention has been paid to culture and institutional tradition. But also, like Hill and Hwang (Chapter Seven), he points rightly to the limitations of cultural explanations, usually in the form of 'Confucianism', and argues convincingly that, instead, what is critical is political ideology – in this case neo-liberalism or the New Right. Thus traditional conservative social organisations and cultural values, especially strong family discipline, provided the basis for political stability and economic growth. These traditional values are emphasised by neo-liberals to support their own ideological policy prescriptions. Kono shows how the shift in Japan's political ideology from traditional conservatism to neo-liberalism has resulted in a change in policy goals – from a militaristic and strongly authoritarian state to a pro-market economy and residual welfare system. Under the influence of neo-liberal globalisation, the residual role of the Japanese welfare system is increasingly becoming emphasised.

In Chapter Seven Michael Hill and Yuan-shie Hwang examine a different Chinese society, Taiwan. They ground their analyses of Taiwan's social policy in the debate about welfare regimes and elaborate some of the points made earlier in this introduction, for example in questioning the classification of East Asian countries as Confucian welfare systems. The chapter includes detailed analyses of the development of health insurance and pensions. Hill and Hwang point to the corporatist Bismarckian origins of Taiwan's social insurance schemes, which coexist with the minimal welfare provision apart from public education. As with the other case studies in this book, they emphasise the key role of the state in the development and maintenance of social policy and the new conditions, especially globalisation, which confront an underdeveloped welfare system.

Chapter Eight focuses on the South Korean welfare system and Sang-hoon Ahn and So-chung Lee first analyse the role of Confucianism in this system. Like the previous case studies, they regard it as only one element contributing to the nature of social policy in South Korea rather than a dominant one. They reveal the crucial role of an authoritarian state dictatorship (backed by the US) in suppressing civil society, partly through the demonisation of the communist north, and forcing the pace of export-oriented industrialisation. Predictably, the same authoritarian governments regarded welfare as residual and mainly a 'regulatory ruling device'. Thus, under the first two authoritarian governments, welfare was based on public assistance programmes adhering strictly to the principle of less eligibility. The second phase of South Korean welfare system building, under the first democratically elected governments, saw substantial expansion and the creation of a welfare state framework. But this structure lacked a unifying philosophy that would ensure long-term survival, because it was in part aimed at neutralising working-class protests. It was thus narrowly aimed at the working class rather than taking a more universal path. The final stage of welfare development, under the People's Government of Kim Dae Jung, is notable for the universalisation of welfare to some extent, despite the economic crisis and a loss of autonomy to the international economic agencies. Today Ahn and Lee argue that the main characteristic of South Korean welfare is selectivity.

Vincent Wijeysingha, in Chapter Nine, adopts an explicit political economy approach towards understanding social policy in Singapore. This entails a combination of political economy, international political economy and historical analysis, which, he argues, is essential to understanding the role of social policy in the making of Singapore and its state following independence in 1959. Singapore emphasises what we see in other East Asian countries: on the one hand, the subordination of public welfare to economic growth and development and, on the other, reliance on the family and, to a greater or lesser extent, the third sector. Wijeysingha traces the development of social policy along with the four phases of economic development in the post-colonial era. At the start this entailed both a focusing of welfare provision on employment by gearing income security to earnings and giving a high priority to social investment, for example in schools. Subsequently, welfare policy was centred on the Central Provident Fund, set up by the British administration, with increasing personal contributions and extension to a wide variety of welfare needs, starting with housing in 1968. Being a highly internationalised economy, globalisation has had a significant impact on Singapore and social policy has been used latterly to upgrade education and skills to increase economic competitiveness. Also, rhetorical appeals to 'Confucianism' and 'Asian values' have been used to demonise western welfare states and to reinforce the authority of the government. The government's response to the global economic recession in the early years of this century was an expansion of welfare provision and, as Wijeysingha notes, this has been accompanied by an easing of the previously strong rhetoric concerning state benevolence and the need to avoid welfare dependency. Whether or not this will have marked the beginning of a new Singaporean welfare state is an open question.

In the conclusion we return to the role of Confucianism in East Asian welfare regimes and characterise it as an adjunct to political ideology. Then, while emphasising the differences between the East Asian welfare regimes in their paths of development, we propose six key factors that are essential to their political economy: development, political ideology, authoritarianism, colonialism, ethnicity and gender. The impact and political function of globalisation are discussed. Finally, in contrast to the almost universal negative rhetoric surrounding welfare in contemporary East Asia, we echo all the contributors to this book by stressing the positive role of social welfare provision as a source of well-being for citizens in the region as well as a major promoter of economic growth.

References

Aspalter, C. (ed) (2001) *Conservative welfare state systems in East Asia*, Singapore: Praeger.

Aspalter, C. (ed) (2002) *Discovering the welfare state in East Asia*, Singapore: Praeger.

Beck, W., van der Maesen, L. and Walker, A. (eds) (1997) *The social quality of Europe*, The Hague and Cambridge, MA: Kluwer Law International.

Berger, P. (1987) *The capitalist revolution*, Hants: Wildwood House.

Central Intelligence Agency, US (2004) *The world fact*, www.odci.gov/cia/publications/factbook

Chan, R., Leung, K. and Ngan, R. (eds) (2002) *Development in Southeast Asia*, Aldershot: Ashgate.

Chen, J. (1999) 'The reform of state-owned enterprises and the establishment of the social insurance system', *Journal of Jiangxi University of Finance and Economic*, Nanchang, no 1, pp 8-12 (in Chinese).

Clammer, J. (1985) *Singapore: Ideology, society, culture*, Singapore: Chopmen Publishers.

Deacon, B. (1992) *The new Eastern European: Social policy past, present and future*, London: Sage Publications.

Digby, A. (1989) *British welfare policy, workhouse to workfare*, London: Faber and Faber.

Dixon, J. (1981) *The Chinese welfare system: 1949-1979*, New York, NY: Praeger.

Dixon, J. and Macarov, D. (eds) (1992) *Social welfare in socialist countries*, London: Routledge.

Doyal, L. and Gough, I. (1991) *A theory of human need*, London: Macmillan.

Esping-Andersen, G. (1990) *The three worlds of welfare capitalism*, Cambridge: Polity Press.

Esping-Andersen, G. (1999) *Social foundations of post-industrial economies*, Oxford: Oxford University Press.

Executive Yuan (2003) *Statistical Yearbook of the Republic of China*, Taipei: Directorate-General of Budget, Accounting & Statistics

George, V. and Wilding, P. (1984) *The impact of social policy*, London: Routledge and Kegan Paul.

Giddens, A. (1998) *The third way: The renewal of social democracy*, Cambridge: Polity Press.

Gintis, H. and Bowles, S. (1982) 'The welfare state and long-term economic growth: Marxism, neoclassical, and Keynesian approaches', *American Economic Review*, vol 72, no 2, pp 341-5.

Goodman, R. and Peng, I. (1996) 'The East Asian welfare states: peripatetic learning, adaptive change, and nation buildings', in G. Esping-Andersen (ed) *Welfare states in transition*, London: Sage Publications, in association with UN Research Institute for Social Development, pp 192-224.

Gough, I. (1979) *The political economy of the welfare state*, London: Macmillan.

Gough, I. (1999) *Welfare regimes: On adapting the framework to developing countries*, Bath: Global Social Policy Programme, Institute for International Policy Analysis, University of Bath.

Gould, A. (1993) *Capitalist welfare systems: A comparison of Japan, Britain and Sweden*, London: Longman.

Hewison, K. (2002) 'Globalisation, inequality and governance', in R. Chan, K. Leung and R. Ngan (eds) *Development in Southeast Asia*, Aldershot: Ashgate, pp 241-56.

Holliday, I. (2000) 'Productivist welfare capitalism: social policy in East Asia', *Political Studies*, vol 48, pp 706-23.

Hort, S. and Kuhnule, S. (2000) 'The coming of East Asia and South-East Asian welfare states', *Journal of European Social Policy*, vol 10, no 2, pp 162-84.

Jacobs, D. (1998) *Social welfare systems in East Asia: A comparative analysis including private welfare*, London: Centre for Analysis of Social Exclusion, London School of Economics and Political Science.

Jones, C. (1990) *Promoting prosperity: The Hong Kong way of social policy*, Hong Kong: Chinese University Press.

Jones, C. (ed) (1993) *New perspectives on the welfare state in Europe*, London: Routledge.

Jones Finer, C. (ed) (2001) *Comparing the social policy experience of Britain and Taiwan*, Aldershot: Ashgate.

Jones Finer, C. (2003) (ed.) *Social policy reform in China*, Aldershot: Ashgate.

Kwon, H.-J. (1997) 'Beyond European welfare regimes: comparative perspectives on East Asian welfare systems', *Journal of Social Policy*, vol 26, no 4, pp 467-84.

Kwon, H.-J. (1998) 'Democracy and the politics of social welfare: a comparative analysis of welfare systems in East Asia', in R. Goodman, G. White and H.-J. Kwon (eds) *The East Asian welfare model: Welfare orientalism and the state*, London: Routledge, pp 27-74.

Liew, K.S. (1993) 'The welfare state in Singapore', unpublished thesis, Singapore: Department of Sociology, National University of Singapore.

Lin, K. (1999) *Confucian welfare cluster: A cultural interpretation of social welfare*, Tampere, Finland: University of Tampere.

Lipset, S.M. (1992) 'The work ethic, then and now', *Journal of Labour Research*, vol 13, no 1, pp 45-54.

McLaughlin, E. (1993) 'Hong Kong: a residual welfare state', in A. Cochrane and J. Clarke (eds) *Comparing welfare states: Britain in international context*, London: Sage Publications and Open University Press, pp 105-40.

Mishra, R. (1999) *Globalisation and the welfare state*, Cheltenham: Edward Elgar.

OECD (2004) *Total public social expenditure (1980-2001)*, http://www.oecd.org/dataoecd/56/37/31613113.xls

O'Connor, J. (1973) *The fiscal crisis of the state*, New York, NY: St. James Press.

Offe, C. (1984) *Contradictions of the welfare state*, London: Hutchinson.

Ornatorwski, G.K. (1996) 'Confucian ethics and economic development: a study of the adaptation of Confucian values to modern Japanese economic ideology and institutions', *Journal of Socio-Economics*, vol 25, no 5, pp 571-90.

Palme, J. (1999) *The Nordic model and the modernisation of social protection in Europe*, Copenhagen: Nordic Council of Ministers.

Ramesh, M. (2004) *Social policy in East and Southeast Asia*, London: Routledge Curzon.

Room, G. (2000) 'Commodification and decommodification: a developmental critique', *Policy & Politics*, vol 28, no 3, pp 331-51.

Rozman, G. (1991) (ed) *The East Asian region: Confucian heritage and its modern adaptation*, Princeton, NJ: Princeton University Press.

Saunders, P. (1996) *Social policy in East Asia and the Pacific area in the twentieth century: Challenges and responses*, SPRC discussion paper, no 74, Sydney: Social Policy Research Centre, University of New South Wales.

Tang, K.L. and Wong, C.K. (eds) (2003) *Poverty monitoring and alleviation in East Asia*, New York, NY: Nova.

United Nations (1984, 1999, 2003) *Statistical Yearbook for Asia and the Pacific*, Bangkok: Economic and Social Commission for Asia and the Pacific.

United Nations Human Development Programme (2004) *Human development report 2004*, http://hdr.undp.org/reports/global/2004/

Walker, A. (1984) *Social planning*, Oxford: Blackwell.

Walker, A. and Wong, C.K. (1996) 'Rethinking the western construction of the welfare state', *International Journal of Health Services*, vol 26, no 1, pp 67-92.

White, G. and Goodman, R. (1998) 'Welfare orientalism and the search for an East Asian welfare model', in R. Goodman, G. White and H.-J. Kwon, *The East Asian welfare model: Welfare orientalism and the state*, London, Routledge, pp 3-24.

Wong, C.K. (1999) 'Reforming China's state socialist workfare system: the cautionary and incremental approach and beyond', *Issues and Studies*, vol 35, no 5, pp 169-94.

Wong, C.K. and Wong, K.Y. (2001) 'Rhetoric and reality of East Asian welfare system: the case of Hong Kong', in Social Policy Research Centre, Hong Kong Polytechnic University, *Repositioning of the state: The experiences and challenges of social policy in Asia-Pacific region*, Hong Kong: Joint Publishing (HK), pp 215-40.

World Bank (2004) *World Bank development report 2004*, www.econ.worldbank.org/wdr/wdr2004/

Yamasuchi, H. (1991) 'Confucianism: pretext for economic success', *Japanese Quarterly*, vol 37, no 3, pp 355-8.

TWO

Is welfare unAsian?

Ruby C.M. Chau and Wai Kam Yu

Introduction

Market ideologies have a significant influence in East Asia (Chau and Yu, 1999). They justify governments' attempts to encourage people to sell their labour as a commodity in the labour market, to see private services as better than statutory and voluntary services in meeting needs, and to believe that creating an attractive investment environment for capitalists is a national goal. Despite their influence, market ideologies fail to fulfil two important functions of a dominant ideology in their application to Asian economies, especially in Hong Kong and mainland China. They are unable to provide a satisfactory explanation for important phenomena such as why some Asian economies had an impressive economic performance over the past few decades until the Asian financial crisis. Nor are they able to provide a clear guide as to how to strengthen Asian people's cultural identity and traditional ideologies in the global age.

This chapter is intended to discuss these inadequacies and the East Asian governments' attitude to them with reference to the view that 'welfare is unAsian'. Four analytical tasks will be conducted. First, we discuss how the basic assumptions underlying the view that 'welfare is unAsian' are related to market ideologies. Second, we challenge the validity of these basic assumptions in order to expose the inadequacies of market ideologies. Third, we explain why some governments are keen to associate their rule with market ideologies despite their inadequacies. We argue that their eagerness to do so is due less to an ideological consideration than to a pragmatic calculation for meeting the requirements of capitalism and pleasing capitalists. Last, we show that their eagerness to strengthen capitalism and promote capitalists' interests is intensified rather than undermined by the Asian crisis. These four tasks will be conducted with reference to Hong Kong and mainland China.

Is social welfare unAsian?

The answer to this question always carries ideological implications. A journalist, writing in the *Far Eastern Economic Review*, asserted that it was unAsian:

> What brought Asia its new-found wealth is not the discovery of some mystical set of new principles, but its faithful adherence to the old verities: hard work, enterprise, family, thrift, responsibility. Today these values may be called 'Asian', but in essence they are also what Sun Yat Sen's generation would have recognised as the 'Protestant work ethic' or 'Victorian virtues' that helped build the West. (Anonymous, 23 June 1994, p 5)

The notion that welfare is unAsian is based on three assumptions: social welfare in Asia is underdeveloped; the underdevelopment of social welfare contributes to the economic success of Asian countries; and 'Asian' values, which are influenced by Chinese culture, specifically Confucianism, do not promote the development of social welfare. Leger (1994, p 43) has illustrated these points even more succinctly by putting forward a formula to explain the economic success of the East Asian countries:

Hard Work + Low Taxes + High Saving Rates + Minimal Government = Economic Boom

It is important to note that these three assumptions are not new. It has long been argued by some economists that the rapid economic growth experienced in some Asian countries is due to the government's emphasis on the private market. Friedman and Friedman (1980) have maintained that those Asian countries putting emphasis on the private market enjoy economic success while those favouring the central planning system have stagnated. When depicting the economic situation of Japan and the four newly industrialising countries, Chen (1979, pp 83-4) pointed out that: "State intervention is largely absent. What the state has provided is a suitable environment for entrepreneurs to perform their functions". These views have been reinforced by cultural studies that intended to reject Weber's view that Confucianism is a stumbling block to modernisation (Chan, 1993). Scholars involved with these projects are keen to prove that the cultural characteristics of Asian countries, especially those characteristics associated with Confucianism, favour the development of a free market philosophy (Henderson, 1993).

If the three assumptions are valid, it will be convincing to argue that Asian countries should promote the importance of the private market as the key mechanism for meeting needs at the expense of welfare institutions, and expect that market values reinforce Asians' cultural values. The validity of these three assumptions, however, is highly questionable, despite their popularity among journalists and some commentators.

Hong Kong and mainland China

The Hong Kong government is often seen as a true believer of laissez-faire values (Rabushka, 1979). For example, Chowdhury and Islam (1993, p 24) have pointed out that: "There is a general consensus among observers of Newly Industrialized Economies (NIEs) that the governments of the NIEs (except in Hong Kong) are interventionists".

Friedman and Friedman have highlighted:

> In today's world big government seems pervasive. We may ask whether there exist any contemporaneous examples of societies that rely primarily on voluntary exchange through the market to organise their economic activity and in which government is limited.... Perhaps the best example is Hong Kong. (1980, p 34)

Based on these views, it is logical to assume that the private market dominates economic development and, consequently, people's lives in Hong Kong.

The economic developments in mainland China over the past two decades have been miraculous. Since Mao, the Chinese government has developed a series of reforms under the banner of socialist marketism (Blecher, 1997). The market economy, as a result, has expanded greatly at the expense of the planned economy. For example, the proportion of people working in the state sector decreased from 76.2% to 40.8% in the period 1980 to 1999 (Leung, 2003).

These massive economic reforms have led to dramatic improvements in economic performance. Direct foreign investment in China increased from US$1.8 billion in 1979 to US$34.61 billion in 1998 (Guan, 2001). Mainland China became the fifth largest trading group in 1995. Its average economic growth rate from 1978 to 2000 was 9.5%. Because of this impressive economic performance, some classical economists use mainland China as an example to illustrate the superiority of the private market and the advantages brought about by reducing government intervention in society (for example, Friedman, 1990).

Certainly there are many differences between Asian countries in terms of both their economic and social development. Moreover, their mainstream values are much more diverse than those simply represented by Chinese cultural values or Confucianism. Hence, Hong Kong and mainland China are far from perfect representatives of the whole of East Asia. However, since they are regarded by many classical economists and journalists as key examples of the Asian formula for economic success (OECD, 1996), they are desirable places for testing the assumptions discussed above.

The first and second assumptions

Studies have shown that the private market does not dominate the economic development of East Asian countries. Vogel (1991) showed that the Taiwanese government is heavily involved in high-tech development and heavy industries such as steel making, shipbuilding and the production of nuclear power. Fong (1990) recorded that Singapore has nearly 500 government-owned companies and statutory boards responsible for steel mills, electronics, oil refining, hotels, shipbuilding, repairing, shipping, financial services, air transport and property development. Hoogvelt (1997) even argued that the East Asian governments not only guide but also distort market decisions. The experiences of Hong Kong and mainland China also show the importance of government intervention in society, especially in the provision of social welfare.

Hong Kong

There are a number of reasons to think that the Hong Kong government believes in laissez-faire values. First, it adopts a free trade policy; tariffs and restrictions on imports and exports are almost non-existent and capital is free to move in and out of the country (Lau, 1982; Castells et al, 1990). Second, there is little protection for labour – there is neither unemployment insurance nor a minimum wage for local workers. Moreover, the labour laws are too harsh for unions to fight effectively for workers' rights (England and Rear, 1975). Third, the government's financial policy is founded on a non-intervention principle. Direct taxation is low and a budget surplus policy is much preferred to a budget deficit policy (Youngson, 1982; Patten, 1998).

However, the government's reluctance to intervene in economic activities is not necessarily associated with the underdevelopment of social welfare. Social welfare in Hong Kong has shown spectacular quantitative growth over the past few decades. There are now comprehensive systems of public education, public healthcare, public housing and social security. Over half the total population is either living in public rental flats or using publicly assisted home purchasing services. There is compulsory education for every child. About 40% of secondary school leavers are provided with access to higher education (Yu, 1996). There are 4.7 beds for every 1,000 people in public hospitals, which are run predominantly on the universalist principle. Ninety-two per cent of inpatient care was provided by the government in the 1990s (Chau and Yu, 2003). A non-contributory, means-tested safety net measure entitled the Comprehensive Social Security Assistance (CSSA) scheme is provided for the poor. In 2001, this scheme had 240,119 active cases.

Social services play an important role in promoting Hong Kong's economic prosperity and political stability. They serve to maintain a stable industrial relationship and nourish a sense of belonging among the people of Hong Kong. The Hong Kong government is not democratic and cannot gain legitimacy by means of a general election (Chau and Yu, 1999). Therefore, its principal way of satisfying the public is to improve their quality of life (Hopkins, 1971; Scott, 1989; Yu, 1996). Moreover, comprehensive health and housing services ensure a satisfactory level of public health and a high-quality labour force (Castells et al, 1990). Social services also help to keep wages at a low enough level to maintain the competitiveness of Hong Kong-manufactured goods in international markets (Schiffer, 1991). In 1995, public housing tenants on average spent 8% of their income on rent, compared with more than 23% spent by those living in private sector accommodation (Castells et al, 1990).

In view of the quantitative developments of social services and their political and economic functions, it is difficult to accept Hong Kong as a showcase of laissez-faire capitalism. To respond to the question 'Is welfare unAsian?' with reference to Hong Kong, perhaps we can borrow a quote from Patten, the last governor of Hong Kong: "What a ridiculous and insulting attack! One of the reasons for the success of the tiger economies was investment in people and in their well-being" (1995, p 13).

Mainland China

China's entry into the capitalist world has not prevented it from developing social welfare. On the contrary, it continually alters the form and function of its welfare regime, in response to the emergence of new needs, in the wake of the market reforms. We illustrate this point by examining why and how the government has changed its method of welfare provision in the post-Mao period.

The mode of welfare provision in Mao's period

Given that 'to each according to need' is the guiding principle of socialism, social welfare in socialist countries should be comprehensive, universal and for the most part free (Mishra, 1981). However, there was an evident gap between this principle and what was practised in mainland China during Mao's period (Chau and Yu, 1998). Since communist China was built out of turmoil, the party leaders were eager to turn it into an economic power within a short period of time. For example, in the late 1950s Mao initiated the 'Great Leap Forward' with the aim of surpassing Britain's steel production within 15 years. His main method of achieving this ambitious economic goal was to make use of human resources and the workers' high morale based on the principle of 'to each according to work'. In order to enable every economically active person to contribute to the economic development, Mao's government tried to practise a policy of full employment.

Against this background, social welfare was seen as an integrated institution of the collective production activities. That is why the production units were assigned the task of running social welfare programmes. As well as wages they provided comprehensive benefits for their workers such as housing, medical care and transportation allowances. In 1958, the government set up the commune system in rural areas, which ran the welfare fund to finance the welfare of peasants. The fund was an important part of the rural social welfare system until 1982.

For those unable to work, the government expected the family to take care of them (Chau and Yu, 2002). Under the Family Law, the family was required to support those in need. The government also educated people to fulfil their role as carers in the family through grassroots organisations such as the street offices and resident committees. If the family failed to meet its responsibility, it was subjected to public criticism by these organisations (Chan and Chow, 1992). In the cities, only those people with no employability, no family and no means of living (the 'three nos') were allowed to receive care from the government. In rural areas, collectives ran the 'five guarantees' scheme to provide clothes, food, housing, medical care, education and funeral services for those with no family. In short, the government did not play a direct role in welfare provision in Mao's period but relied largely on the work units to mobilise people to contribute to economic growth and allocate welfare services.

Social problems in the post-Mao period

A number of social problems have emerged in the wake of the market reforms. These include widespread unemployment, large-scale rural urban migration, widening social inequality and a decline in the credibility of party ideology. These problems, together with the demographic factor, have required both Deng's and Jiang's governments to change the way social welfare is provided.

Unemployment: The reforms within state-owned enterprises are coupled with the emergence of unemployment. In Mao's period, the government utilised state-owned enterprises to absorb young people in the cities. The Organisation for Economic Co-operation and Development (OECD, 1998a) estimated that state-owned enterprises employed two thirds of the urban labour force, although they accounted for less than 20% of GDP. This employment policy made them uneconomic.

Since Mao, the Chinese government has emphasised the need for the state-owned enterprises to meet economic goals rather than fulfil social commitments. In 1984, the Central Committee of the Chinese Communist Party decided that all state-owned enterprises must be profitable. In 1986, the bankruptcy law was passed allowing ineffective state-owned enterprises to be declared bankrupt. Since then, many state-owned enterprises have applied for bankruptcy. The court accepted 428 cases in 1992. This number increased to 710 in 1993 and in 1995 the Beijing government encouraged a further 300 state-owned enterprises to apply for bankruptcy (Chau and Yu, 1999). These changes have caused serious unemployment. In 1998, 12 million workers were laid off (Forney, 1998). In the same year, the unemployment rate was 8.9%, although the government wanted to keep it below 3.5% (Shan, 1996; Mok and Huen, 1999). The future of state-owned enterprises does not look bright. Tang and Ngan (2001) estimated that one third had been loss making since the 1980s. Saunders and Shang (2001) also pointed out that half of all state-owned enterprises either made an operating loss or had become bankrupt. Hence the unemployment problems are expected to continue.

Rural urban migration: Prior to 1979, peasants had not been allowed to move into towns or cities in search of work. But in the 1980s these restrictions were gradually relaxed. As a result, many towns and cities were flooded by migrant workers. The proportion of urban population to total population jumped from 20% to 52% in the period 1981 to 1989. It was officially estimated that 25-30% of the 487.68 million rural labourers were under-employed in 1993 (Wang, 1998). To improve their quality of life, these surplus workers had no choice but to move to other parts of China to seek work. Forney (1998) estimated that, in 1998, 70 million workers attempted to leave their homeland in search of employment. A large migrant population creates significant social and economic repercussions. First, there is no guarantee that the migrant workers will find work in the cities. Even if they are successful in gaining employment, their wages and fringe benefits are usually much lower than those enjoyed by local people. Second, most of them work in the private sector; thus they are not given any social security benefits, and are unfairly treated in comparison with those in the public sector. The situation of those who fail to find work is even worse.

Social inequality: The economic reforms have widened social inequalities. According to the World Bank:

- "the national Gini-coefficient was 0.29 in 1981 and increased to 0.39 in 1995;
- the urban Gini-coefficient increased from 0.18 in 1981 to 0.28 in 1995;
- the rural Gini-coefficient increased from 0.24 in 1981 to 0.33 in 1995". (Atinc, 1997)

Decline in the creditability of party ideology: The replacement of ideological beliefs with material interests as the motivational force has weakened people's loyalty to communist rule. People are no longer as prepared to make sacrifices for the communist ideals as they once were. For example, a survey at Zhongshan University in Guangzhou showed that when choosing a career students considered salary more important than qualifications and social contribution (Chau and Yu, 1999).

Ageing population: In addition to social problems, China is facing the challenge of an ageing population. The proportion of people aged 65 and above is expected to increase to 20% by 2050. The workers to pensioners ratio is projected to decline to about 3:1 by 2050 from 10:1 in 1995 (Tang and Ngan, 2001). Zhang (2003) estimated that three quarters of all care for older people is currently provided by families. However, whether the family has the capacity to take care of its older people is questionable. Statistics show that household size is decreasing. In 1980, rural households averaged 5.5 members and the figure for urban households was 4.4. By 1989, their size had reduced to 4.89 and 3.6 respectively (Davis and Harrell, 1991). Since the government practises a one-child policy, the number of family members available for taking care of older people is further decreasing.

In summary, the economic reforms have created a number of social problems, which have undermined people's quality of life and the government's credibility. The massive social protest which ended in military suppression in Beijing on 4 June 1989 is a reminder that people's dissatisfaction can quickly erupt into a political crisis. Mainland China has recently been troubled by a number of bombing incidents. The government sees these events as an indicator of growing discontent among the poor and socially excluded (Chau and Yu, 1999). Hence, it has actively reformed the social welfare programmes. In 1982, the welfare rights of vulnerable groups were written into the Constitution. The government is also reforming the insurance schemes on health, occupational injury, unemployment and retirement with emphasis on three new features – expanding individual responsibilities, widening coverage, and increasing risk pooling capacity through provincial-level resources management. Thus employees are required to pay a contribution to the insurance fund; the newly designed insurance programmes are aimed at covering all workers regardless of whether the company they work for is state owned or private enterprise; and the provincial governments are encouraged to set up organisations to manage the resources contributed by individual enterprises. These features are exemplified by the establishment in 1999 of unemployment insurance funds at city level and, in 1997, the creation of a unified retirement insurance system (Chau and Yu, 2001, and Chapter Three).

These reforms indicate that the government recognises how important such programmes are in meeting the social costs of economic reforms and satisfying the basic needs of poor people. Hence, it is difficult to accept that social welfare is unAsian in the case of mainland China.

The third assumption

This section examines the relationship between Asian values and the notion of social welfare. We focus briefly on those Asian values influenced by Chinese culture, specifically Confucianism (see Chapters Four and Five for more detail). A number of the East Asian economies with a Confucian background have experienced rapid economic development – namely, Japan, Korea, Singapore, Taiwan and Hong Kong. They share the characteristics of Confucian societies such as 'respect for seniors, filial piety, paternal benevolence, the group before the individual, conflict avoidance, loyalty, dutifulness, lack of complacency, striving for learning, entrepreneurship and meritocracy' (Goodman and Ito, 1996, p 195).

Contrary to common assumptions, we argue that Asian values based on Confucianism are by nature harmonious with the development of social welfare. First, Confucianism is a universal ideology. In fact it shares many ideas with the welfare values of the West. Hence, it has high potential for reinforcing rather than challenging the western welfare institutions. Second, social welfare is an important institution not only in the West but also in the East because it is intended to deal with social problems all around the world rather than just those faced by westerners. Third, some Asian governments use Confucianism as an ideological weapon against the development of social welfare through selectively emphasising those Confucian values favourable to their rule.

The characteristics of Confucianism

Confucius, the founder of Confucianism, was born in 551 BC. He did not invent all 'Confucian' ideas but reinterpreted the traditional principles of behaviour. His aim was to universalise aristocratic codes and restore the social disorder of his time to the peace experienced in the Zhou dynasty. His central doctrine is 'Ren' (humanity), which means goodness, benevolence and humanity (Ching, 1986). It also consists of the utmost self-assertion, sincerity, and forgiveness or sympathy (Hsu, 1995).

Confucius had no intention of prescribing an ideal way of life for just Chinese or Asians. His main aim was to search for universal values. He believed that Ren is a universal virtue, which can guide everybody to perfect their moral life. He also advocated that the virtue of Ren should be manifest in harmonious interpersonal relationships and social order. Hence, it is not surprising that his ideal society, Commonwealth (*Da Tung*), is made up of members who treat each other with love, respect and dignity.

Lin and Liao (1982) identified the characteristics of a Commonwealth as follows:

> The world becomes a commonwealth; men of talent and virtue
> are selected, and mutual confidence and harmony prevail. Then
> people not only love their own parents and care for their own
> children, but also those of others. The aged are able to enjoy

their old age; the youth are able to be fully employed; the juniors respect their elders; widows, orphans, and handicapped are well cared for. (Chung and Haynes, 1993, p 38)

This description indicates that Confucius' Commonwealth has similar elements to the western welfare value system, such as altruism and social integration.

It is undeniable that Confucianism was used as an instrument to lend legitimacy to feudal society, which is characterised by class and gender inequality. This form of society obviously is incongruent with the ideal society promoted by Confucius himself. However, this is not due to any internal contradictions of Confucian ideas but to the fact that the interpretation of Confucianism has been conducted through an unequal social relationship. Few people could afford to receive education in traditional Chinese society. As a result, the interpretation of Confucianism was monopolised by the clan leaders and the official scholars; they were mainly male and members of the upper class. To protect their vested interests, they put forward a number of rules, based on their interpretation of the norms prescribed by Confucius, for people to follow. These rules not only constituted a hierarchical society, but also justified the unequal distribution of resources (Chau and Yu, 1997). However, this hierarchical society is in conflict with Ren and the vision of Confucius. Hence it is the social and political contexts, we argue, that hampered the development of social welfare values and social welfare in the traditional 'Confucian society', rather than the Confucian ideas themselves.

Another point, which shows that Confucianism is a universal ideology, is its dynamic nature. Instead of creating a restrictive dogma for people to follow, Confucius himself reinterpreted the moral principles of the Zhou dynasty in response to daily problems. Following his example, many famous Confucian scholars reinterpreted Confucianism to deal with the problems of their time. Debates between scholars on how to tackle political and social issues were not uncommon. History bears witness to the fact that Confucianism has been revitalised and rejuvenated through reinterpretation of Confucius' ideas. In the search for effective solutions to new social problems, many adopted an absorptive approach in response to foreign ideas instead of strictly following the teachings of Confucius. Beginning in the Han dynasty, Confucianism has incorporated many ideas from Buddhism, Taoism and Methodism (Gernet, 1997). That is why Confucianism is often seen as a combination of ideologies rather than a single one. This characteristic explains why it is able to expand its applicability and influence in different societies.

In the Qing dynasty, Confucian scholars wanted to absorb western ideas into Confucianism. They put forward the theory that the Chinese learning would form the main body of knowledge while western ideas could be used for practical purposes (Levenson, 1958). By making use of the western learning, the scholar officials expected not only to bring back the lost glory of China, but also to further strengthen the Confucian order (Hsu, 1995). However, after the economic and military reforms, starting from the Self-Strengthening Movement (1861-94) until the end of the late Qing reform (1901-11), had failed to strengthen the Qing dynasty against aggressive western powers, scholars began to doubt that China would ever be able to restore its leading position in the world. They even questioned the capacity of Confucian ideas as a leading ideology, and some radical scholars called for Confucian principles to be discarded in order to save China (Hsu, 1995).

The bitter experience of borrowing knowledge from the West and the exposure of Confucianism's ineffectiveness in modernising China in the late Qing dynasty supports the criticism that it is an ineffective modern universal ideology. It cannot be used to justify the view that Confucianism has been transformed from a universal ideology into an Asian ideology. By its nature, Confucianism is a universal ideology without an Asian boundary.

The nature of social welfare

We should not let the diversity of social welfare arrangements obscure its universal characteristics. One of the main aims of social welfare is to solve social problems such as poverty, ill health and bad housing. These problems are always among the top items on political agendas both in the East and the West. As pointed out in Chapter One, it cannot be assumed that solutions can be easily transported from West to East, or vice versa, and the commonality between welfare regimes should not be underestimated. Globalisation may lead to greater similarities.

The Hong Kong and Chinese governments' attitude to Confucianism

Had the Asian governments given sufficient respect to the ideals and characteristics of Confucianism, they would not have overlooked the harmonious relationship between Confucianism and social welfare.

However, many of them regard it mainly as a political instrument for gaining legitimacy. Hence, they only attach importance to those Confucian values that support their rule, instead of fully developing Confucianism. This is demonstrated fully in the case of Hong Kong in Chapters Four and Five. Here we provide some illustrations and also refer to the case of China.

Confucianism and welfare in Hong Kong

In order to lower people's expectations of the government and reduce their reliance on social welfare, the colonial administration always stressed its respect for Chinese traditional values. The White Paper on Social Welfare in 1965 stated:

> ... in Chinese tradition, social welfare measures which individuals may need on account of poverty, delinquency, infirmity, natural disaster and so on are regarded as personal matters which at least in theory ought to be dealt with by the family, if necessary the extended family. It is clearly desirable, on social as well as economic grounds, to do everything possible in Hong Kong to support and strengthen this sense of family responsibility. (Hong Kong Government, 1965, p 6)

By assuming that Chinese people culturally preferred to solve their problems on their own, the colonial administration deliberately limited the development of social welfare even though the expanding economy could support a more vigorous welfare plan. The same view was still evident 25 years later in the social welfare policy paper written in 1991: "The development of social welfare should not be allowed to create the sort of dependency culture that has emerged in some developed industrial societies" (Hong Kong Government, 1991, p 14)

Following the reintegration of Hong Kong into mainland China as a Special Administrative Region (SAR) in 1997, a new administration (the SAR government) was set up to rule Hong Kong. This new administration is enthusiastic about associating its rule with Confucianism. In his millennium address, Mr Tung (the Chief Executive of the SAR government) emphasised:

> In the last 1,000 years, the human race has undergone remarkable changes.... But some fundamental values, like filial piety, mutual respect and the quest for knowledge will endure and will last.... It is my earnest hope that all of us will continue to cherish

these values to build a more united, coherent and harmonious community, so that Hong Kong can scale new heights.... (Yu, 2001, p 29)

At the same time, the Hong Kong SAR government set up the 'teacher day', encouraging the public to learn Mandarin, and initiated discussions on how Hong Kong citizens should contribute to the economic and social development of their motherland.

> It is evident that the government intends to discourage people from relying on social welfare, and to dissuade them from challenging the undemocratic political structure. On a public occasion Mr Tung stressed that: "We must work hard to familiarise ourselves with the Chinese culture and get to know the Chinese values.... I consider that fulfillment of obligation and acceptance of responsibilities, in this context, should be more important than pursuit of their rights. (Chiu and Wong, 1998, pp 238-9)

Although the colonial administration and the Hong Kong SAR government have attempted to associate themselves with Confucian values, Confucianism is not a fully developed ideology. Many aspects of Confucianism have been neglected by these two administrations.

With the emphasis on minimum intervention in society, the colonial administration regarded the development of Confucianism as the Chinese community's own affair rather than the concern of public policy. It did not replace Confucian values with western values, nor did it provide favourable conditions for the development of Confucianism. Unlike the rulers of imperial China, the colonial administration did not recruit civil servants according to their knowledge of Confucianism. Scholars were far less influential than businessmen in the policy-making process. Important consultative posts were filled by the economic elite rather than by moral leaders. In addition, Confucianism only occupied a small part of the primary and secondary education syllabus. In order to avoid arousing the younger generation's discontent with colonial rule, the colonial administration restricted their opportunities to study the contemporary history of China. The people who most wanted to maintain the extended family and Confucian traditions were those living in rural areas. However, since the colonial administration was eager to create a favourable investment environment for capitalists and industrialists, most resources were concentrated on developing the commercial and industrial sectors in the central and suburban districts. Little attention was given to the agricultural sector. As a result, many rural people could not earn a living in the declining agricultural sector and were forced to move out of Hong Kong (Yu, 2000).

It is also important to note that Confucianism is not totally in line with capitalism. Some Confucian practices deteriorated as Hong Kong developed into an advanced capitalist society. An important institution for practising Confucianism's principles is the extended family in which all generations live together with responsibilities and status allocated according to sex and age. However, the extended family has gradually been replaced by the nuclear family with a decrease in the size of the average household.

Moreover, the demand for labour in the capitalist economy leads to a large number of women going out to work. From 1976 to 2000, women's labour participation rate rose from 43.6% to 49%. Because of the difficulties associated with developing a career and performing the role of family carer, there is a trend for women to delay marriage. In 1966, the number of unmarried men aged between 25 and 29 was 63,910. By 1991, this had risen by 197% to 189,995. The number of unmarried women aged between 25 and 29 in 1966 was 12,800. This had increased to 133,723 by 1991 – a growth rate of 944% (Westwood et al, 1995).

The decline of the extended family and the rising number of women taking part in the economy have weakened the family's caring capacity. For example, over one tenth of people aged over 60 were living alone in 1992 (Macpherson, 1993). An increasing number of older people think that they are a burden to the family, rather than a leader. In spite of the colonial administration's expectation that the family should take a caring responsibility, it did not make sufficient efforts to arrest the decline of the extended family. Nor did it provide sufficient support to family carers.

If the Hong Kong SAR government wants to uphold Confucianism as the ruling ideology, it should take an active role in protecting Confucian values and try to remove all barriers to its development. However, there are no signs that the Hong Kong SAR government intends to do so.

Confucianism in Mainland China

In order to promote social cohesion and strengthen the communist rule, the Chinese government has recently tried to associate itself with Confucianism. In 1990, Jiang Zemin, the then Chair of the Chinese

Communist Party, described Confucianism as a fine national tradition (White and Goodman, 1998). He urged the youth to rediscover Beijing opera and openly praised Confucius in 1995 (Pete, 1995). Gu Mu, a very senior party member, stressed the importance of Confucianism at a conference on Confucianism:

> The Chinese nation has had a long history and brilliant ancient culture. For a long period of time in human history, the Chinese culture, with the Confucian school of thought as the main stream, glittered with colourful splendour.... (de Bary, 1995/96, p 483)

There are several reasons for Jiang's government to choose Confucianism as a supplementary ideology. First, Confucianism is seen as a contributory factor to the rapid economic development of East Asian countries, and Jiang wants to gain the same benefits for mainland China. Moreover, the Confucian ideology practised and professed in East Asian countries places emphasis on collective interest, authority and education (Jones, 1993; White and Goodman, 1998). These ideas support the government's campaign against individualism and immorality (Goldman, 1999). Furthermore, as Confucianism is part of Chinese culture, the emphasis on Confucian values helps the government to question the universality of the western standard of human rights, to a certain extent. In reply to the questions raised by Bill Clinton about human rights, Jiang argued that China and the US had different historical traditions and cultural backgrounds, and therefore had different ways of realising human rights and fundamental freedoms.

However, there is no evidence to indicate that Jiang's government intends to uphold Confucianism as an official ideology. As with the SAR government in Hong Kong, it does not recruit civil servants or communist party members according to their knowledge of Confucianism. Though it encourages local governments to teach Confucian values via informal education, no action has been taken to incorporate Confucianism into the syllabus of formal education. Moreover, the development of capitalism undermines Confucian values because it promotes individualism and weakens the extended family, for example by increasing female participation in the labour market. However, the government has not slackened its market reforms to safeguard Confucianism.

Pragmatic considerations

So far we have shown that social welfare at least in quantitative terms is far from underdeveloped in Hong Kong and mainland China. Moreover, it contributes significantly to economic development. Furthermore, the provision of social welfare has great potential for strengthening Confucianism. Hence it is wrong to argue that welfare is unAsian as far as Hong Kong and Mainland China are concerned. It is equally wrong to explain the impressive economic performance of Hong Kong and mainland China solely in terms of the two governments' stress on the private market as the most important mechanism in the allocation and production of resources. Nor is it right to argue that the revival of Confucianism relies solely on the promotion of market values.

However, despite the inadequacies of market ideologies in explaining the rapid economic growth of Hong Kong and mainland China, and guiding people in developing Confucianism, the Beijing and Hong Kong SAR governments are keen to associate their rule with these ideologies. The Hong Kong SAR government identifies itself as the defender of laissez-faire values, while the Beijing government is enthusiastic about launching market reforms under the guidance of market ideologies. It is argued that their eagerness to do so is more out of pragmatic calculation than ideological consideration. Instead of being diehard believers in market ideologies, the governments attach significant importance to the necessity of meeting the requirements of capitalism and advancing capitalists' interests.

A central distinguishing feature of capitalism is an advanced division of labour (Room, 1979). Workers do not directly produce the means for their own existence, but exchange their labour for the other products they need via the medium of money (Giddens, 1985). To promote this kind of coordination between labour and product markets, and thus to facilitate the expansion of commodity production and continuous capital accumulation, the commodification of labour becomes essential in a capitalist society (Forrest and Williams, 1984; Giddens, 1985). In a society dominated by commodity relations, the whole process of producing, consuming and exchanging commodities is ideally conducted in the private market by individual consumers and producers (Room, 1979). On the one hand, the main criterion of access to commodities on the part of consumers is the individual's ability to pay. On the other hand, the main criterion of access to employment is the individual's ability to sell his or her labour power through individual contact (Harloe, 1981). In order to strengthen capitalism, it is thus necessary to make people believe not only that participation in both labour and product markets is important, but also that the private market is the best mechanism in allocating resources and promoting public interests.

Of course, governments are not mere instruments of the capitalist class – they have the autonomy to introduce policies against the interests of capitalists (Ginsberg, 1979; Gough, 1979). However, few governments in the long term can afford to see capitalists withdraw their investments. In order to avoid capitalists exercising the 'veto' power, they find it necessary to provide a favourable investment environment. If the majority of people believe that welfare ideologies are more appealing than market ideologies, and prefer reliance on social welfare to participation in the private market to meet their needs, it will be difficult for the governments to attract capitalists to make long-term investments. Hence it is not surprising to see that some governments such as the Beijing and Hong Kong SAR governments are not interested in challenging the view that welfare is unAsian or market ideologies are flawed. Instead, they are much more concerned with introducing strategies to promote a belief that participation in private markets is the key to economic growth, and East Asian values are well in line with market values.

The Asian crisis

Since the late 1990s, many Asian economies have been troubled by serious economic problems. As a result, there has been an expansion in the volume of research on the reasons for the Asian economic crisis and how to tackle the problem at the expense of research on the Asian miracle. In searching for solutions to the problems arising from the Asian crisis, governments and international economic agencies further stress the supremacy of the private market in the creation and distribution of wealth. The OECD explains the Asian economic crisis in terms of a long list of structural problems within Asian economies, including:

> ... weaknesses in corporate governance arrangements; lack of transparency about business' financial situation and their relationship to government authorities; poor regulatory and supervisory arrangements in the financial sector; and tendencies to high indebtedness and over-leveraging in business sector and to allowing financial institutions to continue operating with high levels of non-performing loans. (OECD, 1998a, p 9)

In fact, the Asian crisis is more than an economic problem, it is concerned with the willingness and ability of governments to govern the financial institutions and the private sector. In addition, these structural deficiencies existed for a long time prior to the outbreak of the crisis. Because many East Asian economies enjoyed impressive economic growth in the past, their governments paid little attention to these problems (OECD, 1998b). These two points imply that East Asian countries need to make serious economic reforms as well as social and political reforms, in order to restore the healthy performance of their economies, and these reforms should have been undertaken long before the Asian crisis.

There is no sign that many East Asian governments have learnt from the crisis. Few show a determination to achieve a better balance between social and economic development. Moreover, instead of tackling the problems brought about by economic globalisation, governments attempt to reconstruct social welfare so as to convince people to accept the problems as a reality and to make individual changes to meet the requirements of the global economy. A striking example is an expansion of welfare-to-work programmes. These programmes represent the governments' intention to deregulate the labour market and to shift its emphasis from creating employment to increasing workers' employability. Furthermore, in order to encourage people to sell their labour as a commodity in the labour market instead of relying on social welfare, some East Asian governments have increased the authoritarian elements of their welfare regimes – for example, they require users of social services to search for work within a short period of time under the supervision of social workers, and to receive some compulsory training. These requirements not only reduce users' freedom in organising their lives, but also make the provision of social services more conditional than if based on social rights.

The Hong Kong economy has been badly hit by the Asian crisis. Hence the Hong Kong SAR government is keen to launch reforms to please capitalists and encourage the public by 'stick and carrot' to take a more active part in the private market so as to rely less on social welfare. Mainland China is one of the few economies able to maintain an impressive growth rate during the Asian crisis. But despite this the Beijing government also tends to attach increasing importance to economic targets at the expense of social ones. On one hand, the Hong Kong SAR government has used public funds to buy shares from the stock market to support big companies, and has stopped selling most of the public housing flats to the public in order to strengthen the attractiveness of private housing to potential customers.

On the other hand, it has added authoritarian elements to its welfare regime and has adopted a supply-side approach to cope with unemployment. In a review report on the Comprehensive Social Security Assistance scheme (CSSA), the government emphasised:

> Obviously, we should avoid the possible emergence of a dependency culture in which there is a tendency for some employable adults to consider reliance on welfare assistance, a preferred option even when there is employment available. International experience tells us that long-term dependency is likely to develop when the benefit level has become equal or close to what can be earned on a job.... (Hong Kong SAR Government, 1999, p 6)

In the 1999 Active Employment Assistance Programme and the Community Work Programme were launched. Under the Active Employment Assistance Programme, CSSA applicants are required to apply for at least two jobs per fortnight, attend fortnightly workplan progress interviews, and update their individual plans. Moreover, they are asked to sign a Job Seeker's Undertaking to acknowledge their obligations. Under the Community Work Programme, CSSA applicants are required to take part in community work for up to one full day or two half-days per week while they are looking for a job. The community work can include jobs such as simple library/clerical work, general counter duties, cleaning country parks, gardening and collecting recycled paper. Both of these schemes convey the message that the CSSA will only provide temporary assistance. At the same time, more than 20 welfare-to-work programmes have been provided for young people (such as Youth Pre-employment Training Programme and Project Yi Jin), focused mainly on employability through the provision of training. These programmes reinforce an individualist explanation for social problems: young people's unemployment is due more to their lack of appropriate skills than lack of jobs.

In response to the Asian crisis, the Beijing government has concentrated on maintaining the GDP growth rate at 8% and strengthening its position in the World Trade Organisation (WTO). These economic targets are seen as criteria for assessing its competence in weathering the crisis and sustaining economic growth. The equalising of this narrow economic target with the national goal emphasises its neglect of the social costs of achieving this target and the disproportionate impacts of these costs on the poor.

Conclusion

We have highlighted the inadequacies of market ideologies, in relation to the view that 'welfare is unAsian', and the attitudes of the Hong Kong and Beijing governments to these inadequacies. In conclusion, it is necessary to highlight the costs of the Hong Kong and Beijing governments' attempts to associate their rule with market ideologies. First, social welfare in these two economies does not receive the recognition that it deserves – this is especially true as far as its economic contribution is concerned. Second, users of social welfare are made vulnerable to stigmatisation. There is too little attention paid to the exploitative nature of the labour market and the failure of the global economy to provide sufficient jobs. Instead, social service users who fail to secure a job in the private market are seen as a social burden. Third, the opportunities are overlooked for developing the cultural identity of East Asian people in general and Confucianism in particular through the provision of social welfare. Worse still, the governments play little heed to the negative effects of capitalism on Confucianism. All these costs, to a great extent, are caused by the governments' attempts to meet the requirements of capitalism and please capitalists through promoting the supremacy of commodity relations and the private market as a mechanism for allocating and producing goods.

References

Anonymous (1994) 'Asia welfare', *Far Eastern Economic Review*, vol 157, issue 25, p 5, June.

Atinc, T. (1997) *Sharing rising incomes: Disparities in China*, Washington, DC: World Bank.

Blecher, M. (1997) *China against the tides*, London: Pinter.

Castells, M., Goh, L. and Kwok, R. (1990) *The Shek Kip Mei syndrome: Economic development and public housing in Hong Kong and Singapore*, London: Pion.

Chan, S. (1993) *East Asian dynamism, growth, order and security in the Pacific region*, Oxford: Westview Press.

Chan, L.W. and Chow, W.S. (1992) *More welfare after the economic reforms*, Centre of Urban Planning and Environment Management, Hong Kong: University of Hong Kong.

Chau, C.M and Yu, W.K. (1997) 'The sexual division of care in mainland China and Hong Kong', *International Journal of Urban and Regional Research*, vol 21, no 4, pp 607-19.

Chau, C.M. and Yu, W.K. (1998) 'Occupational therapy stations in China: economic integration or economic stratification for people with learning difficulties', *International Social Work*, vol 41, no 1, pp 7-21.

Chau, C.M. and Yu, W.K. (1999) 'Social welfare and economic development in China and Hong Kong', *Critical Social Policy*, vol 19, no 1, pp 87-107.

Chau, C.M. and Yu, W.K. (2001) 'Making welfare subordinate to market activities: reconstructing social security in Hong Kong and Mainland China', *European Journal of Social Work*, vol 4, no 3, pp 291-301.

Chau, C.M. and Yu, W.K. (2002) 'Coping with social exclusion: experiences of Chinese women in three societies', *Asian Women*, vol 14, pp 103-27, Winter.

Chau, C.M. and Yu, W.K. (2003) 'Marketisation and residualisation: recent reforms in the medical financing system in Hong Kong', *Social Policy and Society*, vol 2, no 3, pp 199-207.

Chen, E.K.Y. (1979) *Hyper-growth in Asian economics: A comparative study of Hong Kong, Japan, Korea, Singapore and Taiwan*, London: Macmillan.

Ching, J. (1986) 'What is Confucian spirituality?', in I. Eber (ed) *Confucianism: The dynamics of tradition*, London: Collier Macmillan.

Chiu, S. and Wong, V. (1998) 'Social policy in Hong Kong: from British colony to Special Administrative Region of China', *European Journal of Social Work*, vol 1, no 2, pp 231-42.

Chowdhury, A. and Islam, I. (1993) *The newly industrialising economies of East Asia*, London: Routledge.

Chung, D. and Haynes, A. (1993) 'Confucian welfare philosophy and social change technology: an integrated approach for international social development', International Social Work, vol 36, pp 37-46.

Davis, D. and Harrell, S. (1991) 'The impact of post-Mao reforms on family life', in D. Davis and S. Harrell (eds) *Chinese families in the post-Mao era*, London: University of California Press, pp 1-24.

de Bary, W.T. (1995/96) 'The new Confucianism in Beijing', *Cross Currents*, vol 4, no 45, pp 479-87.

England, J. and Rear, J. (1975) *Chinese labour under British rule*, Hong Kong: Oxford.

Fong, P.E. (1990) 'The distinctive features of two city-states development: Hong Kong and Singapore', in P. Berger and H.H. Hsiao (eds) *In search of an East Asian development model*, New Brunswick, NJ: Transaction Publishers.

Forney, M. (1998) 'Who's the boss', *Far Eastern Economic Review*, vol 161, issue 10, pp 10-14, 5 March.

Forrest, R. and Williams, R. (1984) 'Commodification and housing', *Environment and Planning*, vol 16, no 9, pp 1163-80.

Friedman, M. (1990) *Friedman in China*, Hong Kong: The Chinese University Press.

Friedman, M. and Friedman, R. (1980) *Free to choose: A personal statement*, Harmondsworth: Penguin.

Gernet, J. (1997) *A history of Chinese civilisation*, Cambridge: Cambridge University Press.

Giddens, A. (1985) *The nation-state and violence*, Cambridge: Polity Press.

Ginsburg, N. (1979) *Class, capital and social policy*, London: Macmillan.

Goodman, R. and Ito, P. (1996) 'The East Asian welfare states, peripatetic learning, adaptive change, and nation-building', in G. Esping-Andersen (ed) *Welfare states in transition: National adaptations in global economies*, London: Sage Publications. pp 192-224

Gough, I. (1979) *The political economy of the welfare state*, London: Macmillan.

Guan, X.P. (2001) 'Globalisation, inequality and social policy: China on the threshold of entry into the World Trade Organisation', *Social Policy Administration*, vol 35, no 3, pp 242-57.

Harloe, M. (1981) 'The recommodification of housing', in M. Harloe and E. Lebas (eds) *City, class and capital: New developments in the political economy of cities and regions*, London: Edward Arnold, pp 17-50.

Henderson, J. (1993) 'Against the economic orthodoxy: on the making of the East Asian miracle', *Economy and Society*, vol 22, 2 May, pp 200-17.

Hong Kong Government (1965) *Aims and policy for social welfare in Hong Kong* (White Paper), Hong Kong: Hong Kong Government Printer.

Hong Kong Government (1991) *Social welfare into the 1990s and beyond*, Hong Kong: Hong Kong Government Printer.

Hong Kong SAR Government (1999) *Report on review of the comprehensive social security assistance scheme*, Hong Kong: Hong Kong Government Printer.

Hoogvelt, A. (1997) *Globalisation and the post colonial world*, Hong Kong: Macmillan.

Hopkins, K. (1971) 'Housing the poor', in K. Hopkins (ed) *Hong Kong: The industrial colony*, Hong Kong: Oxford University Press, pp 271-326.

Hsu, C.Y. (1995) *The rise of modern China*, New York, NY: Oxford University Press.

Jones, C. (1993) 'The Pacific challenge: Confucian welfare states', in C. Jones *New perspectives on the welfare state in Europe*, London: Routledge, pp 198-217.

Lau, S.K. (1982) *Society and politics in Hong Kong*, Hong Kong: The Chinese University Press.

Leger, J. (1994) 'The boom', *Far Eastern Economic Review*, 24 November, pp 43-7.

Leung, J. (2003) 'Social security in China: issues and prospects', *International Social Welfare*, vol 12, pp 73-85.

Levenson, J. (1958) *Confucian China and its modern fate*, London: Routledge and Kegan Paul.

Lin, P.L. and Liao, L.L. (1982) *Social work education and the professionalization of social work in Taiwan, Republic of China: A sociological analysis*, Indianapolis, IA: Indiana Central University.

Macpherson, S. (1993) 'Social security in Hong Kong', *Social Policy and Administration*, vol 27, no 1, pp 50-7.

Mishra, R. (1981) *Society and social policy*, Hong Kong: Macmillan.

Mok, K.H. and Huen, W.P. (1999) 'Unemployment in China: policy responses, coping strategies and policy implications', *China Development Briefing*, no 1, Hong Kong: City University of Hong Kong, pp 3-18.

OECD (Organisation for Economic Co-operation and Development) (1996) *Economic Outlook*, December, Paris: OECD.

OECD (1998a) *Economic Outlook*, vol 1998, no 1, June, Paris: OECD.

OECD (1998b) *Economic Outlook*, vol 1998, no 2, December, Paris: OECD.

Patten, C. (1995) Speech at the spring reception of the Hong Kong Council of Social Services, 14 February.

Patten, C. (1998) *East and West*, London: Macmillan.

Pete, E. (1995) 'China: move over, Karl Marx – here comes Confucius', *Business Week*, Issue 3426, p 53.

Rabushka, A. (1979) *Hong Kong: A study in economic freedom*, Chicago, IL: University of Chicago, Graduate School of Business.

Room, G. (1979) *The sociology of welfare, social policy, stratification and political order*, Oxford: Blackwell Martin Robertson.

Saunders, P. and Shang, X. (2001) 'Social security reforms in China's transition to a market economy', *Social Policy and Administration*, vol 35, no 3, pp 274-89.

Schiffer, J. (1991) 'State policy and economic growth: a note on the Hong Kong model', *International Journal of Urban and Regional Research*, vol 15, no 2, pp 180-6.

Scott, I. (1989) *Political change and the crisis of legitimacy in Hong Kong*, Hong Kong: Oxford University Press.

Shan, F. (1996) 'Unemployment in mainland China: current situation and possible trend', *Issues and Studies*, October, pp 75-84.

Tang, K.L. and Ngan, R. (2001) 'China: developmentalism and social security', *International Journal of Social Welfare*, vol 10, pp 253-9.

Vogel, E. (1991) *The four little dragons*, Cambridge, MA: Harvard University Press.

Wang, F.L. (1998) 'Floaters, moonlighters, and the under-employed: a national labour market with Chinese characteristics', *Journal of Contemporary China*, vol 7, no 19, pp 459-75.

Westwood, R., Meshrain, T. and Cheung, F. (1995) *Gender and society in Hong Kong: A statistical profile*, Hong Kong Institute of Asia Pacific Studies, Hong Kong: The Chinese University of Hong Kong.

White, G. and Goodman, R. (1998) 'Welfare orientalism and the search for an East Asian welfare model', in R. Goodman, G. White and H.J. Kwon (eds), *The East Asian welfare model: Welfare orientalism and the state*, London: Routledge, pp 3-24.

Youngson, J. (1982) *Hong Kong economic growth and policy*, Hong Kong: Oxford University Press.

Yu, W.K. (1996) 'The nature of social services in Hong Kong', *International Social Work*, vol 39, no 4, pp 411-30.

Yu, W.K. (2000) *Chinese older people: A need for social inclusion in two communities*, Bristol/York: The Policy Press/Joseph Rowntree Foundation.

Yu, W.K. (2001) *Social and public policy analysis*, Hong Kong Division of Social Studies, Hong Kong: City University of Hong Kong.

Zhang, J. (2003) 'China's ageing, risk of the elderly and accounting for aged care', *Managerial Finance*, vol 29, no 5/6, pp 97-110.

Part 2
The East Asian welfare regimes

THREE

Social welfare in China

Joe C.B. Leung

Introduction

Over the past two decades, China has become one of the fastest growing economies in the world. Between 1978 and 1999, China's GDP grew at an average of almost 10% a year, and an average of 6-8% is expected in the coming decade. More significantly, according to the 1998 World Development Report of the World Bank, the per capita GDP of China has reached US$860. Therefore China now ranks for the first time as a middle-income country (the upper limit for low-income countries being set at US$785 per capita). While the phenomenal successes of the economic reforms are substantial and indisputable, they are accompanied by a wide array of mounting social problems and needs. Meanwhile, market-oriented economic reforms have made the traditional socialist social welfare system based on employment increasingly inadequate and inefficient. Indeed, China's accession to the World Trade Organisation (WTO) has further posed a formidable challenge to the traditional welfare system. In the context of a globalised economy, China is now actively in search of a pluralistic, effective and affordable social welfare system that will be compatible with a thriving market economy and a resilient socialist political structure.

China first officially used the term 'social security' in the 7th Five Year Plan (1986-90) to cover social insurance, social assistance, social welfare and preferential treatment. Social insurance refers to employment-based insurance schemes covering old age pensions, medical care, unemployment, work injury and maternity. Social assistance includes relief to those who are poverty stricken due to personal misfortune or natural disasters. Social welfare is services for vulnerable groups such as frail older people, disabled people and orphans. Preferential treatment is special care to disabled servicemen and family members of the revolutionary martyrs and servicemen, and jobs for veterans. The classification was reiterated in the 'Decisions concerning the problems of establishing a socialist market economy' of the Central Committee of the Chinese Communist Party in 1992. Accordingly, China tends to define social welfare from a narrow and remedial perspective. The major functions of social security are to support market-oriented economic reforms through enhancing productivity, and to maintain social stability through mitigating social tensions (Ministry of Labour and Social Security, 1999a). In this chapter the term 'social welfare' is used in a broad sense, equivalent to the Chinese understanding of social security. After outlining the background, strategies and characteristics of the social welfare reform, this chapter reviews the recent development of the three major social welfare sub-systems – namely, social insurance, social welfare and social assistance.

The 'iron rice bowl' under Mao

Under the centrally planned economy modelled after the Soviet Union, the system of public ownership, full and lifelong employment, job creation, job assignment and restricted labour mobility established by Mao Zedong was regarded as a superior feature of socialism. Since social welfare was employment-centred, each work unit functioned as a self-sufficient 'welfare society' within which an individual received employment and income protection, and enjoyed heavily subsidised benefits and services such as housing, food, education and social security benefits for sickness, maternity, work injury, invalidity and death, and old age (Walder, 1986; Leung and Nann, 1995; Lu and Perry, 1997; You, 1998).

While there were substantial differences between rural and urban welfare, and between different work units, the basic policy within each work unit in the urban areas and commune in the rural areas was largely egalitarian, and attempts were made to minimise differences in wages, welfare and employment. Through administrative allocation, a basic security network, the 'iron rice bowl' with 'high employment, high welfare and low wage' was established. While the right to welfare was not based on legal entitlement, the moral obligations and the patron-client relationship of the work units ensured the paternal protection of members in times of difficulty. Under such a system Chinese people had learned to be submissive, dependent and compliant to the benevolent rule of the Communist Party, in return for a protected livelihood with job security and guarantee of basic living standard. Even though China was a low-income country, its level of social welfare for state employees was close to those of middle-income economies

(Ahmad and Hussain, 1991). To the Chinese Communist Party, the welfare system was a political asset that promised social stability and legitimacy. However, it has created a strong sense of dependency among the Chinese on their work units to satisfy their needs and resolve their problems (Mu, 1998).

As this welfare system is 'work unit-centred' rather than 'state-centred', the role of the state at the macro level was to provide a stable order within which the work units could develop and fulfil the functions of political education, economic protection and welfare service provision. For the few people outside a work unit, the state would provide a remedial and limited welfare programme for the 'three nos': those with no family, no source of income and no working ability. The domination of the work unit-centred welfare had rendered unnecessary social services organised by non-governmental charities and government departments.

Under Mao Zedong, social problems such as prostitution, begging, venereal diseases, illiteracy, delinquency, drug addiction and unemployment were either eliminated or substantially reduced. Through the policies of full employment, reduced income differentials, control over wages and prices of essential commodities, China attained high levels of public health, education and social welfare (World Bank, 1992). The Gini coefficient, as a measurement of income inequality, was only 0.31 (0.19 in cities) in 1978 (Griffin and Zhao, 1994). These achievements were better than those of countries with similar levels of economic development. According to estimates by the United Nations, the economic development of China was ranked only 107th among 150 countries in the period 1970-75, but in the Physical Quality of Life Index (literacy rate, infant mortality and life expectancy) it was 68th (Wu, 1995, p 42). These achievements had been made at the expense of relatively sluggish economic growth rates.

Market-oriented welfare reforms

With the introduction of market-oriented economic reforms in 1978, the egalitarian and needs-based social policies have come under severe criticism. The major assaults are on the 'iron rice bowl', or job security, which is regarded as an impediment to the promotion of economic productivity and work incentives. State-owned enterprises are marked by widespread underemployment, mounting welfare burden and escalating losses. It is estimated that one third of them are losing money, and some 20% of their employees are redundant (Leung, 1994a; 1998a).

Under the primacy of economic growth, Deng Xiaoping designed a 'three-stage' development strategy. The first stage was to double the 1980s per capita GNP by the year 1990, and the basic problem of feeding the population should then be resolved. By the year 2000, China, after doubling the 1990s GNP per capita, would attain Xiaokang, a level of living standard marked by a relatively comfortable standard of living with adequate, though not extravagant, food, housing and clothing. The traditional Confucian ideal of Xiaokang refers to a society that has eliminated poverty. In the third step, China aims to become an affluent society comparable to other middle-income nations by the middle of this century (Leung, 1995a; Guo, 1996). In short, China accepts that social development is an integral part of economic development, and that economic growth is a prerequisite to improving the quality of life.

Social and economic development

Distribution, according to Deng Xiaoping, can no longer be based on need, but on labour effort, supplemented by other means of distribution such as ownership of land and capital. Under the market economy, the value of efficiency receives priority over fairness. Furthermore, differences in pay should be widened so as to encourage individual enthusiasm and speed up the development of production, and the major policy is to allow some people to become wealthy first, as part of the goal of common prosperity (*Beijing Review*, 15-21 April 1991, p v).

Based on the Human Development Index (a composite index of achievements in basic capabilities in three fundamental dimensions as measured by life expectancy, school enrolment and real GDP per capita in Purchasing Power Parity), the United Nations Development Programme ranked China 104th among 175 countries in human development in 2003, rising from 111th among 174 countries in 1995 (United Nations Development Programme, 2003, p 235). The compilation indicated that in China in 2001 life expectancy at birth was 70.6 years, adult literacy rate was 85.5%, combined primary, secondary and tertiary gross enrolment ratio was 64%, and GDP per capita in Purchasing Power Parity was US$4,020. According to the compilation by the Chinese Academy of Social Sciences, the areas of social development in which China has done well in are life expectancy (70.8 years), literacy (85%), natural population growth (10.4 per 1,000 population) and per capita food consumption (2,639 calories per day). China has performed poorly in the level of urbanisation (30%), proportion of the labour force in the tertiary industry (26%), and proportion of GDP allocated for education (2.4%) and healthcare (3.2%). These figures are low even when compared with other developing countries (Zhu, 1996).

The reform strategy

On the whole, the Chinese social reform is more guided by pragmatic concerns than by a clear visionary direction and comprehensive developmental blueprint. In launching the reforms, the approach of both Deng Xiaoping and Jiang Zemin was to "grope for stones to cross the river". In China, reform tends to be incremental, trial and error and piecemeal, rather than employing a 'shock therapy' approach based on introducing radical changes. Assuming the role of macro control at the top, the central government delineates broad guiding principles for reform. These principles are indicative rather than mandatory and universal (*Beijing Review*, 18-24 September 1995, p 14). Chinese policy makers have learned actively from overseas welfare experiences and practices. International meetings involving experts from the International Labour Organisation, UN Development Programme and World Bank are frequent, and investigation teams have been sent to countries all over the world. In designing a system of unemployment insurance, the Ministry of Labour has reviewed the experiences of more than 40 countries (White, 1998, p 189).

Local governments are encouraged to experiment with different solutions and models according to local circumstances and capacity. After some years of continuous experimentation and evaluation, the government, through legislation, would attempt to unify diversified practices by promoting one of the more successful models (Guo, 1996). However, models are often found to be impractical for widespread application because of overwhelming government support to make them successful. The strength of this approach is that it can minimise resistance and facilitate readjustments through feedback from programme implementation. The shortcoming is that regional disparities in social welfare development can be substantial.

Impact of the reforms

Market-oriented economic reforms have profound ramifications for the welfare system established by Mao. The disbandment of the communes in 1983 put the collective welfare system in the rural areas in complete disarray. Now the individual family has to bear the brunt of responsibility for protection against contingencies and, as a result, has become more vulnerable to the risk of any loss of income due to a diminution of its labour force and/or damage from natural disasters.

In urban areas, employment guarantees were removed in 1986 through the introduction of the contract worker system, bankruptcy law, open market for labour recruitment and dismissal procedures. Thereafter, lay offs due to redundancy, bankruptcy of the enterprises, termination of contracts and unsatisfactory performance became possible. Now state-owned enterprises are expected to become independent economic entities responsible for their own profits and losses. To enhance efficiency and competitiveness, they have to reduce their welfare responsibilities.

In the 1990s, the central government has issued a rapid series of laws and White Papers related to social welfare. For example, the White Paper on the Development-Oriented Poverty Reduction Programme for Rural China in 2001 showed the commitment of government to eliminate rural poverty. The 9th Five Year Plan on Economic and Social Development and the Long-Term Objectives for the Year 2010 pledged to speed up the reform of the social security system, notably in retirement, unemployment and medical care. In 2002, the White Paper on Labour and Social Security warned that the entrenched problem of rising unemployment would become more critical in the coming decade. (For a detailed description of these recent measures, see the website of the China Internet Information System (www.china.org.cn/e-white/index.htm).

The new laws and plans acknowledge the rights and needs of vulnerable populations. For example, according to the 1994 Labour Law, all enterprises should conform to a prescribed standard in working conditions (minimum wage, holidays, working hours, safety standards and so on), welfare (pensions and unemployment insurance) and protection of women and children. Above all, these laws also prescribe that the primary responsibility for providing care to people in need lies with the family. For example, the 1996 Law on the Protection of the Rights and Interests of the Elderly reiterated the legal obligations of adults to take care of the financial, medical, housing and social needs of their elderly parents and parents-in-law (Leung, 1997). The concepts of individual rights and the rule of law are emerging (Keith, 1997). But, under the Chinese legal system, individual rights are largely subsumed under the interests of the state and the country. Laws on the protection of individual rights, in practice, represent a declaration of government intentions and ideals. Often, they are not strictly enforced.

With the collapse of socialism as the guiding developmental ideology and the emergence of a more pluralistic and market-oriented economy, political ideology has been playing less of a central role in defining social problems and their solutions. The government can no longer rely on vague political promises, political education, propaganda, mass mobilisation or top-down coercive disciplinary action to alleviate social problems and satisfy social needs. Economic decentralisation and marketisation have also reduced the capacity of the central government to control societal resources, and has in a way even discouraged government intervention. Facing perennial budget deficits, soaring international debt, and a declining share of national revenue, the ability of the central government to direct social welfare development in a unified and concerted direction is rapidly eroding. Meanwhile the government, in diminishing its regulatory role in the livelihood of the ordinary people, is more willing to share its responsibility in social welfare with the family, individuals, neighbourhoods and private enterprises. This developmental direction is summarised under the slogans of 'small government and big society' and 'socialisation'. In a loose sense, 'socialisation' refers to the sharing of the welfare responsibility by all the societal sectors (*China Social Work*, 1998, pp 1-21).

Increasingly, the government has to rely more on state-led private charities and philanthropy, NGOs and self-help initiatives to cope with unmet social needs. For example, the China Youth Development Foundation launched Project Hope in 1989 to help dropouts in deprived areas return to school. The China Charity Foundation raises funds for work with orphans and children with disabilities (*Beijing Review*, 25-31 March 1996, pp 13-15). While these emergent charity organisations are primarily under government control, they raise funds mainly from overseas and enterprises (Leung, 1994b; White et al, 1996). One of the more prominent sources of funds for welfare is the introduction of welfare lotteries in 1987. From 1987 to 2002, a total of 25 billion yuan (£1 = 15.2 yuan) has been raised for the renovation of welfare premises, the improvement of welfare facilities and the alleviation of poverty. In 2002, lottery sales amounted to 16.8 billion yuan, representing an increase of 23.3% over the figure in 2001. Among the sales income, 5.9 billion yuan were allocated for welfare programmes (Ministry of Civil Affairs, 2003).

In pursuing an open-door policy, China is linked not only economically and politically to the outside world, but also in social life as well. In abandoning the traditional policy of self-reliance, it is now more open to assistance from international organisations, such as Oxfam, the Red Cross, World Vision and the World Health Organisation, whose programmes include relief in natural calamities, agricultural loans, educational sponsorship, medical operations, staff training, equipment donations and overseas adoption. According to a report from the World Bank, China is now its largest borrower. Funds from the World Bank are used to develop forest and ocean resources, construct infrastructure, improve environmental protection and alleviate poverty (*Beijing Review*, 22-28 June 1998, p 4). Because of the suspicion of the Chinese government towards foreign religious groups, the return of overseas Christian welfare organisations into China has remained slow and hesitant. Finally, the lack of transparency in both organisational structure and accounting procedures inhibits foreign cooperation and indigenous fundraising in China (National Committee on US–China Relations, 1994, p 13).

In receiving outside assistance, the plight of the disadvantaged is open to scrutiny by foreign journalists and human rights groups. China has reiterated that the right to subsistence is regarded as the foremost human right, as compared with political and economic rights (*Beijing Review*, 17-23 November 1997, pp 19-23). Yet because of international pressure, the Chinese government has to pay more attention to the rights of the poor, disabled people, the unemployed, orphans, victims of natural disasters, prisoners and women.

The general trend of social welfare reforms in China is moving towards a pluralistic system, with relatively more diversified funding sources and welfare responsibilities. In turning the enterprise-based insurance into social insurance, the management of social security funds has been shifted to organisations under the Labour and Social Security Departments, independent of the enterprises. Furthermore, employees are encouraged to contribute to social insurance schemes for retirement, unemployment and medical care. Under the 'privatisation' movement, the basis of the pension is now shifting from defined benefit to defined contribution. In the future, a worker's pension will depend on how much he or she paid into the fund and the returns the fund earned. In treating housing as a commodity rather than welfare, the government and enterprises are cutting subsidies. Employees are expected either to buy their own homes or pay much higher rents (Lee, 1996; *South China Morning Post*, 19 July 1998, p 9). In social services, user fees have become the dominant form of revenue for schools, hospitals and homes for elderly people (Henderson, 1990; Phillips, 1998; Wong, 1998). Government allocations only account for 53% of the school expenditures (*Ming Pao*, 21 September 2003, p 8). With the introduction of market-oriented reforms, most government units have turned entrepreneurial with a primary motive of maximising profits. Many of them are involved in profit-seeking businesses directly and indirectly (Duckett, 1998). With few exceptions, creating business ventures are popular among social welfare organisations.

Social insurance

With continual low birth rates and natural growth rates due to the active population control policy for more than two decades (birth rates were 15.2 per 1,000 population and the natural growth rate 8.8 per 1,000 population in 1999), the proportion of the older people (aged 65 and over) in the national population surged from 4.9% in 1982 to 6.96% in 2000. The number of urban retirees soared from only three million in 1978 to 37.2 million in 1999. Pension payments by enterprises increased from only five billion yuan in 1980 to 242 billion yuan in 1999 (State Statistical Bureau, 2001). The demands of an ageing society on the health and social services are substantial.

Despite large social security expenditures, social insurance covers less than 15% of the national population, primarily those working in the state-owned sector. Social security provisions have been extremely limited for the 135 million employees in township enterprises and 62 million employees in the private sector. In particular, there is hardly any state-funded assistance for the 300 million peasants and the 100 million rural migrants living in cities. Currently, only about 15% of the elderly are receiving old age pensions and subsidised medical care (Leung, 2003).

Pension reform

Old age pension reforms focus on three major aspects. First, the coverage of pensions has been extended to other non-state sectors. Second, reforms since the mid-1980s have tried to pool enterprises together to form unified funds. Operated on a pay-as-you-go basis, participating enterprises pay contributions to unified funds at a defined rate, and retirees are to receive their benefits from social insurance funds managed by Labour and Social Security Departments rather than from their employing enterprises. This way, enterprises with different numbers of retirees can share their costs. Third, since the 1990s, employees have to make contributions to unified funds through the establishment of individual accounts. Thereafter, pension benefits would come from multiple sources, including basic pensions and individual accounts. Fourth, unified pension funds should be formed at the provincial level to maximise risk pooling.

With the implementation of reforms, different provinces can adopt a different model with different compositions of unified funds and individual accounts. In 1997, the State Council recommended a unified model in which the total contribution allocated to individual accounts would be equal to 11% of the employee's monthly wages. Currently, the employee contribution is 4% of the monthly wage and would increase by 1% every two years up to a maximum of 8%. Meanwhile, the enterprise contribution to individual accounts would decrease gradually to 3% as individual contribution increases. The rate of enterprise contribution to unified funds has to be decided by the local government, but the maximum rate, together with their contribution to individual accounts, should not exceed 20% of total wages. Current retirees and those with fewer than 15 years of contribution to their individual accounts would continue to receive benefits from unified funds. For those retirees who have contributed to their individual accounts for more than 15 years, their monthly pension benefits would contain a basic part equal to 20% of the local average wage and the accumulated amount in the individual account divided by 120. (With life expectancy at 70 years and the retirement age [for male workers] at 60, it is expected that a retiree on average would live for 10 years or 120 months.) When an employee or retiree dies, the portion of the account contributed by individual payment could be inherited (*China Labour News*, 17 May 1997, p 1; *Beijing Review*, 10-16 September 1997, pp 19-20; Leung, 1998b). Because of the current wide variations in arrangements, it will take more than a decade for China to have a unified retirement insurance system. The proposed new model is a mixed one, compromising the principles of redistribution and efficiency. To facilitate the unification of the social insurance system, a new Ministry of Labour and Social Security was formed in 1998 to take charge of the whole social insurance programme.

In 1999, unified funds covered about 93.2 million employees (44.3% of the urban employee population). Among the working population covered, 68% were from the state sector, 16% from the collectively owned sector and only 9.7% from the privately owned sector. On the whole, unified funds cover 97% of the employees in state-owned enterprises, but only 54% of those working in collectively owned enterprises and 32% in other enterprises (private and foreign-owned enterprises) (Wu, 1999). In September 1998, the premium contribution rate from enterprises was only 88%. Therefore, some pension funds were unable to pay for all the pension benefits, and pension arrears amounted to 8.7 billion yuan (Wu, 1999). With the establishment of pension funds, fund management has become an urgent issue. In 1998, unified fund revenues amounted to 146 billion yuan and expenditures were 151 billion yuan. Over the years, the reserve of the funds has accumulated to 61 billion yuan, an amount insufficient to pay half the annual pension expenditure (*China Labour and Social Security News*, 17 June 1999, p 1). Since property and stock markets in China are still volatile, government regulations stipulated that 80% of the accumulated funds should be invested in government bonds, and the rest should be deposited in banks. Although this arrangement can minimise the risk of mis-investment and corruption, it can hardly protect the fund against losses due to inflation. Even so, state auditors had found out that in the past 12 years, about 10 billion yuan in the pension funds had been misappropriated (Wu, 1999).

According to the World Bank, the major shortcomings of the current pension system include its narrow coverage, high and uneven contribution rates from enterprises, the lack of sufficient accumulation to cope with future liabilities, the heavy welfare responsibilities of the enterprises, and region-based pension funds that do not encourage labour mobility. In particular, the sum of the money in individual accounts and their investment returns are administratively inseparable from the unified funds – they are in reality notional and exist on paper only (World Bank, 1997a). In essence, the present system, with insufficient accumulation, would hardly be able to deliver the promised benefits in the future.

Unemployment insurance

The official unemployment rate in 1999 was only 3.1% (2.5% in 1990), representing 5.75 million people (State Statistical Bureau, 2001, p 80). Unemployed persons are urban registered job seekers, and exclude rural and urban surplus labour, rural migrants and ex-servicemen. In 1986, the government enacted regulations on an unemployment insurance programme for employees working in state-owned enterprises. Under the revised regulations of 1999, unemployment insurance funds, managed by the City Labour and Social Security Bureau, are financed by contributions of 3% of the total wages from participating enterprises (2%) and individual employees (1%). (Before 1998, employee contribution was not required.) The programme provides assistance to employees who are laid off by enterprises or lose their jobs due to mergers, termination or cancellation of contracts, or the bankruptcy or near bankruptcy of enterprises.

The level of unemployment benefits remains flexible and is determined by the provincial governments. In principle, it should be lower than the local minimum wage, but higher than the local level of social assistance. In the revised regulations, the benefits were changed from earnings related to a level close to the local poverty line. The maximum period for receiving benefits is now determined by the length of participation in the insurance programme, rather than the length of employment prescribed in the previous regulations (Leung, 1995b; 1996; *People's Daily*, 29 January 1999, p 8). The maximum period for receiving the benefits is 24 months. After the maximum period, the unemployed have to seek help from the local social assistance programme. The benefit level is on average only 50% of the working wage. By 1999, unemployment insurance covered a total of 96.7 million employees and provided regular assistance to 1.1 million unemployed workers (Song, 2001).

Unemployment insurance does not cover those employees who have been partially laid off by those money-losing enterprises. They are called 'displaced' employees. While they have no need to go to work and receive no wages, they can still obtain a monthly subsistence allowance from their employers, and they can still live in quarters provided by their employers. Because the relationship with their employers has not been cut off completely, they are not officially classified as unemployed (Mo, 1999). This is unemployment with Chinese characteristics.

The number of 'displaced' employees soared from three million in 1994 to 11.7 million in 1999. It was reported that from 1998 to 2001 more than 25.5 million employees had been laid off from state enterprises, of whom more than 16.8 million had been re-employed (*People's Daily*, 30 April 2002, p 6). With the determination of the Chinese leadership to restructure the state-owned enterprises in the coming years, more lay offs are expected. Some 60-70% of the displaced employees were from the state sector. Displaced workers tend to be older, women and low skilled, and the prospect of their re-employment is bleak. Some of them may be forced to leave the workforce altogether (Chinese Academy of Sciences, 1998; Chinese Communist Party Central Party College, 1998). However, it is common practice for displaced workers to be self-employed while maintaining the status of displaced workers so that they are entitled to financial assistance and social security benefits.

The state-owned enterprises are trapped in a dilemma between the irreplaceable and irrevocable socialist obligations to take care of their employees, and the need to lay off redundant staff to maintain their market competitiveness. As massive unemployment would threaten social stability, re-employment projects are launched in most cities to provide assistance to the unemployed. To take over the caring responsibility from the enterprises, 're-employment service centres' are established by local governments and enterprises to provide financial assistance (subsistence allowances, medical care expenses and pension contributions), job retraining and job referrals for the unemployed. Each unemployed person can stay in a re-employment centre for a maximum of three years. These centres are financed by contributions from the government, enterprises, unemployment insurance funds and public donations. By the end of 1998, there were 6.1 million displaced workers being placed in re-employment service centres. With the traditional dependency of workers in state-owned enterprises for living arrangements, and the lack of job security and welfare provisions in non-state sectors, most displaced workers are still reluctant to seek jobs in non-state sectors. Not surprisingly, the re-employment rate in these employment service centres has not been satisfactory (Mo, 1999; Ministry of Labour and Social Security, 1999b).

In 2000, the government announced the gradual closure of these centres, meaning that laid-off employees will now have to seek assistance directly from the unemployment insurance scheme. People who are not eligible for the insurance schemes have to seek help from the social assistance programmes.

Healthcare reform

Only civil servants and employees in state-owned enterprises and their family members can turn to their employers for complete reimbursement of medical expenses. Only 15% of the national population are entitled to subsidised medical care, yet they account for 60% of all the health resources (World Bank, 1997b). Fewer than 10% of the villages, mostly in wealthy areas, operate some form of cooperative medical fund. Without a viable medical insurance scheme in the rural areas, peasants cannot even afford to pay for the most basic medical treatment (*Beijing Review*, 3-9 March 1997, p 23). As medical care expenses for employees in state-owned enterprises are mounting, unified medical insurance funds are being created. Furthermore, individual accounts are being introduced gradually in some cities. According to the model proposed by the government, enterprises have to contribute 6% of total wages and individual employees 2% of their wages to independent medical insurance funds. Employee contributions and 30% of the enterprise contributions would form the individual accounts. Medical expenses covering outpatient services and hospitalisation would be paid first from individual accounts. Only after individual accounts became insufficient to pay for the expenses would the unified funds share part of the costs (Leung, 1998b; *China Daily*, 23 July 1999, p 4; Chinese Academy of Social Sciences, 1999). It is envisaged that medical costs can be shared through a system of co-payment. By 1998, only four million people had joined the unified medical insurance programmes with individual accounts, and another 11 million had joined the unified programmes for hospitalisation (*China Labour and Social Security News*, 17 June 1999, p 1).

The Ministry of Labour and Social Security has summarised the major tasks of social security reform as 'three emphases, two guarantees and one unification'. The 'three emphases' are the work of re-employment of laid-off workers, medical insurance reforms and deepening the reforms of retirement insurance. The 'two guarantees' are the basic living standards for laid-off workers and pension benefits for retirees. The 'one unification' is to unify the management of social insurance programmes (Ministry of Labour and Social Security, 1999b). In 2000, the State Council set up a National Social Security Foundation funded by central government to subsidise local authorities that were facing difficulties in making payments to those laid off and the retired. In 2001, the Ministry of Labour and Social Security announced the launch of a three-year experiment in Liaoning province on the reform of the social insurance system (Leung, 2003).

Social welfare

Traditionally, work units shouldered the total responsibility for providing social care to their employees. They operated a wide variety of social services for their employees, such as nurseries, schools, homes for elderly people, hospitals, dining halls, cultural centres and sports stadia. The responsibility of the government was to take care of those without work units and family support. With the economic reforms, this responsibility is expected to shift gradually to local governments and neighbourhoods (*China Daily*, 27 December 1999, p 3).

Social welfare services consist of welfare institutions and welfare factories. Welfare institutions provide residential care for the 'three nos' – those without the ability to work, a source of income and family support. They include mental health services users, people with learning disabilities, orphans and childless elderly people. In 2002, they provided residential care to 1.25 million residents. Some 90% of these are in homes for elderly people. In addition, some 77.7% of residential places, 1.25 million were operated by neighbourhood governments (street offices in the cities and township governments in the rural areas), 2.7% were run by private organisations and the rest by Civil Affairs Departments (Ministry of Civil Affairs, 2003). (The Ministry of Civil Affairs is the policy making ministry at the national level. At the provincial and city level, the Civil Affairs Departments of the local governments provide the welfare services.) Since 1983, those institutions operated by the Civil Affairs Departments have been opened to people who can afford to pay the market fees. The occupancy rate of these homes is only 76%, reflecting the traditional reluctance of older people in China to live in institutions.

Welfare factories provide employment for people with disabilities – in 2003 about 690,000 persons. Some 84% of these welfare factories are operated by neighbourhood governments (Ministry of Civil Affairs, 2003). Facing strong competition from the private sector, many welfare factories have begun to lose money. Their losses are due to a number of factors, including weak markets, together with the lack of capital, energy, raw materials, credit and transportation support. More importantly, the government is becoming reluctant to grant welfare enterprises tax exemption for employing people with disabilities, and the jobs provided for them are declining.

In the 1990s, community-based welfare services for vulnerable populations in cities have been enthusiastically promoted by the government. In China an urban neighbourhood of about 50,000 residents is administered by a street office, an extension of the district people's government. The street office is responsible for the provision of a variety of public and social services including fire and crime patrols, marriage registration, household registration, sanitation, supervision of delinquents, nurseries, recreational and cultural activities, family planning and mediation, management of parks and public toilets, and so on. Specifically, community services include welfare provision for the vulnerable populations; public services for general residents; and job placements for the unemployed and retirees. A typical street office provides a home for older people, day care centres for frail elderly people and children with disabilities, and shelter workshops for disabled people and mental health service users. Recent emphasis is on the development of volunteer services. Community-based services are regarded as an emergent and vital source of personal social services, particularly for the vulnerable populations, such as frail and single older people, those with physical or learning disabilities, ex-servicemen, the unemployed, low-income families, youth at risk and rural migrants (Leung and Wong, 2002).

In 2002, there was a total of 8,820 community service centres with some 750,000 employees and 3.8 million volunteers (Ministry of Civil Affairs, 2003). With limited financial support from city governments, each neighbourhood has to rely on its own efforts to develop public and welfare services. In the case of Guangzhou city, the public allocation for community service accounts for only 30% of the total cost. Profits derived from commercial enterprises (factories, restaurants and guest houses) and fee-charging public and welfare services managed by the street offices are used to finance overall operations. As such, it is exceedingly difficult to separate the welfare and profit-making commercial functions of community services. Because the provision of welfare services is largely dependent on the ability of the street office to develop a profitable local economy, the quality and quantity of the welfare services provided can vary substantially from neighbourhood to neighbourhood. Often street offices in commercial districts and city centres tend to have much higher revenues. In some street offices, charity funds for welfare are established with revenue from public donations, profits in welfare enterprises and street office allocations. In general, community services are both informal and loosely structured, and the quality of services is not standardised.

Social assistance

Under the rule of Mao poverty was not considered a problem at all. In fact, Mao tended to glorify poverty as a necessary condition to maintain the revolutionary spirit of the people. In contrast, the issue of poverty has received growing attention from the Chinese government since the mid-1980s, and the government is proud to claim that it has effectively reduced the number of people living in absolute poverty from 250 million people in 1978 to only 30 million in 2002. According to surveys, 80% of the poor live in the western and central provinces. Ethnic minorities constitute less than 8% of the national population, but they account for 40% of the poor (World Bank, 1992, 1997c; Kang, 1996, p 5).

In 1986, the State Council established the Leading Group Office of Poverty Alleviation and Development with the primary task of formulating policies and plans to assist underdeveloped regions. The coordinating work of the office at the national level, which focuses on regional poverty alleviation, is described as 'macro-level poverty alleviation'. The work with poor households is the responsibility of the Civil Affairs Departments (which, at the provincial and city level, provide the welfare services), and is called 'micro-level poverty alleviation'. The work of the government in poverty-stricken regions includes investment in transportation, industrialisation, electrification and irrigation work. Assistance to individual poor households includes the provision of loans, information, technologies, training and employment, tax exemption and reduction, and subsidised education.

In urban areas, the number of people in poverty had reached 11.8 million in the late 1990s, or 3.3% of the urban population. Some 85% of these urban poor lived in economically backward cities in central and western regions. Some 84% of them became poverty stricken because of unemployment (*Beijing Review*, 19–25 May 1997, p 6; State Council Research Office, 1997). In the past, the Civil Affairs Departments operated a limited social assistance programme catering only for the 'three nos', those with no income, no family support and no working ability. As a last-resort welfare safety net in cities, the government restructured the traditional social assistance programmes in 1993 to extend their coverage, raise the level of benefits and secure financial commitment from local governments. According to the regulations, assistance is provided to those with urban household registration status and excludes those rural migrants living in cities. For those with connections to their work units, these would be primarily responsible for providing the assistance. This means–tested programme is an attempt to fill the gap between the inadequacy of the social insurance programmes and the falling ability of families to provide support.

The assistance line is calculated according to the minimum living standard, often based on expenditure surveys of low-income households, and the financial capacity of the local governments. It should be lower than the city minimum wage and the unemployment benefits. At a minimum level, the assistance would merely cover subsistence food and clothing costs, excluding rent, medical care and school fees. The payment from the programme may be supplemented by other charity activities, such as the delivery of food and fuel, fee reduction for hospitalisation, and scholarships from street offices, unions and city charity foundations.

By 1999, all cities had implemented the programmes and, by early 2001, there were only 4.16 million recipients. But with the pledges from the government leadership to cover all those eligible, the number of recipients jumped to 21.82 million in June 2003. These recipients comprised 8.8% low-income employees, 24.1% laid-off employees, 4.6% retirees, 18.1% unemployed and 4.7% 'three nos', the rest being family members (Ministry of Civil Affairs, 2003). Most recipients are found in the north-east and central provinces where unemployment is becoming critical. The total expenditure on the programme soared from only 1.5 billion yuan in 1999 to 10.9 billion yuan in 2002, while the central government subsidy increased from 26% in 1999 to 42% in 2002. The assistance levels vary significantly from city to city, ranging from the highest of around 300 yuan (£19.74) per person each month in Beijing, Guangzhou, Shanghai and Shenzhen to the lowest of around 160 yuan (£10.53) in Xining, Hohhot and Xian in the central provinces. In terms of actual payments, the national average was only 55 yuan (£3.62) per person each month (Ministry of Civil Affairs, 2003). The difference between the theoretical minimum and average is explained by the fact that some household members are not eligible (for example, wives who have a rural registration status).

Street office cadres are responsible for carrying out the investigations, delivering the benefits and reviewing the situation of recipients periodically (Leung and Wong, 1999). To facilitate 'public monitoring' of the situation of the recipients, their names and the amount of benefits received are publicised on the neighbourhood bulletin boards. To the West, this practice violates individual rights, but to the Chinese government it is a necessary way of preventing fraud, so that assistance is only given to the deserving poor. Based on the principle of 'deterrence', the provision is rendered so unpleasant and harsh as to deter all save the most desperate. Also the low level of benefits and the stringent eligibility criteria are intended to ensure that this assistance will never be a disincentive or a barrier to employment. This reflects a reliance on public pressures based on the traditional values of the Chinese to keep 'face' and avoid committing 'shameful' acts.

Conclusion

For decades Chinese people learned not to make demands on the state for welfare. Under the 'corporatist system', the state acts as the paternal and benevolent guardian of the interests of the people in the name of national interests (Unger and Chan, 1996). However, economic reforms have left more people either outside the safety net or facing inadequate protection. Work unit commitment towards welfare is rapidly eroding and is becoming both inadequate and unreliable. People now can enjoy more freedom of movement, employment and life chances; yet, at the same time, these new freedoms expose them to the risks and contingencies of the market economy. Under a globalised economy, insecurity in employment and livelihood is perceived by the government as the price to be paid for moving China towards a market economy. Moreover, to maintain its competitive advantages, China has to keep welfare and labour costs low.

The role of the state as the paternal protector of the livelihood of the people remains significant. Because of the traditional commitment of the state to industrial workers in state-owned enterprises in cities and the threat of instability by laid-off workers, welfare has been primarily targeted towards this group of people. With the decline of the appeal of the socialist ideology, the Chinese government has to resort to the use of traditional Confucian ideals and virtues to meet social needs. The Confucian ideal of 'Xiaokang' society, a well-off society, has been reiterated in the 16th National Congress of the Communist Party of China in 2002 as the blueprint for economic and social development. The legal enforcement of the filial obligations in the care of older adults emphasises the traditional family values of inter-generational support. In the social assistance programme, the use of 'public monitoring' of the recipients creates stigma and discourages reliance on the government. The fear of the 'loss of face' has been an effective traditional tool of social control.

Given the incremental nature of welfare reforms, the emerging social welfare system is highly decentralised and segmented. Access to social services and social security benefits is primarily differentiated among occupational groups, economic sectors and geographical regions. An underclass has emerged made up of peasants, low-income families, the unemployed, rural migrants, the sick and people with disabilities. Despite financial difficulties, the Chinese government has to strengthen its remedial role of providing means-tested and neighbourhood-based social assistance to those in desperate need.

Economic reforms create social tensions and threaten social stability. In particular, income disparities have widened significantly between rural and urban areas, geographical regions and economic sectors. The Gini coefficient, as a measurement of income inequalities, has increased from 0.288 in 1988 to 0.388 in 1995. The level of inequality in China is now similar to that in the US, and higher than those in Asian countries such as India, Pakistan and Indonesia (World Bank, 1997c; Khan and Riskin, 1998). Not surprisingly, industrial and rural unrest has been reported from time to time. In the countryside, peasants complain about excessive taxes, fees and fines, as well as the government's inability to pay contracted prices for their grain. In cities, workers protest against massive lay offs, delayed payment of wages and pensions, soaring food prices and land requisitions for redevelopment. Welfare reforms dictated by market principles are regressive in nature and often further accentuate existing inequalities. Caught between the conflicting goals of marketisation and political stability, the Chinese government can only inch forward cautiously in social welfare development so as to minimise the risk of social unrest.

References

Ahmad, E. and Hussain, A. (1991) 'Social security in China: a historical perspective', in E. Ahmad, J. Dreeze, J. Hills and A. Sen (eds) *Social security in developing countries*, Oxford: Clarendon Press, pp 247-304.

China Internet Information System (www.china.org.cn/e-white/index.htm)

Chinese Academy of Sciences (1998) *Employment and development (Jiuye yu fazhan)*, Shenyang: Liaoning People's Publishers.

Chinese Academy of Social Sciences (1999) 'Study on the social security system in China', *China Social Sciences (Zhongguo shehui kexue)*, vol 4, pp 72-86.

Chinese Communist Party Central Party College (1998) 'Study on the problem of redirecting and re-employing *xiagang* workers in state owned enterprises', *Journal of the Chinese Communist Party Central Party College (Zhonggong zhongyang dangxiao xuebao)*, vol 4, pp 45-54.

China Social Work (Zhongguo shehui gongzuo) (1998) vol 4, Beijing: Ministry of Civil Affairs.

Duckett, J. (1998) *The entrepreneurial state in China*, London: Routledge.

Griffin, K. and Zhao, R.W. (1994) *The distribution of income in China*, New York, NY: St. Martin's Press.

Guo, J.Y. (1996) *Social development in China: The blueprint (Zhongquo shehui fazhen lanpian)*, Kunming: Yunnan People's Publishers.

Henderson, G. (1990) 'Increased inequality in health care in China', in D. Davis and E. Vogel (eds) *China on the eve of Tiananmen: The impact of reform*, Cambridge, MA: Harvard University Press.

Kang, X.G. (1996) *The problem of poverty in China and anti-poverty theories (Zhongguo pinkun yu fan pinkun lilun)*, Nanning: Guangxi People's Publishers.

Keith, R. (1997) 'Legislating women's and children's rights and interests in the PRC', *The China Quarterly*, no 144, pp 29-55.

Khan, A.R. and Riskin, C. (1998) 'Income inequality in China: composition, distribution and growth of household income, 1988 to 1995', *The China Quarterly*, no 149, pp 29-55.

Lee, P. (1996) 'Housing privatization with Chinese characteristics', in L. Wong and S. MacPherson (eds) *Social change and social policy in contemporary China*, Aldershot: Avebury, pp 113-39.

Leung, J. (1994a) 'Dismantling the iron rice bowl: welfare reforms in the PRC', *Journal of Social Policy*, vol 23, no 3, pp 341-61.

Leung, J. (1994b) 'The emergence of non-governmental organisations in China: problems and issues', *Asian Journal of Public Administration*, vol 4, pp 83-95.

Leung, J. (1995a) 'From subsistence to *xiaokang*: social development in the PRC', *Social Development Issues*, vol 17, no 3, pp 104-14.

Leung, J. (1995b) 'The political economy of unemployment and unemployment insurance in the PRC', *International Social Work*, vol 38, pp 123-33.

Leung, J. (1996) 'The emergence of unemployment insurance in China: problems and issues', *Canadian Review of Social Policy*, vol 38, pp 5-17.

Leung, J. (1997) 'Family support for the elderly in China: issues and challenges', *Journal of Aging and Social Policy*, vol 9, no 3, pp 87-101.

Leung, J. (1998a) 'The transformation of social welfare policy: the restructuring of the iron rice bowl', in J. Cheng (ed) *China in the post-Deng era*, Hong Kong: The Chinese University Press, pp 617-44.

Leung, J. (1998b) 'Social security reforms: a long and winding road', in J. Cheng (ed) *China Review 1998*, Hong Kong: The Chinese University Press, pp 480-99.

Leung, J. and Nann, R. (1995) *Authority and benevolence: Social welfare in China*, New York, NY: St. Martin's Press.

Leung, J. and Wong, H. (1999) 'The emergence of a community-based social assistance programme in urban China', *Social Policy and Administration*, vol 33, no 1, pp 39-54.

Leung, J. and Wong, Y.C. (2002) 'Community service for the frail elderly in China', *International Social Work*, vol 45, no 2, pp 205-16.

Leung, J. (2003) 'Social security reforms in China: issues and prospects', *International Journal of Social Welfare*, vol 12, no 2, pp 73-85.

Lu, X.B. and Perry, E. (eds) (1997) *Danwei: The changing Chinese workplace in historical and comparative perspective*, Armonk, NY: M.E. Sharpe.

Ministry of Civil Affairs (2003) www.mca.gov.cn

Ministry of Labour and Social Security (1999a) 'Overall development direction for labour and social security tasks in 1998-2002', *China Labour Human Resources Development (Zhongguo renli ziyuan kaifa)*, vol 7, pp 4-7.

Ministry of Labour and Social Security (1999b) *The foremost task, the number one work: Guidelines for re-employment work and livelihood guarantee for xiagang workers* (*Toudeng daishi, diyiwei de gongzuo – Guoyou qiye xiagang zhigong jiben shenghuo baozhang he zaijiuye gongzuo zhidao*), Beijing: Economic Science Publishers.

Mo, R. (1999) 'The prospect of the employment situation in China in 1998-1999', in X. Ru, X.Y. Lu and T.L. Shan (eds) *The analysis and forecast of the social situation in China in 1999* (*1999 Zhongguo shehui xingshi fenxi yu yuce*), Beijing: Social Science Publishers, pp 231-42.

Mu, H.Z. (1998) *The study on the appropriate level of social security in China* (*Zhongguo shehui baozhang shidu shuipin yanjiu*), Shenyang: Liaoning University Publishers.

National Committee on US–China Relations (1994) *Rise of nongovernmental organizations in China: Implications for Americans*, New York, NY: National Committee on US–China Relations.

Phillips, M. (1998) 'The transformation of China's mental health services', *The China Journal*, vol 39, no 1, pp 1-36.

Song, X.W. (2001) *Report on the reform and development of China's social security system* (*Zhongguo shehui baozheng xidong gaige yu fazhen baogao*), Beijing: People's University Press.

State Council Research Office (1997) 'Concerning the analysis and recommendations on the issue of income disparities among urban residents', *Economic Research* (*Jingji yanjiu*), vol 8, pp 3-10.

State Statistical Bureau (2001) *China statistical yearbook 2001* (*Zhongguo tongji nianjian 2001*), Beijing: State Statistical Publishers.

Unger, J. and Chan, A. (1996) 'Corporatism in China: a developmental state in an East Asian context,' in B. McCormick and J. Unger (eds) *China after socialism: In the footsteps of Eastern Europe or East Asia*, Armonk, NY: M.E. Sharpe, pp 95-129.

United Nations Development Programme (2003) *World development report*, Oxford: Oxford University Press.

Walder, A. (1986) *Communist neo-traditionalism: Work and authority in China's industry*, Berkeley, CA: University of California Press.

White, G. (1998) 'Social security reforms in China: towards an East Asian model', in R. Goodman, G. White and H.J. Kwon (eds) *The East Asian welfare model: Welfare orientalism and the state*, London: Routledge, pp 175-97.

White, G., Howell, J. and Shang, X.Y. (eds) (1996) *In search of civil society: Market reform and social change in contemporary China*, Oxford: Clarendon Press.

Wong, L. (1998) *Marginalization and social welfare in China*, London: Routledge.

World Bank (1992) *China, strategies for reducing poverty in the 1990s*, Washington, DC: The World Bank.

World Bank (1997a) *Old age security: Pension reform in China*, Washington, DC: The World Bank.

World Bank (1997b) *Financing health care: Issues and options for China*, Washington, DC: The World Bank.

World Bank (1997c), *Sharing rising incomes: Disparities in China*, Washington, DC: The World Bank.

Wu, C.P. (1995) *The report on changing population and development in China (Zhuanbian zhong de zhongguo renkuo yu fazhan zong baogao)*, Beijing: Higher Education Publishers.

Wu, X.Y. (1999) 'China's social insurance situation and reforms in 1998-1999', in X. Ru, X.Y. Lu and T.L. Shan (eds) *China's social situation analysis and forecast in 1999 (1999 nian zhongguo shehui xingshi fenxi yu yuci)*, Beijing: China Social Science Publishers, pp 147-64.

You, J. (1998) *China's enterprise reform: Changing state/society relations after Mao*, London: Routledge.

Zhu, Q.F. (1996) 'An assessment on the level of socio-economic development in 188 cities in China', *City Problems (Chengshi wenti)*, vol 1, pp 38-42.

FOUR

Hong Kong: from familistic to Confucian welfare

Sammy Chiu and Victor Wong

Introduction

In the words of Mr Tung Chee Hwa, Chief Executive of Hong Kong Special Administrative Region (SAR), "Hong Kong opened a new chapter in history" on 1 July 1997 (Tung, 1997a). Hong Kong was reunited with China after more than 150 years of British colonial rule and began a new identity of being China's first special administrative region. According to the Joint Declaration signed by the British and Chinese governments in 1984, the Hong Kong SAR will enjoy a high degree of autonomy in all its domestic management, yet China will be responsible for its foreign and defence affairs. Under the concept of 'one country, two systems', the Basic Law provides a constitutional framework whereby Hong Kong is allowed to preserve its capitalist system and lifestyle, which are different from those of mainland China.

The framework provided by the Joint Declaration and the Basic Law is a blueprint for change, but at the same time it is an assurance of preservation. On the one hand, it governs the change of sovereignty and, perhaps to a certain extent, the way in which Hong Kong is to be administered. On the other hand, however, it also stipulates the continuation of the capitalist system, its distributive machinery and, above all, the status quo. Paradoxically, the momentous historical event of resuming national sovereignty seems to rely mainly on the reproduction of the previous colonial rule. For example, in addressing an international audience two months before the handover, the then Chief Secretary of the Hong Kong Government maintained publicly that continuity was the key to Hong Kong's future, and that Hong Kong was to continue in virtually the same way after the handover to China (Chan, 1997a). Likewise, the Chief Executive himself also made a number of similar reassurances on different important occasions that it would be 'business as usual' in Hong Kong after the establishment of the SAR (Tung, 1997b; 1997c).

However, it was important for the new SAR government and the Chief Executive himself to establish their own identity and legitimacy by distancing themselves from former colonial rule. The urgent need for a new identity and a new legitimacy was voiced by the Chief Executive in his first policy address: "Hong Kong has finally broken free from the psychological constraints brought about by the colonial era" (Tung, 1997d, p 1). As a result, the community was asked to have the courage to set aside past modes of thought and plan Hong Kong's long-term future with a new vision. What the Chief Executive had in mind for the new vision for Hong Kong, which he later substantiated, is essentially an amalgamation of Confucian values and the free market economy. This is the first time in Hong Kong since British colonial rule that Confucianism has been explicitly adopted as a guiding principle for the government in managing the society. In this chapter we examine the Hong Kong version of Confucian welfare and the way in which the new SAR government selectively uses Confucianism to support its own ruling legitimacy and, specifically, to legitimise residualism.

The legacy of colonial social policy

Positive non-intervention and the emergence of consensus capitalism

Hong Kong's colonial government was always proud of its non-intervention and minimalist welfare regime. The typical welfare discourse constructed primarily by the colonial government reflected and perpetuated the belief that excessive public provisions could disrupt the traditional family values of self-reliance and would jeopardise the economy (Hong Kong Government, 1965, 1973). Non-intervention by the government was not to be taken to mean passivity. Rather it was construed as an active measure to refrain from 'improper' interference with the market, while at the same time it directed people to believe that the government was positive in helping those who were in genuine need. The positive non-interventionist regime was built on three formulations. First, there was the sense of crisis among the population, the majority of whom moved to Hong Kong from South East China to avoid the Japanese invasion and the civil war. Hong Kong was increasingly not a transient but a permanent home for these migrants. Having experienced prolonged social and political turbulence and material deprivation, most people tended to take Hong Kong as their last refuge and developed an anxiety about the boat being rocked. Thus the unpredictable economic prospects of Hong Kong warranted prudent financial management by the government. Second, there was the reproduction of a traditional moral discourse that public support was a symbol of guilt and shame. Since it was suggested that public provision was incompatible with Chinese traditional values, it was believed that the government should do only the minimum. Third, positive non-interventionism was made possible by continuous economic growth in the territory, so that even with very minimum state support, the public was able to benefit in real terms, though certainly to varying degrees.

As noted by Chan (1997b), the Hong Kong colonial government had always refrained from playing a proactive role in providing social services, and had from the outset restricted its role in redistributing wealth. Instead it was primarily concerned with the creation of wealth, albeit for a small number of capitalists and entrepreneurs. The distribution of wealth through fiscal policy and social welfare would mean interference to the free market and would discourage foreign investment. As a matter of fact, the commitment of the Hong Kong government to free trade has a strong colonial origin. In 1843, a year after Hong Kong was ceded to Britain, the then British Foreign Secretary, Lord Aberdeen, instructed the first Hong Kong Governor that the intention of Her Majesty's Government was to use Hong Kong as a free port, and that the harbour dues should be as light as possible so as to encourage commerce (Tsang, 1995). Similarly, the tight fiscal discipline was also set up as a measure to prevent colonies from becoming economic burdens on Great Britain (Lau, 1997). As recorded by Tang (1997), the colonial regulations set up by the Colonial Office in London stipulated that the total expenditure of the government in any particular year should not in ordinary circumstances be allowed to exceed the total estimated revenue. This regulation imposed stringent control over the fiscal strategy of the Hong Kong government before the Second World War, and became an important parameter for financial management when Hong Kong gained financial autonomy from British control in the 1950s. Sir John Cowperwaite, the Financial Secretary of the colony in the 1960s, laid down an iron rule that any increase in public provision could only be realised if it were funded by sustained revenue growth. This rule has, in effect, set a clear boundary for the role and size of the government, and has successfully curbed public expectations for welfare expansion and for social policy to be redistributive.

Sir Philip Haddon-Cave, who was the Financial Secretary of the colony in the 1970s, coined the government strategies in economic and social affairs as 'positive non-interventionism' (Hong Kong Government, 1978, p 813).

The strategy of positive non-interventionism gave the government good justification for not providing adequate social services not only in the 1950s and the 1960s, but also when the economy was experiencing continuous growth in the 1970s and the 1980s. It consisted of several elements, the most important of which was the low tax rate. The colonial government saw tax as an evil, which was necessary only when it could not be avoided. So tax rates have always been kept to a minimum. Furthermore, the government reiterated at different times that the revenues generated from taxation served only to support essential public expenditure that, again, had to be kept as modest as possible. Thus the idea of using taxation as a means to redistribute wealth and to promote social justice was regarded as impossible (Hong Kong Government, 1977a). In Hong Kong raising the tax rate is the major 'prohibited area' in social policy (Chiu et al, 1997).

Consensus capitalism

The conservative budgetary approach established early in colonial rule was maintained by the Hong Kong government for its entire life (Tang, 1997). In 1995, when colonial rule was approaching an end, this policy principle was still reaffirmed by the then Financial Secretary, Sir Hamish Macleod. However, considering the change of socio-political context in late colonial Hong Kong where party and pressure group politics became more active, the government found it increasingly necessary to gain popular support for the status quo from a wider spectrum of the society. Hence the concept of 'consensus capitalism' was coined by Macleod (1995) to characterise the Hong Kong brand of capitalism: "[There is] a consensus about the need to encourage free enterprise and competition, while promoting equity and assistance for those who need it. Enterprise, because that is what gives dynamism to our economy" (Macleod, 1995).

Beyond the jargon, consensus capitalism seems to have deviated little from the early principles. The promotion of equity and assistance for the needy was more rhetoric than reality. Social welfare expansion remained possible only through budget surpluses. Taxation reforms in the direction of wealth redistribution were unequivocally refused despite the widening of income inequality (Chiu, 1996).

In sum, the colonial government successfully constructed an ideological consensus in social policy, whereby it was believed that the welfare of the citizens was best brought about by the non-intervention of the state. This thesis has gone almost totally unchallenged for several decades, and has resulted in a severe restriction on the role of the government in providing social welfare.

Familistic residualism

The term 'residual model of social policy' was first coined by Titmuss (1974) to mean that welfare is arranged only as a stop gap measure provided temporarily to the needy when private means break down. Based on the circumstances of American society, Wilensky (1975) saw residual welfare as coming into play only when the normal structures of supply, such as the family and the market, break down. In this light, residual welfare implies, on the one hand, that self-reliance is the ultimate ideal of welfare arrangements. Residual social policy therefore reflects an individualistic understanding of social needs and social problems (Spicker, 1995). On the other hand, residualism implies an active role for the market in distributing welfare and in meeting needs. This implies, first, that the normal way for individuals to secure their welfare is to participate in the market, either through labour or capital; and, second, that private welfare is morally more appropriate than public provision.

Hong Kong has demonstrated a classical example of residualism where economic growth was seen as the best solution to poverty and other related problems, and the market the best place to satisfy needs. This philosophy of welfare was clearly expressed in the first colonial welfare policy White Paper, entitled *Aims and policy for social welfare in Hong Kong*, published in 1965:

> The economic well being of any community demands that as far as possible every resident contributes to, rather than draws upon, its resources. In other words, quite apart from the obvious dictates of humanitarianism, it is poor economy to sustain non-productive members of the community if by rehabilitation measures they can become partially or fully productive; it is poor economy to have families broken up and members cared for at the expense of the public purse if by preventive measures they can be held together … it is poor economy to neglect the constructive character building measures available to individuals, groups and communities … when such measures could forestall

> or avert unrest or loss of life and property and serve to reduce the pressure on police, prison and probation services. (Hong Kong Government, 1965)

The fact that social services have been maintained at a basic minimum level in Hong Kong is well known. In the field of social welfare, which covers social security, services for older people, services for family and young people, and rehabilitation and other social work services, government spending as a percentage of GDP had been kept within the region of 5% before 1995, and only as a result of the ageing of the population in recent years has social security expenditure begun to increase. The Hong Kong government's total spending, and welfare spending in particular, is much lower than many of the western countries with comparable economic performance.

The main feature of residual welfare in colonial Hong Kong is that it was developed, reinforced and legitimised by a strong sense of traditional Chinese familism. Thus the first port of call, when unmet needs arise, has always been the immediate family, with the state only a distant supporter. Between the family and the state, the market has, in the Chinese sense, not played an important mediating role. Rather, the extended family, the clan and the philanthropic associations were encouraged, and these operated on the traditional Chinese assumption of benevolence rather than on the assumption of welfare rights. A classic argument that supports the notion of familistic residualism in Hong Kong is that the western concept of welfare, which stresses the notion of rights, is not compatible with Chinese culture, which emphasises the aspect of obligation (Tao, 1991). Tao believes (1991, p 24) that Hong Kong people have their "cultural roots deeply engrained in the long enduring tradition of Confucian moral values and beliefs" (see Chapter Two, p 33). The locus of the philosophy is that the self in Chinese culture is seen as a relational being rather than an independent entity. What the culture suggests is not therefore a fulfilment of individual rights, but primarily a fulfilment of one's own role obligations.

The Hong Kong brand of residualism has been strongly supported by traditional Chinese family values selectively manipulated by the colonial government. The role of the Chinese family in providing care has all along been placed at the centre of the stage in social policy in Hong Kong. The Chinese family is seen as a natural mutual-aid unit where members naturally engage in mutual help when needs arise. It is not only filial piety that is assumed to be naturally active – horizontal care between family members is also regarded as one of the

Chinese family traits. The government holds several assumptions about the Chinese family. First, it has been the site for the personalisation of social needs. It had been assumed by the colonial government since the early development of social welfare that needs with regard to poverty, old age and delinquency as well as natural disaster were all personal matters that should be settled within the family (Hong Kong Government, 1965). Second, there is the assumption that the Chinese family remained intact and its caring function effective (Hong Kong Government, 1977b, 1991). Third, owing to the above two assumptions, the primary objective of the government in social welfare in Hong Kong is not to provide services to replace the function of the family, but rather to preserve and to strengthen the family function. This objective has been in force from the 1960s to the present day. In the first social welfare White Paper it was stated that:

> It is of the greatest importance that social welfare services should not be organised in such a way as to make it easier for socially disruptive influences to gain a hold over the community, or to accelerate the breakdown of the natural or traditional sense of responsibility – for example by encouraging the natural family unit to shed on to social welfare agencies, public or private, its moral responsibility to care for the aged or infirm. (Hong Kong Government, 1965, p 5)

The paradox of new visions

The SAR version of conservatism

The last British governor regretted the "irony of handing a free Chinese city to a totalitarian Chinese State", and the fact that "the last British colony was to be surrendered to the last communist tyranny" (Patten, 1998, p 13). The new regime sees the colonial history as being undignified, and thus changes are inevitable, although it is also necessary to preserve economic success:

> For the first time in history, we, the people of Hong Kong, will be masters of our own destiny. The Special Administrative Region government is fully committed to preserve the Hong Kong way of life, maintaining Hong Kong's free and open economic system.... We will be compassionate to those in need.... I understand the hopes and aspirations of Hong Kong people ... [and] will lead the 6.5 million people of Hong Kong, along

> with our indomitable spirit, towards the future. As part of China, we will move forward as one inseparable nation with two distinct systems. (Tung, 1997a)

Ironically though, change in the Hong Kong SAR has to be established on the confidence of preservation. No matter how much the British rule was undignified and disgraceful, the SAR government has followed the colonial legacy, especially concerning the role of the state in social policy. The Chief Executive has declared openly his version of conservatism:

> As many people know, I am conservative. But conservatism – wanting to sustain things that you know and value – does not mean standing still or turning back the clock. Sustaining a wonderfully complex and exciting community like Hong Kong requires constant, judicious movement and sometimes pre-emptive adjustment.... (Tung, 1997b)

What the Chief Executive wants to sustain is the prudent and conservative financial management strategy of the government (Tung, 1997d). It is not only that the size of the public sector has to kept to a minimum; it is also essential for the government as well as the subvented sector to constantly review their efficiency so as to ensure minimum spending. Thus the Chief Executive demanded that all the government departments and the NGOs under its financial subsidy, with the exception of the Education Department, enhance their productivity by cutting 5% off their recurrent expenditure over the next three years (Tung, 1998a). In addition, selected areas of social services are required to conduct Fundamental Efficiency Reviews (FERs), whereby 'inefficient' services have to be curbed or close down. It is stressed by the Chief Executive that the Enhanced Productivity Programme (EPP) is not a temporary measure of the government to cope with economic downturn, but a long-term policy to rectify the problem of an overweight government created by Patten's administration (Tung, 1998a). Beyond conservative financial management, however, consensus capitalism appears to have been retuned, so that seeking consensus from among political parties and pressure groups has given way to the need for a strong administration. Positive non-interventionism seems to have been reduced to mean merely minimal social programmes. According to the SAR government, it was the colonial social and economic policy that led Hong Kong into the present deep water, and this must be rectified:

> People from various sectors have told me that the speculative
> atmosphere created by the formerly prevalent 'bubble economy'
> had seriously undermined people's work ethics and attitudes
> towards learning. (Tung, 1999a, paragraph 34)

In a nutshell, there is an active role for the government to play in
leading and coordinating the efforts of the private sector in developing
the economy. Tax must continue to be kept to the minimum so as to
maintain a favourable infrastructure for business, and the size of the
public sector must be further reduced to avoid competition with the
private sector, which is the locomotive for economic growth.
Correspondingly, social services must be reconfigured so as to halt the
'unhealthy' demand for welfare rights stirred up by the former
government, and to prevent the pressure on the government. While
there are administrative measures such as the EPP to curb the size of
the government, one of the most important steps taken by the SAR is
to redirect the mentality of the people from being concerned about
their rights to focus on their obligations and responsibilities. This is
nothing new for societies where state spending is being cut back.
However, in Hong Kong, this has been taken to an ideological level
where the change of mentality is equated with the restoration of
traditional Chinese values and self-government.

Restoration of Chinese values

The SAR government sees the traditional role and function of the
family and its affiliated values, such as filial piety and respect for older
people, as important to continue but not quite enough. The scope of
value restoration has been expanded from the family domain to that
of the social – that is, in other words, from the private to the public.
Indeed, filial piety and the caring function of the family are the basic
imperatives for care. For example, in the opening address at the
Conference for the Year of the Older Persons, the Chief Executive
made it clear that care for older people is, in his view, primarily a
family responsibility, and that it is a good tradition for Hong Kong to
maintain (Tung, 1999b). In addition, Hong Kong people must
familiarise themselves with Chinese culture and traditional Chinese
values and be proud of being Chinese: "As I have always said, the
Chinese in Hong Kong should be proud of being a Chinese. We must
work hard to familiarise ourselves with the Chinese culture and get to
know the Chinese values" (Tung, 1997a).

While very few people would reject the part on national sentiment, the comments of the Chief Executive on the contents of Chinese culture and Chinese values were rather selective. In the ceremony establishing the Hong Kong SAR on 1 July 1997, the Chief Executive emphasised the need to strengthen traditional cultural values in Hong Kong (Tung, 1997a). The traditional Chinese values that the Chief Executive selected as being of major importance included not only familial values, such as filial piety and love for one's family, but also those that govern social and political relationships, such as conformity, obedience, being self-restrained, and shouldering collective responsibility. The priority to promote a strong sense of Chinese values has been stressed in other speeches, for example:

> ... I consider that fulfilment of obligations and acceptance of responsibilities, in this context, should be more important than pursuit of their rights. This does not simply concern the right way to enhance self accomplishment, develop one's potentials, and make one's dream come true. More importantly, it is to create an atmosphere and promote an attitude of correctness and vitality in the local community, thereby resolving satisfactorily the unhealthy problems prevailing in Hong Kong and among the youth. (Tung, 1997e)

The contrast between 'eastern' and 'western' values by means of a simple distinction between the 'fulfilment of responsibility' and the 'pursuit of rights', at best, is over-simplified (White and Goodman, 1998). Viewed from a traditional Confucian perspective, the core of Confucianism lies within the practice of *jen*, which means benevolence. It requires the rulers to limit their extension of power and to develop a caring heart for the people (Tu, 1991). Of course, the practice of *jen* does not only apply to the rulers, but it is important for the rulers to lead by example, and thus to be followed by the gentry and fellow citizens. Corresponding to the practice of *jen*, Confucianism also promotes the practice of *li*, which means rites or proper behaviour. Tu (1991) suggests that the essence of *li* is a distinction, which divides human society into superiors and inferiors, and a class of nobles and a class of commoners. So *li* is about the establishment and maintenance of a social order, according to which different classes have to follow certain rites or proper behaviour. In short, *li* is about the way to rule in harmony. But the prerequisite for harmony is *jen*, which is the self-restraint of the rulers. Unfortunately, what the Chief Executive suggests for the Hong Kong SAR is a one-sided view of Confucian values: citizens should refrain from demanding, conform and be submissive by not confronting the government. The extent to which this could lead to social unity as proposed by the Chief Executive is rather doubtful. Even if it does, it is obviously a unity based not on equal citizenship, but rather on *li* and on the promotion of rhetorical nationhood.

Confucian welfare: familial or political?

As was made clear in Chapter One, minimal welfare backed up by traditional Chinese values has been construed as culturally unique for Chinese communities in East Asia and described by Jones (1993) as the 'Confucian welfare state'. Similarly, Dixon (1981), in his early study of Chinese welfare, suggested that social welfare in China is embedded with a strong Confucian welfare legacy. The prevalence of family care is taken as an important indicator of Confucian welfare, which is underpinned by the emphasis placed on paternalistic, patriarchal and filial forms of care.

In practice, it was the Chief Executive of the Hong Kong SAR who first used Confucianism explicitly as the ruling principle for Hong Kong. In his election platform prepared for the campaign in 1997, he suggested that the traditional Chinese values developed from the core of Confucianism should be upheld, and that the society of Hong Kong needed to be united by its traditional values. In fact, the Chief Executive suggested an extension of Confucianism to cover a wide range of social values and practices, including the submission to authority, politics by consensus, individual obligations and responsibilities over one's rights and entitlements, and so on. Indeed, Confucianism is not purely concerned with the practice of filial piety and family responsibility; it is fundamentally about the establishment of social order based on a set of hierarchical relationships. As pointed out in the Analects (1996): "Let the ruler be ruler, the minister minister, the father father, and the son son".

According to the Confucian teachings, it is only through the rectification of names, by which proper people are put in proper places performing proper duties, that an orderly society can be established. Guiding the rectification of names, according to Confucius, were the cardinal relationships, which included governmental, parental, conjugal and fraternal relationships, as well as friendship (Chai and Chai, 1962). According to these five cardinal guiding principles, for example, the Monarch was to guide the subject; the father was to guide the son, and the husband was to guide the wife. In other words, the monarch, the father or the husband is obliged to set himself as a model or example for his subject, son or wife to follow. In return, the latter has to be loyal, submissive or obedient to the social or familial duties prescribed to them. So, the promotion of the five cardinal principles is but a call to follow the rules of the social hierarchy. This pattern of relationships that formed the basis of social order in Chinese society was not one aimed at promoting equality. Rather it implied and possibly constructed sets of superior and subordinate relationships. In this context, filial piety and loyalty can be understood as an effective and legitimate means to reinforce the patriarchal system and the ruling regime, through its requirements for complete obedience, harmony, discipline and the proper order of seniority (Kiang, 1982; Trauzettel, 1991; White and Goodman, 1998). In the following sections we discuss the way in which the SAR government reproduces the Confucian welfare ideology.

The position of the self in the Confucian context

Alongside the importance attached to familial and social hierarchy of relations and obligations, traditional Confucian values place much emphasis on the spirit of self-cultivation, self-reliance and self-sacrifice. An ideal moral character is demonstrated by a strong work ethic, perseverance against personal ups and downs, and being capable of working for the interests of the vast majority of the society apart from following the rules of a hierarchical order of social relations. For example, in the case of learning and education, Confucius did not favour unconditional respect for teachers, but encouraged his disciples to develop critical thinking on their own. Confucius was not pleased with Yanhui, his favourite disciple, because he raised no criticism or comments on his teachings, nor tried to express different opinions. Confucius reproached him, saying "Yanhui is not helping me; he is never displeased with what I say" (quoted in Cheng, 1991, p 195). When confronted with troubles and difficulties, instead of giving up and being disheartened, one has to show courage and make unceasing efforts to improve oneself and struggle on and on. Persons of such high moral calibre will ultimately gain respect from others and even from the whole of society, despite the fact that they may not get any rewards or make any improvement in a material sense. However, the traditional Confucian sense of self-improvement is not something equivalent to Maslow's hierarchy of needs in which self-actualisation is placed at the top of the pyramid. The Confucian notion of self is still circumscribed by the politics of consensus and a wider network of familial and community obligations or duties, of which the self is not viewed as an independent subject but a relational being.

The Chief Executive has been fully aware of the difficulties and challenges the Asian financial crisis and economic downturn have brought to the people of Hong Kong. Bank credit has not risen significantly over the past two years, and the unemployment rate has reached the region of 6%, which is the highest for the past two decades. He frequently cites examples of people with traditional virtues demonstrated by their diligence, hard work, perseverance and, most important of all, their simple but determined belief to ride out the storms by making unceasing efforts on their own. The pictures of hardship are not haunting but memorable, and are interpreted as providing opportunities for people to make continuous self-improvement, and build up remarkable qualities, all of which are deemed desirable to lead to success. Under the heading of 'Moral values' in his 1999 Policy Address, he outlined his political philosophy:

> I believe we all desire a society of greater harmony, in which everybody respects and treats others well. We should carry forward our traditional virtues, such as filial piety, humanity, importance attached to education, and diligence. We favour consultation, not confrontation. We seek protection of the rights of the individual, yet we should also fulfil our social responsibilities and obligations. (Tung, 1999a, para 167)

Confucian moral values serve not only to mobilise cultural resources to cope with severe hardship, but also to provide legitimacy for the residual welfare regime. There is a longstanding government anxiety that traditional virtues of self and family reliance might be weakened by disruptive social forces, such as divorce and dependency on welfare. The major difference between the colonial and the new ruling regimes is the explicit promotion of Confucian moral values, which serves to rationalise the inadequacy of state support to individuals and to the family. Consequently, any individuals or families failing to take up the challenges of severe hardship, or not succeeding in meeting the needs of family members will be liable to shoulder the guilt and shame by themselves. Rather than the provision of social welfare by the government, economic growth plus the continuation of traditional Chinese culture are seen as the only ways to address important social issues like unemployment. Framed by Confucian moral values, it is not difficult to understand why the Chief Executive is optimistic in believing that "Hong Kong people are accustomed to working hard and earning their own living, and do not like to depend on public assistance" (Tung, 1999a, para 28).

The government's role is to provide only the safety net for those who are in genuine need or for whom public assistance is the last resort. Thus the Hong Kong welfare regime emphasises traditional moral values to foster self-help and family care.

Young people and Confucian virtues

Young people with remarkable qualities are cited by the Chief Executive as good examples to follow:

> Youth development has always been one of my major concerns. Whenever I read about outstanding young people like Kwong Lai Yin who sacrificed herself to save others and Chan Man Fong and Yeung Yan Yan who have attained remarkable academic achievements despite their physical disability, I am very touched and have great admiration for them. On the other hand, I am deeply distressed to read news such as large numbers of young students obtaining poor grades in public examinations, juveniles involved in gang activities, and the youth unemployment rate reaching 29%. (Tung, 1999a, para 79)

So far, in the Hong Kong context, it is rare for an important official document like the Policy Address of the Chief Executive to mention the names of lay people and even rarer to mention young people. The three young ladies were named individually not so much for their self-cultivation and self-sacrificing behaviour, but also for the underlying political purpose of attaching great importance to traditional Confucian values in youth development. Among others, the Chief Executive is deeply distressed by dropout students, juveniles and unemployed youths. By highly commending the virtues and qualities of able-bodied and disabled young people, expectations of the younger generation are implicitly set up for wider community reference, particularly around the virtues of self-sacrifice, hard work and perseverance. However, a demarcation between the well socialised and the marginal is not only arbitrary but also undesirable, particularly in the sense of strengthening the stereotypical and stigmatising biases against those young people who are on the margins, socially or economically (Wong and Chiu, 1998). The Chief Executive is not unaware of the fact that the young are acquiring western culture and values in Hong Kong, where East meets West; and that, like their adult counterparts, they also suffer much from the economic downturn in the region (Tung, 2002). On at least two different occasions he has emphasised Chinese values to a young audience. For example:

> ... education is not just about knowledge but also about values. A proper set of values is vital for the new generation to handle challenges and to cope with both successes and adversities: trust, love and respect for our family and our elders; integrity, honesty and respect for all; commitment to education; preference for consultation rather than confrontation; emphasis on our obligations to the community as a whole rather than just our rights as individuals. These values have been with us and with our community for thousands of years and are as relevant today as they have ever been. I hope you will hold these values dear to you in your journey through life. (Tung, 1998b; also Tung, 1997e)

What is expected of young people is for them to "take pride in their Chinese heritage" (Tung, 1998a, para 111), to "learn to put aside immediate interests" (Tung, 2001) and to develop a sense of self-sacrifice and self-cultivation in the face of hardship. The priority is successful socialisation and internalisation of Confucian moral values, and the pursuit of young people's rights is secondary.

Confucianism lays down very clearly the importance of developing a sense of self-sacrifice, self-examination and self-cultivation and, at the same time, a sense of duty towards the family, the community and the nation at large. In the words of the Chief Executive, "Our students need to learn how to become responsible and caring individuals" (Tung, 1999a, para 55). This may explain why the state has been eager to promote a sense of volunteerism among unemployed school-leavers by encouraging them to take part in volunteer schemes organised by social welfare agencies. The provision of incentives to this group of young people in the form of small allowances for transport and meals is to provide them with an opportunity to learn to serve the community and to acquire proper social manners and skills. Recently, the government has also launched a youth pre-employment training programme, which does not emphasise skills training but, rather, the instilling of proper attitudes towards a job and in the world of work. But will all these schemes turn out to be social control measures to discipline the young who are neither in school nor in work, particularly in view of the very high unemployment rate, which reached 32.8% among young people aged 15-19 in the second quarter of 2003 (Census and Statistics Department, 2003)? Will these measures be used to obscure the severity of youth unemployment as the scheme participants are counted as economically inactive people? Will they obscure the government's responsibility to provide formal training packages to this group of young people, who are highly frustrated by the sluggish job market and the prevalent ageist practices of employers? Within an environment where there is an increasing level of competition and hardship, the measures taken to promote a successful internalisation of Confucian moral values is more about paternalistic control and discipline than social welfare.

Ageing and Confucian ethics

Care for older people was announced as one of the top priorities of the new Hong Kong SAR government in 1997 and the Chief Executive emphasised that: "[C]aring for the elderly is the responsibility of every family…" (Tung, 1997d, para 114). Promoting family care for older people has always been a central concern in social policy in Hong Kong. It is assumed to be entirely legitimate to expect each family to take care of their frail members in line with the tradition of filial piety. Moreover, the Chief Executive also asked people to respect and care for the senior members of other families (Tung, 1999b). Confucian ideology has legitimised the government's policy of mobilising familial and community resources to meet the needs of an ageing population. Care for older people therefore is primarily a family responsibility, the community comes second, and the government is again the last resort for those who are in genuine need.

Rather than focusing on the input of professional resources, the government has continued to place emphasis on the mobilisation of the community. The volunteers, neighbours and the older people themselves are all portrayed as important community carers participating in the process of providing care. As a result, a number of services that are aimed at encouraging informal support have been set up or are at an experimental stage, including the Volunteer Workers Programme, Older Volunteers Programme and the recently established Support Teams for the Elderly in multi-service centres for older people. From the government's perspective, community carers contribute to three important purposes: to further expand the informal support network for older people in need; to keep older people in the community (family) as long as possible; and to give healthier older people an opportunity to serve as volunteers and set a good example for the younger generation to follow. Unfortunately, without sufficient state support provided to the community, community care for older people would simply end up as care by the community (Chiu and Wong, 1998a).

Moreover, the government's emphasis on family responsibility in the care of older people has perpetuated the domestication of such care in at least three senses. First, the site of such care is the family, which is the only available resort for many older people. The family is not only a place of residence but also a workplace catering for the physical, health and social needs of older family members. Second, the caring labour performed by the family supplements the provision of formal care for older people. Over the past few years, community-based geriatric outreach teams have been set up to provide support to the community and family carers. However, because of their bias towards providing support to paid carers in hostels and residential homes, the family is usually left to provide care alone for their older members. Another worrying example is the case of respite services for the older people. At present there are less than 20 places available for all family carers in Hong Kong. Finally, the domestication of care also means the shifting of costs from the public sector to the family, both in terms of unpaid caring labour and the finance of care (Chiu and Wong, 1998b; Wong, 1999). Within the Hong Kong SAR, the domestication of care for older people is largely operated on the basis of Confucian ethics of filial piety and respect for older people on a wider community level. However, it is doubtful whether the needs of older people can be met by the promotion of Confucian and filial ethics without sacrificing the interests of the family and its female members in particular.

Conclusion

Confucian welfare ideology has been used by the Hong Kong SAR government not only as a means to contain social welfare costs, but also as an instrument to strengthen social control and the prevailing hierarchical order of relations. The reproduction of Confucian ethics has witnessed a growing penetration of conservative political ideas into the moral fabric of the society. Without a democratic mandate, the further strengthening of traditional Chinese culture and Confucian virtues, whether by means of policy making or story telling by the Chief Executive, may turn social and welfare demands into personal and family issues. However, the people of Hong Kong are well aware of their social and political rights, and there is an ongoing protest against the inadequacy of social policy. The ways in which the SAR government can successfully mediate the contradiction between residual welfare and economic supremacy, uphold Confucian moral values and consequently strengthen the legitimacy of its welfare regime are all important issues that must be addressed in the near future.

References

Analects of Confucius (1996) English and modern Chinese versions, *Confucian Bible*, Book I, Hong Kong: The Chinese University Press.

Chai, C. and Chai, W. (1962) *The changing society of China*, Hong Kong: Montor Books.

Chan, A. (1997a) Speech by the Acting Chief Executive, Mrs Anson Chan, to the 30th international general meeting of the Pacific Basic Economic Council in Manila, 19 May 1997, Hong Kong (www.info.gov.hk/ce/speech/cesp.htm).

Chan, R. (1997b) *Welfare in newly industrialised society: The construction of welfare state in Hong Kong*, London: Avebury.

Cheng, H.B. (1991) 'Confucian ethics and moral education of contemporary students', in S. Krieger and R. Trauzett (eds) *Confucianism and the modernization of China*, Germany: v.Hase and Koehler Verlang Mainz, pp 193-202.

Chiu, S. (1996) 'Social welfare', in M.K. Nyaw and S.M. Li (eds) *The other Hong Kong report 1996*, Hong Kong: The Chinese University Press, pp 431-48.

Chiu, S. and Wong, V. (1998a) 'Community care for older people in Hong Kong: from policy to politics', *Social Policy and Social Work*, vol 2, no 2, pp 101-37.

Chiu, S. and Wong, V. (1998b) 'Social policy in Hong Kong: from British colony to Special Administrative Region of China', *European Journal of Social Work*, vol 1, no 2, pp 231-42.

Chiu, S., Yu, S., Shiu, W. and Lai, D. (1997) 'Seven challenges of the policy analysts', in S. Chiu, S. Yu, W. Shiu and D. Lai (eds) *Social policy in Hong Kong in the 1990s: An alternative analysis*, Hong Kong: Hong Kong Policy Viewers, pp 3-12.

Dixon, J. (1981) *The Chinese welfare system, 1949-1979*, New York, NY: Praeger Publishers.

Hong Kong Government (1965) *Aims and policy for social welfare in Hong Kong: A White Paper*, Hong Kong: Government Printer.

Hong Kong Government (1973) *Social welfare in Hong Kong: The way ahead*, Hong Kong: Government Printer.

Hong Kong Government (1977a) *The personal social work among young people*, Hong Kong: Government Printer.

Hong Kong Government (1977b) *Services for the elderly: A Green Paper*, Hong Kong: Government Printer.

Hong Kong Government (1978) *Hong Kong Hansard 1977-78*, Hong Kong: Government Printer, p 813.

Hong Kong Government (1991) *Social welfare into the 1990s and beyond: A White Paper*, Hong Kong: Government Printer.

Jones, C. (1993) 'The Pacific challenge', in C. Jones (ed) *New perspectives on the welfare state in Europe*, London: Routledge, pp 198-217.

Kiang, K.H. (1982) 'The Chinese family system', *The Annals of the American Academy of Political and Social Science*, vol 52, New York, NY: Garland Publishing Inc.

Lau, C.K. (1997) *Hong Kong's colonial legacy: A Hong Kong Chinese's view of the British heritage*, Hong Kong: The Chinese University Press.

Macleod, Sir Hamish (1995) Speech of the Financial Secretary at the budget debate in the Legislative Council, 29 March 1995, Hong Kong: Government Printer.

Patten, C. (1998) *East and West*, London: Macmillan.

Spicker, P. (1995) *Social policy: Themes and approaches*, London: Prentice Hall and Harvester Wheatsheaf.

Tang, S.H. (1997) 'The Hong Kong fiscal policy: Continuity or redirection', in P.W. Lee (ed) *Political order and power transition in Hong Kong*, Hong Kong: The Chinese University Press, pp 187-230.

Tao, J. (1991) 'The moral foundation of welfare: a comparative study of Chinese Confucianism and deontological liberalism: a case study of Hong Kong', unpublished PhD thesis: University of East Anglia.

Titmuss, R. (1974) *Social policy: An introduction*, London: George Allen and Unwin.

Trauzettel, R. (1991) 'On the problem of the universal applicability of Confucianism', in S. Krieger and R. Trauzettel (eds) *Confucianism and the modernization of China*, Germany: v. Hase and Koehler Verlang Mainz, pp 42-50.

Tsang, S. (1995) *Government and politics: Documentary history of Hong Kong*, Hong Kong: Hong Kong University Press.

Tu, W.M. (1991) 'A Confucian perspective on the rise of industrial East Asia', in S. Krieger and R. Trauzettel (eds) *Confucianism and the modernization of China,* Germany: v. Hase and Koehler Verlang Mainz, pp 29-41.

Tung, C.H. (1997a) Speech by the Chief Executive, the Hon. Tung Chee Hwa, at the ceremony to celebrate the establishment of the Hong Kong SAR of the People's Republic of China, 1 July 1997, *Speeches and statements of the Chief Executive of the Hong Kong SAR*, Hong Kong (www.info.gov.hk/ce/speech/cesp.htm).

Tung, C.H. (1997b) Speech by the Chief Executive, Mr Tung Chee Hwa, to the Royal Institute of International Affairs in London, 22 October 1997, *Speeches and statements of the Chief Executive of the Hong Kong SAR*, Hong Kong (www.info.gov.hk/ce/speech/cesp.htm).

Tung, C.H. (1997c) Speech by the Chief Executive at the luncheon hosted by the Asia Society, New York Society, USA, 12 September 1997, *Speeches and statements of the Chief Executive of the Hong Kong SAR*, Hong Kong (www.info.gov.hk/ce/speech/cesp.htm).

Tung, C.H. (1997d) *Building Hong Kong for a new era: Policy Address of the Chief Executive of the SAR to the provisional Legislative Council*, Hong Kong: Government Printer.

Tung, C.H. (1997e) Speech by the Chief Executive, Mr Tung Chee Hwa, at the Conference on the Review of the Implementation of the Charter for Youth, 20 December 1997, *Speeches and statements of the Chief Executive of the Hong Kong SAR*, Hong Kong (www.info.gov.hk/ce/speech/cesp.htm).

Tung, C.H. (1998a) *The 1998 Policy Address*, Hong Kong: Government Printer.

Tung, C.H. (1998b) Speech by the Chief Executive at DGS Annual Speech Day, 27 November 1998, *Speeches and statements of the Chief Executive of the Hong Kong SAR*, Hong Kong (www.info.gov.hk/ce/speech/cesp.htm).

Tung, C.H. (1999a) *The 1999 Policy Address*, Hong Kong: Government Printer.

Tung, C.H. (1999b) Chief Executive's opening address at Conference for Year of Older Persons, 26 April 1999, *Speeches and statements of the Chief Executive of the Hong Kong SAR*, Hong Kong (www.info.gov.hk/ce/speech/cesp.htm).

Tung, C.H. (2001) Speech by the Chief Executive at the kick-off ceremony of the 'Better World', 10 April 2001, *Speeches and statements of the Chief Executive of the Hong Kong SAR*, Hong Kong (www.info.gov.hk/ce/speech/cesp.htm).

Tung, C.H. (2002) Speech by the Chief Executive at the opening ceremony of Youth Summit, 14 September 2002, *Speeches and statements of the Chief Executive of the Hong Kong SAR*, Hong Kong (www.info.gov.hk/ce/speech/cesp.htm).

White, G. and Goodman, R. (1998) 'Welfare orientalism and the search for an East Asian welfare model', in R. Goodman, G. White and H.J. Kwon (eds) *The East Asian welfare model: Welfare orientalism and the state*, London: Routledge, pp 3-24.

Wilensky, H.L. (1975) *The welfare state and equality*, Berkeley, CA: University of California Press.

Wong, V. (1999) *The political economy of health care development and reforms in Hong Kong*, London: Ashgate.

Wong, V. and Chiu, S. (1998) 'In the eyes of social workers: the social production of marginality of youth in Hong Kong', *Youth Studies Australia*, vol 17, no 1, pp 36-42.

FIVE

Managing welfare in post-colonial Hong Kong

Chak Kwan Chan

Introduction

The Chief Executive of the Hong Kong Special Administrative Region (SAR), Mr Tung Chee Hwa, announced (1997a) several welfare measures that brought new hope for Hong Kong people who had been living under a colonial welfare system for over 150 years. As Tung (1997a, para 12) declared at his first Policy Address, "to promote the well being of the people is the most fundamental task of a responsible government". In response to the housing problem, the new regime had three commitments: "to build at least 85,000 flats a year in the public and private sectors; to achieve a home ownership rate of 70% in 10 years; and to reduce the average waiting time for public rental housing to three years" (Tung, 1997a, para 52). Concerning the financial needs of older people, he increased the Comprehensive Social Security Assistance (CSSA) scheme monthly payment for older claimants by HK$380. Regarding education, he planned to change all primary schools from half-day to whole-day schooling, and also introduced a non-means-tested loan scheme to benefit 50,000 full-time tertiary students. However, the Hong Kong government suddenly changed these policies following the outbreak of the East Asian economic crisis. In response to rising social needs caused by Hong Kong's economic downturn, the Hong Kong SAR even cut public expenditure, withdrawing its housing commitments, and reduced the level of social security benefits. Against this background, this chapter analyses the underlying causes, patterns and basis of Hong Kong's welfare management.

Socioeconomic pressures on welfare provision

Socioeconomic changes have put tremendous pressures on the Hong Kong SAR. In the field of housing there are a large number of "less fortunate households in the private sector who have pressing housing needs" (Fung, 1996). There are 150,000 applicants on the waiting list for public rented housing and the number increases at the rate of 2,000 per month. The average waiting time for an application, however, can be as long as seven years. In addition, 620,000 people in temporary housing and squatter areas are seeking permanent public housing (*Eastern Express*, 21 May 1996). Thus, many households have long been living in overcrowded and poor housing.

At the same time soaring property prices have weakened the affordability of private housing for ordinary households. Between 1985 and 1991, the prices tripled. The housing expenditure of one-person households and four-person households increased by 122.6% and 84.7% respectively between 1989/90 and 1994/95 (Wong and Choi, 1996).

With regard to population ageing, between 1991 and 2001, the number of people aged 65 or above increased by 55%, from 482,040 to 747,052 (11% of the total population) (CSD, 2001). However, only one third of the labour force is protected by some kind of retirement scheme (Patten, 1992). As a result, some older people have to live on means-tested social security benefits, which are too low to give them a decent living (MacPherson, 1994; Hong Kong Polytechnic University, 1995; MacPherson and Chan, 1996).

With regard to health services, the government has to face various pressures such as higher public expectations of the quality of medical care, rising medical costs and the rapid increase in medical consumption of an ageing population. For example, public expenditure on healthcare tripled between 1987/88 and 1992/93, representing an increase per capita from HK$883 to HK$2,529 (Hong Kong Government, 1993). This increase has had little impact on the improvement of health services. In fact, the system is overloaded. Many hospitals are often lined with camp beds and there are long waiting times at specialist outpatient clinics and for hospital admission or surgery (Hong Kong Government, 1993).

The Hong Kong SAR's economy was badly hit by the Asian economic crisis in 1998 (CSD, 1998b; Tung, 1998). Hong Kong's GDP for the third quarter of 1998 fell by 5.2% in real terms compared with the previous year (CSD, 1998c). As a consequence, the unemployment rate has risen sharply: from July to September 1998 the unemployment rate was 5% (174,900 persons) while the underemployed rate was 2.6% (86,400 persons). Also, labour earnings in wholesale, retail and import/export trades and financing, insurance, real estate and business between the first quarter of 1997 and the first quarter of 1998 fell by 4.2% and 2.2% respectively (CSD, 1998a). A survey showed that about 20% of workers in the retail trade have been forced to accept salary reductions of between 10% and 40% (*Ming Pao*, 3 August 1998). The Financial Secretary (Tsang, 2001, p 1) admitted that Hong Kong has experienced "some extraordinary ebbs and flows of the economy tide", "buffeted by a series of unprecedented shockwaves that threatened our very economic survival". Since then things have worsened, the economy was hit by the outbreak of SARS (Severe Acute Respiratory Syndrome) and the unemployment rate in August 2003 was 8.6% (309,000 persons) (CSD, 2003). In the past, Hong Kong's welfare development was the result of economic growth. Now, the government needs to tackle the welfare needs of the public in an adverse economic environment.

Welfare management: from intervention to contraction

In response to these pressing social needs, the government at first tried to play a more active role in welfare provision, particularly in housing. However, it suddenly shifted its policies after the decline of the property market and the increasing pressure on public finance.

Welfare to develop the economy

While facing the public's demands for more social welfare, the Hong Kong government firmly upholds the principle that social welfare should facilitate economic development. Tung (2003b) announced that the direction of his economic policy was to build up Hong Kong as "a highly developed knowledge-based society". Thus education is the government's "top priority" (Tung, 1998). In fact, his first Policy Address stressed that the purpose of his administration was to ensure "the private sector has an open market and a well developed skills base which it can use to build on its head start in the field of the hardware of information technology infrastructure" (Tung, 1997a). Accordingly, the government's expenditure on education from 1996/97 to 2001/02 increased by 46% (Tung, 2001). The government also aims to increase the number of senior secondary school students receiving higher education from 30% to 60% within 10 years.

The relationship between social welfare and the economy is further revealed by the introduction of the Mandatory Provident Fund (MPF) on 1 December 2000. Against the financial needs of retired workers, many labour organisations and the directly elected members of the Legislative Council (Legco) demanded that the government set up an Old Age Pension Scheme to provide financial support for all older people. However, the government, together with the Legco members coming from the business community, rejected the public's demands and introduced the MPF, which was supported by only 7% of respondents (Legislative Council [Legco] Paper No.CB(1) 1265/96-97). The MPF was severely criticised by democrats and unionists for failing to provide financial protection for a large number of citizens such as older workers, low-income earners, housewives and people with disabilities.

However, the implementation of the MPF will boost the activities of the financial sector. As the largest venture capital market in Asia, Hong Kong manages 32% of the total capital pool of the region. The assets from provident funds are easily channelled to support local economic growth, especially to the long term pension business (Ruyter, 1998; Global Economic Forum, 2000; Wong, 2000). The *Hang Seng Economic Monthly* (2000) estimated that the asset size of the MPF funds would exceed HK$10 billion in the first year, and grow to HK$70 billion and HK$170 billion by the end of the fifth and 10th years respectively. The MPF is "a boon not only for the savings industry in Hong Kong but also for the local financial services industry" and for enhancing market stability in Hong Kong in the long term (Global Economic Forum, 2000; Adams, 2001). Obviously, the economic objectives of the MPF are more important than its welfare objectives. Labour welfare not only becomes a means to develop Hong Kong's financial market, it also helps socialise the whole working population to investment activities.

Intervention for stability and withdrawal for market activities

Turning to the social policy domain of housing, Hong Kong's housing policy reveals that the government's primary aim is to protect the business community and not to tackle the housing needs of the public. The Hong Kong SAR followed its colonial counterpart in creating a 'secondary property market'. The expansion of the Home Ownership Scheme (HOS) for the lower middle class and the building of Sandwich Class Housing (SCH) for the middle-class were two typical examples. The 'secondary property market' had two functions: providing cheap housing for some income groups and financing the housing costs of the working class. Because of sky-high housing prices since the mid-1980s, many lower-middle and even middle-class families are unable to purchase flats on the open market. The government, through the Housing Authority (HA) and Housing Society (HS), built and sold flats to eligible applicants at prices that not only covered the building costs but also obtained profits with which to subsidise public rental flats. In 1995, for example, the HA got about HK$15 billion from the sale of HOS flats in contrast to HK$8.9 billion from rental flats and HK$4.9 billion from commercial premises. After 1997, the SAR continued this policy by increasing HOS housing. The HA was accused by housing activists of building more flats for sale rather than reducing the waiting time of public rental housing. By selling more HOS flats, the government was able to meet the housing needs of the middle class without changing its low taxation policy.

Although the Hong Kong government constantly reiterates its commitment to the market economy and consistently promotes its free market image, public and private housing has been heavily subsidised. The purchasing power of the lower middle and middle classes with regard to private property was enhanced by various types of government loans and grants. Several initiatives were taken by the government to help lower middle and middle-class households to buy property, including the Home Purchase Loan Scheme (HPLS), SCH programme, and Home Starter Loan Scheme (HSLS). As *Finance Asia* (2001) points out: "To some, Hong Kong is the ultimate example of the free market economy, while to others it is just a myth which hides the basic truth that Hong Kong is as open to government intervention as anywhere else".

The HPLS was operated by the HA, which provided either a low-interest loan of HK$600,000 or a monthly subsidy of HK$5,100 for households with a monthly income below HK$30,000 so that they could buy private flats. As for the SCH, it included a main scheme and a loan scheme. According to the main scheme, the Housing Society was responsible for building flats for sale at discounted prices to households with incomes between HK$30,001 and HK$60,000. Under the Sandwich Class Housing Loan Scheme (SCHLS), the government provided a low-interest loan of HK$550,000 or 25% of the flat price for eligible families purchasing private housing. The HSLS provided a low-interest loan of up to $600,000 or 30% of the purchase price of property for households with a monthly income between HK$30,001 and HK$70,000. The government estimated that applicants of HSLS would take up 17% of the annual 35,000 new flats from the private sector (Finance Committee of the Legislative Council, 1998).

The above measures clearly show that the government is eager to sustain the private market as the key housing provider even though "home ownership in the private sector" was "beyond the reach of many families", and even though many young managerial and professional couples lacked the resources to purchase reasonable accommodation on the open market (Hong Kong Government, 1998, p 20). Obviously, the main beneficiaries of the government's interventions, instead of being the very poor who are living in extremely overcrowded and low-quality housing, were middle-class households, bankers and property developers. It is also evident that the Hong Kong government, instead of refraining from involvement in economic affairs, plays an active role in strengthening the operation of the private market. Thus the key issues of social policy in Hong Kong concern the strategies adopted and the forces behind them as well as the social and economic consequences of the government's interventions.

The government's determination to safeguard the property market was further reflected in its housing measures following the East Asian financial crisis. In response to the decline of property prices (for example, small and medium residential properties fell in value by 40% between October 1997 and June 1998), the government doubled the quota of HSLSs from 6,000 to 12,000 and increased the quota of HPLSs from 4,500 to 10,000. Also, the HSLS was extended to 660,000 families living in public rented flats. All land sales by auction and public tender were suspended between 22 June 1998 and 31 March 1999. After these measures the property prices increased by more than 15% (*Ming Pao*, 17 November 1998). By providing financial assistance for home buyers, the Hong Kong government subsidises the operation of the free market.

To further sustain housing prices, the Hong Kong SAR withdrew its commitment to the provision of 85,000 flats a year. In response to property developers' complaints about the negative effect of subsidised public housing on the private market, the government also suspended the sale of HOS and HS flats. The Hong Kong General Chamber of Commerce (2001) pointed out that "the government's decisions are in line with the policy recommendations the Chamber has been making in various submissions to the SAR Administration over recent months". Later the Hong Kong SAR terminated the HOS, which had successfully provided housing for lower-income families for more than 20 years. It was explained that the HOS had already completed its historical task and that it was an appropriate time to end it. The above measures will reduce total public housing provision by 17% within five years. This also implies that the government is not likely to fulfil its promise made in 1997 to reduce the waiting time for public housing to three years. The Hong Kong government's actions were criticised as "an unholy alliance" with property developers and banks to keep the property prices as high as possible (Hong Kong Democratic Foundation, 1996). The Chief Executive of the Hong Kong People's Council on Public Housing also said that "the government only looks at the developers' point of view when drafting policies" (*South China Morning Post*, 26 August 1998). The Chief Executive and the Financial Secretary defended their decisions, claiming that the property market is in "Hong Kong's long term interest" (*Daily Information Bulletin*, 22-23 June 1998). As Tung (2003a, p 10) explained: "A stable property market is one of the important elements in revitalising Hong Kong's economy. At this stage, to restore interest in investment and consumption requires the restoration of confidence in property ownership".

The shift in government housing policy reflected the needs of public finance. The previous colonial low taxation system was partly supported by revenues from land sales. But the decrease in the property market caused "the drop in revenue from land sales and related sources" (Tung, 2003a, p 16). As a consequence, the fiscal deficit hit a record high of more than HK$70 billion, about 5% of Hong Kong's GDP. This violated the principle of a balanced budget stated in the Basic Law, which was also pursued by the old colonial regime. Thus, resolving the fiscal deficit became the government's top priority (Tung, 2003a, p 18). Its latest objective is to boost the property market rather than to meet the housing needs of the public. In Tung's words:

> We will make full use of this opportunity to reduce the size of government, redefining its responsibilities, reducing unnecessary intervention, streamlining and reorganising work procedures and departmental structures. We will also carefully review our social welfare policies, reprioritise the provision of public services and give full play to market forces. In short, our moves to tackle the deficit problem will expedite the return to a small, lean government, which is more energetic, more sharply focussed on its priorities, more efficient and better able to make optimum use of resources. (2003a, p 18)

The Hong Kong government's welfare commitments are constrained by its principles of low taxation and a free economy. It will play an active role in social welfare only when such provision will not threaten the capital accumulation of the business community.

The renewal of colonial welfare principles

Seeing the decline in property prices and also the seriousness of the fiscal deficits, the government renewed its commitments to the colonial economic principles. First, promoting market forces is considered the most effective strategy to restructure the economy. As the Financial Secretary (Leung, 2003, para 24) states: "We believe that a free market will lead to optimal distribution of resources, promote economic growth and create employment opportunities". Thus, "small government, big market" is definitely the way to go (Leung, 2003). The government's top priority is therefore to create an infrastructure facilitating economic growth, rather than one to remove the wealth gap (Tsang, 2001). Second, public expenditure should be reduced to 20% of Hong Kong's GDP or less. In this way "the public sector will not become a burden on the community" and sufficient room can be left for private activities (Leung, 2003, para 25). Third, a balanced budget should be achieved so that the growth of public expenditure "does not outstrip GDP growth over time" (Tsang, 2001, para 75). Fourth, fiscal reserves are considered to be essential to Hong Kong's financial stability and these should be equal to 12 months of government expenditure.

The above measures show that the Hong Kong SAR has changed its welfare role and, as argued in Chapter Four, has adopted the British colonial social policy in response to dissatisfaction from property developers and from people suffering negative equity as a result of falling housing prices. Welfare contraction and market expansion have become the Hong Kong SAR's new guiding welfare philosophy.

Promoting the work ethic and limiting welfare needs

The rapidly increasing number of unemployed recipients threatens the affordability of the CSSA, which is financed by general revenues. For example, the unemployment rate reached a record high of 8.7% (309,000 persons) in July 2003 following the outbreak of SARS (*Ming Pao*, 18 August 2003). Also, the CSSA has to cope with the increasing number of older and low-income claimants. As a result, the original estimated social security expenditure was insufficient to meet these demands. The Social Welfare Department (SWD) had to approach the government to provide extra resources. Thus the containment of social security expenditure became the primary task of the SWD. Several measures have been implemented to reduce the level of assistance, limit the number of eligible applicants, and enhance the work ethic of recipients.

First, the Hong Kong SAR cut the amount of CSSA payments in 1998 and 2003 respectively. In 1998, the government argued that the level of CSSA assistance was higher than that of low-income earners. To prevent welfare dependency and preserve work incentives, the standard rate for families with three members or more was cut by 20%, and some special grants and supplements for able-bodied adults and children, such as dentures and spectacles, were cancelled. In 2003, the government claimed that the purchasing power of CSSA recipients had been raised by deflation over several years, and it reduced the level of CSSA by 11%; saving as much as HK$19.6 billion a year. In fact, before these cuts in welfare benefits, research had reported that the amount of CSSA was inadequate for claimants to live on (MacPherson, 1994; Liu et al, 1996; Wong and Choi, 1996).

Second, citizenship is used to exclude new arrivals from public welfare. The residency requirement for CSSA applications was changed from one year to seven years in 2003. In this way, a large number of immigrants, especially those from Mainland China, have been excluded from the basic public financial protection. They are also the most likely to be subject to discrimination in the labour market. The extension of the residency requirement implies that welfare rights are only awarded to citizens who make longer-term contributions to Hong Kong's economy.

Third, CSSA unemployed recipients are required to participate in a Support for Self-Reliance Scheme (SSRS) as a condition for receiving assistance. According to this scheme, a job seeker has to apply for at least two jobs per fortnight, develop and update an individual work plan, and write job-seeking diaries as well as attending regular work plan interviews. Further, he or she cannot decline any job offered on account of the mode of work (full-time, part-time or casual jobs), working hours, or wages. Added to this, they have to do voluntary work such as cleaning country parks, gardening, collecting recycled paper, general counter duties and laundry work. Such 'voluntary work' is supposed to help recipients enhance their self-confidence and develop work habits (SWD, 1998). In short, the life of unemployed recipients has been made uncomfortable. They have to earn their benefits by participating in non-paid voluntary jobs and also to demonstrate their willingness to rejoin the labour market.

After implementing the above measures, the SWD boasted about its success in helping CSSA recipients to get jobs. However, it was reported that most CSSA recipients could only get temporary and low-income jobs (Hong Kong Council of Social Services and Hong Kong Oxfam, 1998). This means that there is a high probability that these workers will reapply for government assistance. From 2001 to 2002, the number of low-income CSSA cases increased by 17% (SWD, 2002). Thus the SWD mainly aims to control the CSSA expenditure by forcing recipients temporarily out of the welfare system. Limited work has been done to address the long-term employment needs of disadvantaged groups such as single parents, women and older workers.

In sum, a discouraging social security system matches Hong Kong's market-oriented welfare regime by providing only temporary assistance to poor people.

The use of statutory and voluntary bodies

The voluntary sector and statutory bodies play a crucial role in welfare provision. As early as the 1980s, the Hong Kong government had already created several statutory welfare institutions based on the principles of efficiency and cost-effectiveness. For example, the HA was made a financially autonomous body in April 1988, responsible for building and managing public housing. Recent government policy on terminating the HOS implies that the HA might have to increase the rents of public housing. This is because the HA can no longer sell flats to finance its public rental housing for lower-income groups. Thus, the financial pressures on the HA might create more conflicts between public housing tenants and the government in the future.

Similarly, the management of public and government-subsidised hospitals was taken over by the Hong Kong Hospital Authority in 1990. The Authority considers managerialism as the guiding principle in running health services, and the concept of Continuous Quality Improvement through the vehicle of Quality Assurance has been promoted since 1993 (Hong Kong Hospital Authority, 1994, p 61). Also more private wards and itemised charging were introduced to raise revenue. Owing to the government's budget deficit, the Hospital Authority asked patients to make higher financial contributions to their treatment by introducing new charges. For example, patients now have to pay for prescriptions and those receiving treatment at Emergency and Accident services have to pay HK$100 per attendance.

The voluntary sector plays an important role in social services: in 1996/97, nearly 90% of direct welfare services were provided by 173 subsidised voluntary organisations. In order to control the amount of financial support for voluntary organisations, the SWD introduced a fixed funding formula. Under the new arrangement, the government no longer pays for the actual expenses of voluntary organisations but provides a lump sum instead. This creates big challenges for voluntary organisations and some welfare professionals are worried that the new funding formula will lower service quality. Added to this, the government has set Service Quality Standards to enhance NGOs' 'management responsibility' and to monitor their services (Health and Welfare Bureau, 1998). According to Leung (2000), former Director of the SWD, these measures are aimed at "enhancing accountability, efficiency and cost-effectiveness in public spending".

Contracting public sector services and reducing welfare costs

In the face of the budget deficit, the government plans to cut the civil service by 10% by 2006-07 (Tung, 2003a). This means that the total number of civil servants will be reduced from more than 180,000 to 160,000. Such a large reduction may adversely affect the quality of public services and, in response to such a possible negative impact, the government carried out an Enhanced Productivity Programme to raise the productivity of existing staff. It is estimated that HK$6 billion a year could be saved (Tung, 2001).

In order to minimise the cost of welfare provision the government has increased the involvement of the private sector in the delivery of public services (Tsang, 2001). More and more government departments are encouraged to contract out their services to private companies. Workers in private companies receive lower salaries and have to work for longer hours. For example, a private sector cleaner only receives 45% of the salary of their counterparts in the civil service and 21% have no paid leave (*Ming Pao*, 18 March 2002). Some companies even ask their workers to sign a 'self-employment contract' so that they do not need to pay for their holidays and pensions. This policy is supported by the absence of protection for the working class: no minimum wage policy, the suppression of labour organisations and constraints on collective bargaining and strikes.

In summary, the expansion of social welfare in Hong Kong immediately following the end of British rule was partial, minimal and short-term. The most obvious welfare commitments of the government were in housing with the objectives of boosting home ownership and shortening the waiting time of public housing. However, these policies were built on financially and politically weak foundations: their successful implementation depends on the growth of the economy and the favourable attitudes of the business community. After the Asian economic crisis, these policies threatened the private property market and, in return, reduced the government's revenues from land sales. Consequently, the Hong Kong SAR suddenly changed its policies and put emphases on reviving the property market and balancing the budget. Public expenditure was cut to maintain the low taxation environment.

The basis of welfare management: free market, Chinese familism, and administrative-led government

Free enterprise, Chinese familism and an undemocratic polity are the three fundamental forces that facilitate the Hong Kong SAR's welfare strategies. Hong Kong was created as a free port in 1842 and the laissez-faire economy is said to be the key to its economic success (Patten, 1995). According to the Hong Kong Annual Report, "It is probably the only territory still completely faithful to liberal economic policies of free enterprise and free trade" (Hong Kong Government, 1973, p 12; see also Hong Kong Government, 1995, p 7). It has been rated as the freest economy in the world for eight successive years by the US Heritage Foundation (Hong Kong Government, 2002).

After 1997, the government continued to preserve the image of the freest economy, especially as it was facing strong competition from other East Asian countries. As Tung (2000, p 16) stated, "We remain firmly committed to upholding our system of free enterprise and will adhere steadfastly to the philosophy of small government with prudent fiscal management". The Financial Secretary also stressed that it is vital to maintain the "reputation for fiscal prudence" (Tsang, 1999). Thus the government reduced the Corporate Profits Tax rate from 16.5% to 16% even though Hong Kong's tax rate is very low compared with other East Asian countries. The pursuit of a free economy seems to be a strategy to keep up the confidence of the public in the new regime and to attract foreign investment. Thus Hong Kong's historical burden of laissez-faire, and the coincidence of the free market and economic success, have strongly constrained its fiscal and welfare policies (Chapter Two).

In Hong Kong, as Chiu and Wong have pointed out (Chapter Four), Chinese familism has always been manipulated in line with government social policies. For example, the waiting time for public housing applicants is reduced by three times if one of their household members is aged 60 or over. As a matter of social policy traditional Chinese familism has been preserved to be the dominant welfare ideology. Wong (1995) reported that more than two thirds of his survey respondents disagreed that "the traditional virtue of filial piety is outdated", while the majority of respondents (80.1%) rejected the idea that "nowadays, children have no or little responsibility for the caring of their old age parent". Similarly, Chan (1999) found that more than three fifths of 764 respondents in his survey of public opinion agreed with the statement that "in caring for old people's financial needs, the children should play the primary role". This suggests that filial piety is still upheld by the majority of people and family care is commonly regarded as the most respectable means of caring.

Chinese familism has been further consolidated by the government since 1997. For example, Tung Chee Hwa believes that filial piety is the most effective means of meeting older people's needs (see Chapter Four for more detail). His first policy address emphasised that "caring for the elderly is the responsibility of every family" (Tung, 1997a). Accordingly, tax incentives encouraging the family care of older people were introduced in 1998. For example, the basic allowance for a dependent parent or grandparent was increased by 11.1%, while the additional allowance for taxpayers living with a dependent parent or grandparent was increased by 275%. Children who provide financial support for their parents in private homes can also get a new Salaries Tax deduction of up to HK$60,000 a year (Tsang, 1998).

The implementation of the MPF can be seen as a long-term utilisation of the family's resources. First, because at least 30 years of operation are needed to yield benefits under the MPF, the majority of older people have to continue seeking financial support from their families. Also, a maximum contribution of HK$1,000 is set for employees with a monthly income of more than HK$20,000. Although workers with a monthly income of less than HK$4,000 do not need to pay contributions, they only get a 5% contribution from their employers. Given the low rate of contributions, one expert has concluded that "an MPF might not be the best answer to an ageing population" because workers aged 45 would not have a sufficient retirement income. Clearly, the MPF is not generous and is poorer than many existing retirement schemes (*Hong Kong Economic Journal*, 6 May 1995). Thus the MPF provides only limited financial support for a limited number of older people over a limited period. This implies that the family will continue to be the basic source of financial security for older people.

In short, Chinese familism not only encourages welfare contributions from individuals and the family, but also helps to minimise the state's welfare spending (Chan, 1997).

Success in promoting a market economy and putting the responsibility for welfare on the community depends on a polity's capacity to monopolise the ideologies of civic society and to police the working class. Hong Kong's undemocratic polity serves these purposes. The British administration limited the power of Legco. For example, the government withdrew a bill improving labour welfare even though Legco had already passed it! Government officials have always objected to proposals for raising taxation and increasing welfare expenditure. To rebuff demands for higher CSSA rates, the government even compared the expenditure patterns of CSSA recipients with those of the lowest 5% of households and concluded that people living on benefits had a better standard of living.

The political rights of the public have improved little after the establishment of the Hong Kong SAR. An Election Committee composed of only 800 social and economic elite members elects the Chief Executive, the most powerful figure in Hong Kong. Also, members of the Executive Council, assisting the Chief Executive in making decisions, are only appointed by the Chief Executive (The Consultative Committee for the Basic Law of the Hong Kong SAR of the People's Republic of China, 1990). The appointed members are mainly senior officials, businessmen and professionals. Among the 11 unofficial members of the first Exco of Hong Kong SAR, five were businessmen, two were key figures of public statutory bodies, two were professionals, one was a retired Chief Justice and one an officer of a pro-China labour organisation. This composition suggests that former colonial co-option politics have been adopted by the Hong Kong SAR.

Due to disagreements between the British government and the Chinese government over the composition of the first Legislature of the SAR, the old Legco (many of its members were elected by over two million voters) was dispersed and a Provisional Legislative Council (PLC) was formed with members elected by a small elite. Since members of the PLC were mainly representatives of the business community and pro-China's labour unions as well as members of pro-China political parties, they supported the Chinese government's principles of a free economy and strong administrative government. Later, the PLC became a mechanism for passing legislation in the interests of the bureaucrats and capitalists. For example, the main body of legislation concerning the implementation of the MPF, affecting the long-term benefits of the working population, was passed by the PLC (*Ming Pao*, 25 February 1998). In this way the previous colonial regime's conservative economic ideology has been preserved. Tsang (1997a) emphasised that nothing has changed after the transition, the SAR's economic philosophy is still "minimal government intervention and maximum private sector", and the new government will continue to maintain "a low, simple and predictable tax regime" (see also Tsang, 1997a, 1997b; Tung, 1997a, 1997b, 1997c, 1997d). Tsang (*Daily Information Bureau*, 14 October 1998) declared that in Hong Kong the free market is a law because the SAR has a constitutional duty to develop itself as an international financial centre according to the Basic Law.

In addition, the new Exco and the PLC passed measures to limit freedom of demonstration and to suppress the interests of the working class. According to the amended Public Order Ordinances, the public has to inform the police about the place of demonstrations as well as the number of participants. Very often, the police set up 'demonstration zones' restricting the activities of demonstrators. Also a strong police force has been used to monitor small-scale protects. It is believed that the Hong Kong police always keep a close eye on some activists and use strong force, as many as 10 times the number of demonstrators, to keep demonstrations under control (*Ming Pao*, 6 October 1997). Moreover, seven labour ordinances passed by the old Legco, granting employees more power over collective bargaining, were abolished by the PLC. The former Chief Secretary of the Administration explained that these ordinances would adversely affect "harmonious labour relations" and "Hong Kong's economic competitiveness and attractiveness to overseas investments" (Chan, 1997). The government has also proposed a Construction Labour Importation Scheme allowing employers to hire low-cost workers from China. It was widely believed that the scheme would push down local wages and endanger local workers' livelihoods.

Compared to the Legco during Patten's administration, the current Legco is too weak to check the government's power. The publicly elected members are in a small minority. Among the 60 Legco members, 30 are representative of functional constituencies, 10 are elected by an Election Committee composed of 800 elite members and only one third (20) is directly elected by the general public. The Basic Law constitutionally suppresses the power of public representatives in putting forward bills. Although the members can introduce private bills, only those which are not related to public expenditure, political structure and the operation of the government are allowed. Moreover, written consent from the Chief Executive is required for bills related to government policies (The Consultative Committee for the Basic Law of the Hong Kong SAR of the People's Republic of China, 1990). Added to this, bills introduced by individual members have to get a majority vote from two groups of Legco members: those from functional constituencies and from direct elections, and the Election Committee. Because the members of functional constituencies mainly represent the interests of the business community and professional bodies, it is unlikely that they will support legislation improving the welfare of the working class. Thus the Basic Law has institutionalised the interests of the business community and professional groups, consolidated the principle of 'administrative-led government', and kept the working class under control. As the Chief Executive of the Monetary Authority admitted, Hong Kong's politicians do not have the authority to direct government policies (*Daily Information Bureau*, 20 October 1998). In fact, the Legco is merely a place where public representatives express their opposition to government policies.

Conclusion

Hong Kong's experience reveals that state intervention is essential to the operation of even the 'freest' capitalist economy because the state has to facilitate economic development and secure a stable social and political environment. The importance of the state's activities in the market economy was revealed by the Hong Kong government's intervention in the property and stock and future markets by buying more than HK$160 billion shares. Then, the Hong Kong Monetary Authority announced a 30-point programme in order to tighten up the disciplines in the securities and futures markets (*Daily Information Bureau*, 7 September 1998). The concept of 'positive non-interventionism' was used to justify Hong Kong's approach to the market economy (Chapter Four). The Hong Kong government had already recognised the necessity of state intervention in the 1970s, and the SAR continues with this approach. The true purpose of positive non-interventionism is to safeguard the interests of big business, especially the property market and the banking system. This is because its development affects the stability of the SAR's budget. Thus key issues for Hong Kong's social policy and its welfare regime are not only non-interventionism, but the nature, objectives and strategies of interventions and their impact on class relations and business opportunities. The residual welfare regime is sustained by an undemocratic political economy.

Recent welfare reforms in Hong Kong not only suppress the welfare rights of the working class but also undermine the interests of the middle class. Traditionally, the Hong Kong colonial regime rewarded the middle class with high salaries and co-opted them into key advisory bodies. For example, the salary of Hong Kong university academics is 141% and 109% greater than their counterparts in the UK and US (*The Standard*, 2 May 2003). In addition, they are entitled to occupational benefits such as a pension, medical treatment, housing and children's education allowances. As for senior civil servants, their fringe benefits include a travel allowance and education allowance for their children studying overseas. Moreover, the middle class in Hong Kong only has to pay 15% of its incomes in taxation. Obviously, the middle class is one of the main interested parties in Hong Kong's residual welfare regime. The stability of the Hong Kong colonial regime, to some extent, was due to its education and reward policy that had successfully integrated the middle class into its market-oriented welfare system.

However, the problem of the budget deficit forces the Hong Kong SAR government to reduce public expenditure and enhance the efficiency of welfare workers. These measures directly threaten the benefits of civil servants and welfare professionals. For example, the monthly salary of a contracted accountant was HK$31,500, compared with HK$52,705 for a permanent accountant in the civil service. Also, university lecturers, especially those who are teaching on diploma and associate degree courses, are experiencing job losses or reduced salaries. The SWD's fixed funding policy forces the subsidised welfare organisations to employ young workers on lower salaries. Medical professionals are also employed on fixed-term contracts. The implementation of 'efficiency' and 'accountability' puts a lot of pressures on school teachers, nurses, social workers and doctors, who used to face only inadequate manpower and heavy workloads. Recent government demands for assessments, reporting and paperwork have created a lot of resentment among the welfare professionals. Furthermore, a lot of homeowners accuse the government of causing the decline in housing prices. As a result, more and more middle-class people are openly expressing their dissatisfaction.

The Hong Kong SAR's recent welfare reforms threaten the interests of both the working and the middle class. Unlike its colonial counterpart, which only had to tackle the welfare demands of the former, the Hong Kong SAR has to manage the needs of both. For example, 1,600 welfare recipients and low-income earners held a demonstration opposing reductions in the CSSA (*Ming Pao*, 3 March 2003). As for the middle class, 73 university academics signed a petition criticising the government for cutting higher education expenditure (*Ming Pao*, 9 September 2003). Welfare professionals also held a joint campaign about cuts in health, social security and education. Most importantly, a large demonstration involving more than half a million people was held on 1 July 2003. A survey found that nearly 60% of the demonstrators were middle class (Chan and Chung, 2003). The welfare reforms launched by the SAR show that a residual welfare regime has to have support from the middle class. In other words, the successful implementation of 'big market and small government' by the Hong Kong government depends on how it safeguards the interests of the middle class. That will be a key factor shaping Hong Kong's future welfare. On the other hand, with little political and economic power, the welfare rights of the unemployed, the sick and new immigrants will continue to be neglected by a regime that always claims that "Hong Kong people are ruling Hong Kong" (Tung, 1997a, para 145).

References

Adams, D. (2001) 'Mandatory Provident Fund system given go-ahead', *The global employer: Global labour, employment, and employee benefits bulletin*, Baker and Mckenzie (www.shrmglobal.org/publications/baker/1098glob/home/htm).

Chan, C.K. (1997) 'The socio-political basis of Hong Kong's residual welfare system – bureaucratic-capitalist state and Chinese familism', *The Journal of Applied Social Sciences*, vol 22, no 1, pp 3-17.

Chan, F.O.S. (1997) Speech by the Chief Secretary for Administration in moving the Second Reading of the Legislative Provisions (Suspension of Operation) Bill 1997 at the Provisional Legislative Council, 9 July.

Chan T.M. and Chung, T.Y. (2003) 'Demonstrators opposed article 23 and Tung Chee Hwa', *Ming Pao*, 7 July.

CSD (1998a) *Payroll and wage statistics for first quarter 1998*, Press release, 17 July.

CSD (1998b) *Unemployment and underemployment statistics for March-May 1998 and April-June 1998*, Press release, 20 July.

CSD (1998c) *Estimates of gross domestic product for second quarter of 1998*, Press release, 20 July.

CSD (2001) *Statistical table on population by age by sex* (www.info.gov.hk/censtatd/eng/hkstat/fas/pop/by_age_sex.htm).

CSD (2003) *Unemployment and underemployment statistics for June-August 2003*, Press release, 18 September.

Finance Asia (2001) *Property guru tells HK government to stay out of property market* (www.financeasia.com/articles/96517310-9557-11D5-81D00090277E174B.cfm).

Finance Committee of the Legislative Council (1998) *Loan Fund*, 9 January, Hong Kong: Hong Kong SAR Legislative Council.

Fung, T. (1996) 'The housing challenge ahead: Hong Kong', *Housing for millions the challenge ahead,* Hong Kong conference, 20-23 May.

Global Economic Forum (2000) *Hong Kong: Coping with ageing: The implications of the MPF* (www.morganstanley.com/GEFdata/digests/20000228-mon.html).

Health and Welfare Bureau (1998) *Policy programmes* (www.info.gov.hk/hwb/english/policy/21cent.htm).

Hong Kong Council of Social Services and Hong Kong Oxfam (1998) *A study on recipients leaving and re-applying CSSA*, Hong Kong: Hong Kong Council of Social Services and Hong Kong Oxfam.

Hong Kong Democratic Foundation (1996) *'Land tax' and high land prices in Hong Kong* (www.hkdf.org/papers/9601landtax.htm).

Hong Kong General Chamber of Commerce (2001) *Housing measures to promote confidence, stability,* Press release (www.chamber.org.hk/info/press_release/2001/01090301.asp).

Hong Kong Government (1973) *Hong Kong: Report for the year 1972*, Hong Kong: Hong Kong Government Printer.

Hong Kong Government (1993) *Towards better health*, Hong Kong: Hong Kong Government Printer.

Hong Kong Government (1995) *Safeguarding rational allocation of public housing resources: Consultation document*, Hong Kong: Hong Kong Government Printer.

Hong Kong Government (1998) *Homes for Hong Kong: Hong Kong people into the 21st century: A White Paper on long term housing strategy in Hong Kong*, Hong Kong: Hong Kong Government Printer.

Hong Kong Government (2002) *The world's freest economy* (www.info.gov.hk/info/Hkbus/eecon.htm).

Hong Kong Hospital Authority (1994) *Hong Kong Hospital Authority business plan 1994-1995,* Hong Kong: Public Affairs Division of Hospital Authority.

Hong Kong Polytechnic University (1995) *A study of CSSA special grants users*, Department of Applied Social Studies, Hong Kong: Hong Kong Polytechnic University (in Chinese).

Legislative Council Paper No.CB(1) 1265/96-97 – *Subcommittee on Mandatory Provident Fund System*, Hong Kong: Hong Kong SAR Legislative Council.

Leung, A. (2003) *The 2003-2004 Budget by the Financial Secretary to the Legislative Council on 5 March 2003*, Hong Kong: Hong Kong Government Printer.

Leung, K.P. (2000) *Social welfare subvention reform (SWD 1/128/73C V)*, 10 February, Hong Kong: Hong Kong SAR Social Welfare Department.

Liu, K.K., Yue, S.J. and Lee, M.Y. (1996) *A research on the determinants for the social assistance scale in Hong Kong and selected countries*, Hong Kong: Research and Library Services Division, Hong Kong Legislative Council Secretariat.

MacPherson, S. (1994) *A measure of dignity: Report on the adequacy of public assistance rates in Hong Kong*, Hong Kong: Department of Public and Social Administration, the City Polytechnic of Hong Kong.

MacPherson, S. and Chan, C.K. (1996) *Preliminary report on the lifestyles of low-income households in Sham Shui Po*, Hong Kong: Department of Public and Social Administration, City University of Hong Kong.

Patten, C. (1992) *Policy Address by the Governor to the Legislative Council*, 7 October, Hong Kong: Hong Kong Government Printer.

Patten, C. (1995) *Policy Address by the Governor to the Legislative Council*, 11 October, Hong Kong: Hong Kong Government Printer.

Ruyter, T. (1998) 'Mandatory options: comparing the provident fund pension model with defined contribution alternatives', *Asia Pensions*, summer, Asset International.

SWD (Social Welfare Department) (1998) *Support for self-reliance: Report on review of the Comprehensive Social Security Assistance Scheme*, Hong Kong: Hong Kong Government Printer.

SWD (2002) *Figures on social security* (www.info.gov.hk/swd/heml_eng/ser_sec/main.html).

The Consultative Committee for the Basic Law of the Hong Kong SAR of the People's Republic of China (1990) *The Basic Law of the Hong Kong SAR of the People's Republic of China*.

Tsang, Y.K. (1997a) *Hong Kong: Looking towards the future*, Speech by the Financial Secretary at a dinner hosted by the Committee for Economic Development in Australia (CEDA), Melbourne, Australia, 28 August.

Tsang, Y.K. (1997b) Speech at the 11th International Investment Funds Conference, 27 October.

Tsang, Y.K. (1998) *The 1998-99 Budget by the Financial Secretary to the Legislative Council*, 18 February, Hong Kong: Hong Kong Government Printer.

Tsang, Y.K. (1999) *The 1999-2000 Budget by the Financial Secretary to the Legislative Council*, 3 March, Hong Kong: Hong Kong Government Printer.

Tsang, Y.K. (2001) *The 2001-02 Budget by the Financial Secretary to the Legislative Council*, 7 March, Hong Kong: Hong Kong Government Printer.

Tung, C.H. (1997a) *Policy Address by the Chief Executive to the Provisional Legislative Council*, 8 October, Hong Kong: Hong Kong Government Printer.

Tung, C.H. (1997b) Speech at the Hong Kong General Chamber of Commerce Luncheon, 9 October.

Tung, C.H. (1997c) Speech at the Official Opening Dinner of 1997 East Asia Economic Summit, World Economic Forum, 13 October.

Tung, C.H. (1997d) Speech at the APEC CEO Summit, Vancouver, 23 November.

Tung, C.H. (1998) *Policy Address by the Chief Executive to the Legislative Council*, 7 October, Hong Kong: Hong Kong Government Printer.

Tung, C.H. (2000) *Policy Address by the Chief Executive to the Legislative Council*, 11 October, Hong Kong: Hong Kong Government Printer.

Tung, C.H. (2001) *Policy Address by the Chief Executive to the Legislative Council*, 10 October, Hong Kong: Hong Kong Government Printer.

Tung, C.H. (2003a) *Policy Address by the Chief Executive to the Legislative Council*, 8 January, Hong Kong: Hong Kong Government Printer.

Tung, C.H. (2003b) Speech by the Chief Executive at the reception of the 6th anniversary of the establishment of the Hong Kong SAR, 1 July.

Wong, C.K. (1995) 'Welfare attitudes: one way of explaining the laggard welfare state phenomenon', in S.K. Lau, K.M. Lee, P.S. Wong and S.L. Wong (eds) *Indicators of social development: Hong Kong 1993*, Hong Kong: Chinese University Press, pp 205-27.

Wong, H. and Choi, W.S. (1996) *The study of the expenditure patterns of low-expenditure households in Hong Kong: A mid-term report*, Hong Kong: Hong Kong Council of Social Service and Oxfam.

Wong. I. (2000) 'Hong Kong insurance market — what the future holds', *Newsletter*, October, The Insurance Institute of Hong Kong.

SIX

The welfare regime in Japan

Makoto Kono

Introduction

Japanese welfare has increasingly attracted the interest of western scholars, yet they "have approached this topic mainly in brief overview chapters, or as an example within some broader interpretation of post-war public policy" (Campbell, 1992, p 22). In general, as Goodman and Peng (1996, p 193) suggest, Japan is regarded as "a variety of pre-existing social welfare models conceptualised from a western framework" and is sometimes seen as "an 'exception' to the rule rather than as a new pattern".

The relatively inferior standard of Japanese welfare services has often been described in recent studies of welfare states; yet many of them have overlooked some of the distinctive aspects of Japanese welfare development. This chapter will highlight the special features of Japanese welfare production and its background factors, such as rapid economic development and the traditional values deeply embedded in its social system. Beginning with an examination of the welfare regime in Japan, it will show that industrialisation, as a causal factor behind Japanese welfare development, has different implications than those assumed by conventional industrialisation theory. It will also explore the relationship between culture and political ideology, particularly the political utilisation of culture.

Japanese-type welfare society

Emergence of the 'Japanese-type welfare society'

In terms of economic development, Japan achieved tremendous success over the post-war period and became the country with the second largest Gross National Product (GNP) in the world. In striking contrast to its economic eminence, Japan's achievements in the field of welfare development are poor. Comparative studies of the welfare state normally describe Japan's status as 'residual'. For example, Hill (1996) regards it as "a low performing welfare state". Table 6.1 substantiates this. Apart from its residual nature, the Japanese welfare system may be characterised by:

1. active informal welfare practices;
2. high economic performance substituting for state welfare;
3. a status-segregated, social insurance system;
4. occupational welfare for 'core' workers;
5. low spending on personal social services (Bryson, 1992; Esping-Andersen, 1996a, 1996b, 1997; Goodman and Peng, 1996; Hill, 1996; Jacobs, 1998).

These characteristics of the Japanese welfare system were formulated in accordance with the concept of the 'Japanese-type welfare society' in the first half of the 1970s.

Urban migration and a large shift in the industrial structure, beginning in the mid-1950s, increased the need for welfare. At the same time these factors undermined the bases of active informal welfare practices, such as the extended family and local community systems (Harada, 1988; Abe et al, 1990). However, rapid economic development also increased national income, which provided room for expanding state welfare services. As the industrial theory of welfare state development assumes (see later), basic Japanese welfare systems were formulated during the 1950s and the 1960s as the demand for welfare and the supply capacity both increased. The social security and the healthcare insurance systems were widened to accept those who had been previously excluded, such as the self-employed workers in small companies and their families, culminating in universal coverage by

Table 6.1: Social security expenditure as a percentage of GDP in selected countries

	Healthcare		Pensions		Social services and other		Total	
Japan (2004)	5.5	(32.4)	9.0	(52.9)	2.5	(14.7)	17.0	(100.0)
Japan (1998)	5.7	(37.7)	7.3	(48.3)	2.1	(13.9)	15.1	(100.0)
USA (1998)	6.0	(40.0)	6.8	(45.3)	2.1	(14.0)	15.0	(100.0)
UK (1998)	5.6	(22.1)	11.0	(43.5)	8.8	(34.8)	25.3	(100.0)
Germany (1998)	7.8	(26.6)	12.3	(42.0)	9.2	(31.4)	29.3	(100.0)
France (1998)	7.3	(24.7)	12.7	(43.1)	9.6	(32.5)	29.5	(100.0)
Sweden (1998)	6.6	(19.4)	10.2	(29.9)	17.3	(50.7)	34.1	(100.0)

Source: MHLW (2004b)

the beginning of the 1960s. Until then, the provision for personal social services was limited to the poor (starting in 1946), children (1947), and people with physical disabilities (1949). Later on, the scope was extended to people with learning disabilities (1960), older people (1963), widows and single-parent families (1964). The government still recognised that there was a positive relationship between the economy and welfare, namely that increasing the supply of public welfare would facilitate economic growth.[1] Along the lines of the "handmaiden model" of social welfare (Titmuss, 1974), welfare policy in Japan was given a role as an adjunct to the economy.

High economic growth had dual effects: it improved people's living standards but it also created social problems, including environmental disruption and increased disparity in incomes and working conditions. By the beginning of the 1970s, the public demand for improvements in welfare services had increased dramatically. This stimulated the mass media and activated left-wing political parties, local governments and labour organisations. They became more critical about the production-first policies and demanded an improvement in state welfare. Welfare reforms inevitably became an issue for conservative rulers as they attempted to avoid a political crisis. Moreover, it was clear that Japan lagged far behind western countries in state welfare expenditure. This backwardness may also have created a sense of international inferiority in government circles, which led the authorities to increase welfare spending (Kato, 1991; Watanabe, 1991; Gould, 1993; Shinkawa, 1993; Goodman et al, 1997, 1998).

Some authors (for example, Shinkawa, 1993) suggest another factor lay behind this policy change: the rapidly developing Japanese capitalist system was likely to reach a stage where structural adjustment was required in its socioeconomic domain. So the political right, including conservative politicians, business leaders and the economic bureaucracy, compromised welfare expansion in order to maintain the capitalist system. This change was not opposed to their ideological beliefs and political interests, but can be seen as a form of 'risk management' in the development of the capitalist system (Kato, 1991; Shinkawa, 1993). The Japanese government finally decided to improve its major welfare systems[2] and announced that 1973 was the 'First Year of the Welfare Era'. However, this policy change was soon repealed.

The Japanese economy was hit by the world oil crisis in 1973 and soon after by serious stagflation. Ironically, 1973 became the final year of the period of high economic growth and the beginning of the 'low economic growth era'. These changes in economic circumstances "convinced the Japanese authorities that the welfare state had become a disadvantage to the competitiveness of other advanced capitalist countries" (Gould, 1993, p 6), and led them to return to the residual approach. Their objectives shifted to the promotion of informal and private welfare, namely the establishment of the Japanese-type welfare society. This notion was a version of the New Right's strategy for rolling back the development of a western style welfare state (Shinkawa, 1997; Goodman et al, 1998). It was officially adopted as the guiding principle of welfare policies in the 'New Economic and Social Seven Year Plan':

> [The] new welfare society that Japan should aim at will be a 'Japanese type welfare society' in which – while founded on the self-help efforts of individuals and the solidarity of families and neighbourhood communities that the Japanese possess – an efficient government guarantees appropriate public welfare according to priorities. (EPA, 1979, p 11)

The key characteristics of the Japanese-type welfare society: the roles of informal welfare and enterprise welfare

On the basis of the concept of the Japanese-type welfare society, residual public welfare provision was justified again and the standards of some welfare services were downgraded – for example, the age limit for receiving pension benefits was raised and benefit levels were cut. The free healthcare system for older people was abolished, whereas healthcare insurance contributions and personal social service fees were increased.

The concept of the Japanese-type welfare society takes for granted that the process of Japanese modernisation is different from those found in western-societies. It advocates that welfare policies should not follow a western-style welfare model but instead emphasises self-help, mutual aid, market welfare activities and enterprise welfare. The Japanese-type welfare society suppresses any increase of state welfare by enhancing the roles of other sectors. This kind of residual approach to welfare reform is found in some right-wing welfare reforms in other countries. However, the distinctive feature of this Japanese version of the New Right strategy is its endeavour to highlight the country's own culture and traditions. The Japanese welfare regime can be characterised in part as a familist welfare approach. Although its preconditions have declined in relation to the modernisation of society, the significance of informal welfare has been re-emphasised in the political domain, and the major role borne by the family is now recognised as orthodoxy.

The growth of the nuclear family contributed to rapid economic development in Japan, but it was expected to weaken social cohesion. Although public welfare services complementing family functions were introduced, mainly in order to promote further economic development, the family was understood as an 'objective' of social support until the early 1970s. However, after this change of policy, the family would be seen as a 'cooperator' to restrain the increase of public expenditure, and finally it would be regarded as the main source of welfare provision (Harada, 1988). For example, contemporary community care policy defines domiciliary services as those supporting family carers rather than caring for older people directly, based on the assumption that a majority of older people live with their children and are cared for informally (Kono, 2003).

In the Japanese-type welfare society, traditional values, such as the obligation to care for older relatives, are expected to be unchanged in the future. As such, state welfare services play only a subsidiary role to the informal welfare practices (Hori, 1981; Harada, 1988; Abe et al, 1990; Campbell, 1992; Oda, 1992; Okuma, 1993; Shinkawa, 1993, 1997). In addition, enterprise welfare has been accentuated in the Japanese welfare regime.[3] Let us now examine the implications of enterprise welfare and its role.

The Japanese style of enterprise management emphasises solidarity among workers, between workers and enterprises, and between trade unions and enterprises. It also stimulates keen competition among workers. These apparently contradictory principles of management are harmonised through at least six different mechanisms (Baba, 1991; Saito, 1991; Wakamori, 1991; Watanabe, 1991; Hirao, 1993; Stockman et al, 1995). First, ownership and management are thoroughly separated and an enterprise is not recognised as a possession of stockholders but as a community of workers. Second, the structure of wages and promotion is connected from the bottom to the top of the workforce, and there is only a small gap between white-collar and blue-collar workers. Third, workers obtain skills by on-the-job training and frequent redeployment over a period of lifetime employment. Fourth, employees' lifestyles are closely linked to their involvement in enterprises through lifetime employment and the seniority rule of promotion. Industrial relations transcend general relationships between employers and employees, and are tightly bound by the concept of loyalty/group cohesiveness. Fifth, under these circumstances, male workers are subjected to the super-exploitative demands of their enterprises. Japanese women are forced to support the male workforce and make up for male absence from the domestic sphere. Moreover, Japanese women are regarded as cheap, low-skilled and obedient labour and are utilised for enterprise development. Sixth, these mechanisms of the Japanese-style management system can only work when a trade union has negligible power and lacks a strong coalition with other unions at a national level. Therefore, a precondition of this model is enterprise unionism and a low level of organised labour.

Enterprise welfare (for example, earnings-related pensions, individual retirement accounts and housing services) plays a significant role in enterprise management. Enterprise welfare supports workers who devote themselves to their work, and their life chances are affected largely by the standard of enterprise welfare. It is not given as a right to workers but functions to increase their productivity (Saito, 1991; Wakamori, 1991). Since these services are a kind of reward system, the level of enterprise welfare varies. Higher-standard services are provided to those who occupy relatively higher positions. Moreover, enterprise welfare schemes are not even in their coverage, and the level of enterprise welfare is closely linked to the size of enterprise and worker's employment status (that is, full-time or part-time). Only those who are in large enterprises (and who are normally male and full-time) enjoy high enterprise welfare services (Yamada, 1991; Gould, 1993; Esping-Andersen, 1997; Shinkawa, 1997). Gould points out, for example, that:

> Members of the Japanese labour aristocracy were not decommodified by high welfare benefits but remained highly dependent on their employers. The rest of the labour force was entitled to benefits and services ranging from the inferior to the non existent. (1993, p 236)

Thus, Japanese companies use enterprise welfare as a managerial device. At the same time, it is a significant element of the Japanese welfare system as a whole. Enterprise welfare has provided substantial services to company workers instead of residual public welfare. Miyamoto (1997) suggests that enterprise welfare services, together with informal welfare practices, have taken the place of residual state welfare. Accordingly, the government could resist an expansion of state welfare, as occurred in the 1970s. The government reinforced enterprise welfare programmes through tax deductions and state subsidies in order to prevent state welfare development.

Shinkawa (1997) argues that some parts of the state welfare system in Japan were originally designed to cover those who could not receive enterprise welfare. Since the state played a subsidiary role to enterprise welfare, there were large gaps between different groups in receipt of public welfare. For example, the systems of social security and health insurance were fragmented and their benefit levels varied according to the working status of the beneficiary.

Figure 6.1 shows the structure of the national pension scheme in Japan. Although pensions for both self-employed and salaried workers provide additional benefits to their members, there are large gaps in their coverage. Japanese health insurance programmes have a similar structure to the pension schemes. They consist of Employee Health Insurance (EHI) and National Health Insurance (NHI). The EHI primarily covers company and factory workers and their families, and the NHI covers persons outside the EHI, such as farmers, retired employees below the age of 75 and workers in small companies (those with less than five employees). The benefit levels of the NHI and the EHI were originally different, with the latter providing the higher benefits. Although this disparity was removed in 2003, the EHI programme provides additional benefits to its members. According to a survey of the joint committee of health insurance societies, in 2002 approximately 90% of the EHI societies (more than 1,500 out of 1,700 societies) provided such additional benefits.

Full-time workers in large enterprises receive the highest benefits because state services are supplemented by additional benefits from their enterprises (Ishida, 1992). Thus there is little reason for them to press for improvements in the benefits of others. This section of the labour force sometimes objected to the improvement of state welfare services because it would necessitate tax increases (Gould, 1993; Shinkawa, 1997) and, therefore, help to keep state welfare services at a residual level.

Globally, right-wing welfare reforms promote either 'the residual model' of welfare or a more sophisticated welfare–market relationship based on the 'industrial achievement performance model', which assumes that social needs are met on the basis of merit, work performance and productivity (Titmuss, 1974). In other words, welfare is seen as supporting the economy and is controlled in accordance with market requirements (Titmuss, 1974; Goodman et al, 1997, 1998; Kwon, 1999). Jessop (1994) counterposes the Schumpeterian Workfare State (SWS) with the Keynesian Welfare State. One of the distinctive objectives of the SWS is to promote innovation to strengthen the competitiveness of the national economy via supply-side interventions. Thus, the SWS not only restrains social policy but also restructures

Figure 6.1: Structure of the pension scheme

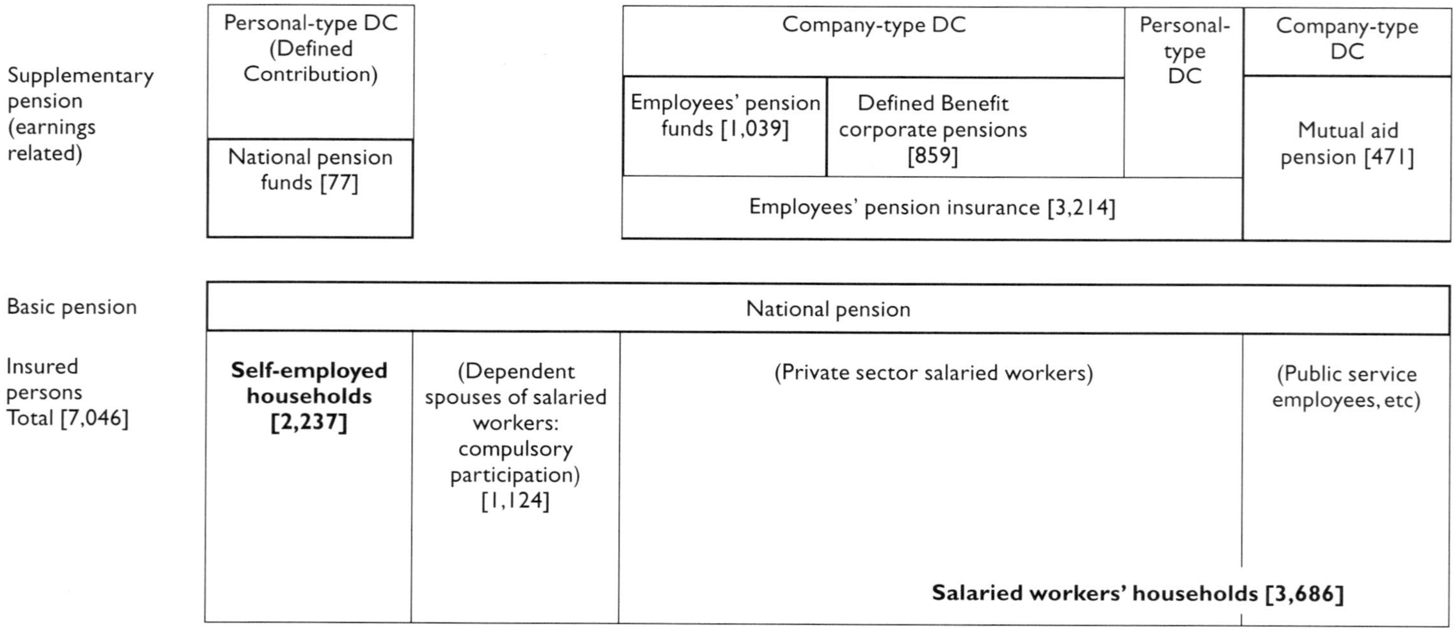

	Personal-type DC (Defined Contribution)	Company-type DC		Personal-type DC	Company-type DC
Supplementary pension (earnings related)	National pension funds [77]	Employees' pension funds [1,039]	Defined Benefit corporate pensions [859]		Mutual aid pension [471]
		Employees' pension insurance [3,214]			
Basic pension	National pension				
Insured persons Total [7,046]	**Self-employed households [2,237]**	(Dependent spouses of salaried workers: compulsory participation) [1,124]	(Private sector salaried workers)		(Public service employees, etc)
			Salaried workers' households [3,686]		

Note: Figures in brackets are the number of insured ten thousand persons in 2003.
Source: MHLW (2004a)

and subordinates it to market forces (Jessop, 1994). It is clear that the SWS is more compatible with the industrial achievement performance model than the residual one.

The Japanese welfare regime has elements of residualism and, at the same time, characteristics of the industrial achievement performance model. It is not only enterprise welfare services but also state services that are likely to be allocated on the basis of the principle of industrial achievement performance, within the framework of the SWS. Recent changes in Japanese society, such as population ageing and the impact of globalisation upon the national economy, undermine the preconditions of the Japanese welfare regime. At present, market welfare is being emphasised more strongly than ever in the Japanese welfare regime (Esping-Andersen, 1997, 1999; Mishra, 1999). It may become a new strategy of the Japanese government to ensure residual state welfare, an issue I will return to later.

The impact of rapid industrialisation upon Japanese welfare production

Japanese welfare provision expanded alongside economic development. Thus the hypotheses posed by traditional industrialisation theory (for example, Cutright, 1965; Jackman, 1975; Wilensky, 1975; Haniff, 1976; Flora and Heidenheimer, 1981; Alber, 1982) seem to be applicable to Japan's welfare development. However, the explanatory power of industrialisation theory is diminished in relation to highly developed countries partly because excessive significance is attached to economic growth as an explanation of welfare state development (Uusitalo, 1984). In the Japanese case, although industrialisation theory can explain the relationship between developments in the economy and welfare at an early stage, it cannot explain Japan's disproportionately low level of welfare in relation to its present economic performance. In this case industrialisation theory has neglected the influence of culture and political ideology. Moreover, it overemphasises irreversibility and the stability of welfare state institutions, which oversimplifies the pattern of welfare state development (Mishra, 1990; Wong, 1991).

Another methodological limitation to industrialisation theory is that its description of the relationship between industrialisation and welfare state development is static. By drawing attention to the dynamic nature of industrialisation, especially its pace of change, we may find that industrialisation has varying implications in terms of our understanding of welfare state development. Rapid industrialisation leads to high economic growth, while, at the same time, it probably allows a society to retain its cultural values and traditional customs (possibly because of the continuing influence of the older generation). Therefore, modern economic features and pre-modern social conditions may coexist in rapidly industrialised countries.

This cultural context supports a high level of consensus about the potential of informal welfare as a substitute for state welfare provision, which allows a government to maintain the latter at a low level. For example, in Japan a significant part of personal care for older people is provided by the informal sector. In addition, other preconditions for active informal care, such as the high percentage of intergenerational co-residence, still remain. Although this combination of socioeconomic and political circumstances is not common in western societies, it is a standard feature of East Asian countries including Japan. This cannot be revealed by an approach that focuses only on the degree of industrialisation and its impact on welfare state development, but it can be highlighted when the pace of industrialisation is analysed.

This approach, which attaches special importance to the 'late start effect' of industrialisation (Oda, 1992), suggests that the gap between developments in the economy and society will be reduced and finally disappear as the preconditions supporting pre-modernity in a society decline. Accordingly, the necessity for public welfare provision will increase. However the distinctive features of Japanese welfare production were deliberately maintained and traditional values mobilised politically, although the preconditions for the traditional approach to welfare activities were significantly undermined. In Japan the ruling political ideology and its influence on the cultural legacy play a significant role in keeping state welfare residual.

The cultural background to the Japanese welfare regime

A new paradigm in comparative studies

There is a new cluster of modernisation studies that places importance on cultural values (So, 1990, quoted in Sonoda, 1993, p 142) and looks not only at the relationship between tradition and modernity but also argues that traditional institutions have played a positive role in facilitating modernisation. Moreover, they do not regard the process of modernisation as an inevitable part of westernisation, but assume instead that non-western societies can develop in a manner different from that described in theories of westernisation (Tai, 1991). As shown in Chapter One, this paradigm has developed in comparative social policy and, with reference to East Asia, usually emphasises the key role of Confucianism.

The theory of the Japanese-type welfare society, which attempts to describe the socioeconomic circumstances of Japan's welfare regime by focusing on its unique culture, is an example of this new cluster of welfare state studies. It stresses the heterogeneous pattern of Japanese development and assumes that its traditional societal relationships – for example, active informal welfare practices – are part of the nature of Japanese society and, therefore, will not disappear. Furthermore, social policies should assume the maintenance of active informal welfare practices. Family functions are strengthened not to support the family as a unit for satisfying emotional aspects of welfare needs (Morioka and Aoi, 1985) but to reinforce its capacity as a direct service provider.

One strength of this paradigm is recognition of the relevance of culture in Japan and other East Asian societies, which have previously been regarded as backward. However, as pointed out in Chapter One, this approach risks falling into a culturally deterministic explanation of state policy (Fukuyama, 1995). Those based on a culturally deterministic model may interpret the general differences between cultures, but they often have blind faith in its relevance and tend to deliberately ignore other important factors. Cultural factors are necessary, but not sufficient, conditions for shaping state policy (Tai, 1991). The overemphasis on cultural structures as determinants of reality may obscure underlying power relationships and the possibility that traditional values might be ideological devices (Dale, 1986; Gould, 1993; Goodman et al, 1997, 1998; Kwon, 1999).

Ambiguities of Confucianism

Confucian teachings support a hierarchical authoritarian socio-political system, in which the emperor is regarded as the son of heaven and has absolute authority over his people. The family is considered to be one unit of a hierarchically constructed authoritarian state; parental power is also based on a doctrine that emphasises the virtue of loyalty and obedience to authority. Confucian teachings justify unequal relationships between people and legitimate the obedience of women to men, the young to older people and the lower status to the higher (Fukuyama, 1995; Chan 1996).

Japan's socioeconomic development is often introduced as an ideal example of a Confucian model. However, the dominant feeling binding Japanese people together is somewhat different from those found in traditional Confucian society. For instance, loyalty, a value derived from the Confucian ethical code and reinforced by feudalism, is a major factor in Japanese society. In contrast to other Confucian countries, the vertical dimension of human relationships has been emphasised more in Japanese society.

Sonoda (1993) criticises previous research on Confucianism in East Asia. He argues, first, that it asserts that all East Asian societies share Confucian traditions without demonstrating this empirically. Second, these studies do not give an account of the reasons why the Confucian traditions have changed. Third, they do not take on board that there may be more influential factors accounting for the unique pattern of development found in the East Asian societies. In accordance with this critique, it is necessary to examine the relationship between political intentions and Confucian traditions.

Confucianism is an important facet of East Asian culture. It is best described as an ideology that, to some extent, rules the activities of individuals and social organisations. But, with regard to Japan, Confucianism is not powerful enough to control a whole range of state policies. Unlike political ideologies such as neo-liberalism, which can largely determine the direction of state policies, Confucianism's influence is more indirect.

Confucianism is a historical legacy but, in Japan, it does not have a legitimate representative such as a political party or an interest group to represent it. It may be utilised by organisations to promote their political ideologies.[4] As indicated earlier, various Confucian ethics were contained in the notion of the Japanese-type welfare society and have played a significant role in residualising state welfare. However, they were not naturally preserved in society but were selected and amplified to fit specific political intentions.

Culture and political ideology

It is necessary to examine the relationship between Confucianism and political ideology in order to identify their influence on welfare policy making in Japan and other East Asian societies. Jones (1993) attempted to deal with this issue by introducing the label 'Confucian welfare state', but, as argued in Chapter One, this confuses Confucianism with political ideology. However, her study does make a helpful suggestion, namely that East Asian capitalist societies share conservatism as the most influential political ideology. This implies that conservative forces, which have drawn on Confucian traditions, shape the formative stages of East Asian welfare states. Along similar lines, Winckler (1988) argues that traditional social organisations and cultural values in the East Asian societies, represented by strong family discipline, provide the foundations for political stability and economic growth. These are then emphasised by neo-conservatives to support policies based on their ideological preferences (Kwon, 1999).

From a traditional liberal perspective, cultural traditions obstruct the development of a capitalist political economy and should therefore be removed through the process of modernisation. Liberals hold the view that the modernisation of society is the result of domestic industrialisation, which imitates developed societies. Therefore the modernisation process displays a tendency towards convergence and westernisation. Classical liberalism is unlikely to utilise traditional culture to realise the development of a capitalist society. However, in practice, liberals now "recognise(s) that tradition can contribute to modernisation" (Winckler, 1988, p 33). They concede that a strong state is required to preserve the freedom of the market and, in combination with conservatism, this creates 'the New Right' philosophy (Gamble, 1988; Pierson, 1991; Bryson, 1992; Hewitt, 1992; George and Wilding, 1994). The liberal strand believes that a strong state promotes a free economy, although it is cautious about the intervention of the state in other spheres of social life. Its conservative counterpart regards a free economy as the main force behind a strong state (King, 1987; Gamble, 1988; Pierson, 1991). Thus, there are some parallels between liberal and conservative thought in terms of their policy goals, although their respective notions of the good society, human nature, and the relationship between individual and society are opposed to each other (Hewitt, 1992, p 57).

East Asian societies rely on the expansion of international trade to improve their national economies. There are also tendencies towards strengthening individualism among younger generations. However, these tendencies cannot be observed to the same degree in all East Asian societies. With the increased influence of the New Right, state policies become more compatible with free market principles, which also reflect the adoption of Confucianism in policy making. As noted earlier, there are differences in the Confucian customs retained by different East Asian societies. Some variations may be explained by disparities in the strength of Confucianism in the history of each society, but they are also a reflection of differences in the strength of New Right ideology, or the kind of blends of conservatism and liberalism in each society.

The disparate styles of company management in Chinese and Japanese societies is an example of this diversification. Tai (1991) argues that Chinese companies were normally directly owned and managed by families and hence often encountered problems such as the demoralisation of employees. Japanese companies have avoided these problems by separating capital from management and by establishing a para-family system that fosters employees' loyalty to the company instead of direct management by family-owned companies. Lifetime employment, the seniority rule of promotion, equalisation of working conditions and enterprise unionism were not originated in the post-war concept of modern management but were created unevenly, beginning with a traditional management system. It is no wonder, therefore, that the system reflects Japanese traditional values, such as group/community-oriented activities, the patriarchal system, the concept of loyalty and gender inequality. These traditional elements were reorganised into the modern management system, and have emphasised the unity of workers in order to facilitate the productivity and competitiveness of enterprises (Baba, 1991; Shinkawa, 1997).

Japanese-style company management is not the result of retaining traditions and values in social institutions, nor of a policy that encourages traditional values in enterprise governance. Rather it is a reflection of the strong influence of New Right tendencies in the shape of strong pro-market liberal orientations associated with Japanese enterprise administration.

Transition of traditional values in Japan

According to Morishima (1982), Japan was strongly exposed to Chinese culture from the sixth century until the end of the feudal period in 1868. It absorbed this foreign culture both actively and passively, consolidating certain values such as loyalty. Yet Confucianism was moderated by the Japanese to suit its native traditions: the "effect of Confucianism is not as dominant a force in Japan's religio-ethical framework" (Pally and Usui 1995, p 246). It is implicit rather than explicit; a distinctively Japanese interpretation of Confucianism was developed during the feudalist period to establish a sense of loyalty as the paramount rule for governing society. In this society a relational tradition was formed, in which people in superior positions would look after the welfare of those in subordinate positions and, in turn, people in subordinate positions would faithfully serve their masters. Thus Confucianism by itself was not the ethical code that underpinned social relations in Japan, but rather a sense of loyalty based on the principles of Japanese feudalism combined with Confucianism (Pally and Usui, 1995).

Stockman et al (1995) note that this moral code was only understood in terms appropriate to the life of the warrior class (*samurai*). Therefore it only influenced the elite group and their families. They also suggest that "Confucian ethics, with its strict gender segregation and subordination of women, was not dominant over the entire population of pre-modern Japan as it was in China", and "the lives of men and women were by contrast more equal and less segregated" among the majority of people (Stockman et al, 1995, p 155). Thus in the feudal period Confucian ethics were interpreted on the Japanese's own terms which formed some unique traditional customs. Loyalty and gender segregation were rooted in Japanese social ethics, but they did not control the behaviour of the general public; influence was limited to specific spheres of society during the feudal period.

Social ethics extracted from Confucianism infiltrated the whole of Japanese society following the establishment of the first modern government in 1868. The overwhelming majority of the new elite in the government came from the former warrior class and they opened the gateway to the world and started to adopt the culture and technology found in the advanced western nations. At the same time they established the Constitution and the Civil Code based on loyalty, obedience to authority and gender inequality. Consequently, the warrior class' traditional values were generalised and became the moral precepts of the Japanese people. In a rigid hierarchical society, in which the emperor was granted absolute authority, these legislated rules were useful instruments for a political elite with a conservative orientation to upholding a strong state. They propagated and reproduced the above values and utilised them to develop the capitalist economy, govern the people and strengthen militarism in an authoritarian way until the end of the Second World War (Fukutake, 1987).

Not surprisingly, the Japanese family system prescribed by the former Civil Code, which had been taking effect until the end of the Second World War, clearly displayed its pre-modern and semi feudalistic characteristics (JNC, 1986). In the family system, the head of a family (that is, the father) possessed exclusive authority over property, and the eldest son inherited this privilege. The head of the family was obliged to take care of family members (JNC, 1986; Kinjo, 1992). The concentration of power and financial means in the hands of the eldest son forced other offspring to support themselves. Many immigrated to urban areas and became wage earners in modern industries. Women and young children, obliged to support their family budgets under patriarchal rules, also joined the labour force. Their working conditions were normally very bad with only limited legal protection. Taking care of exhausted labourers was not regarded as a social responsibility but an obligation of the family. The government, therefore, could concentrate on the development of a capitalist economy and militarism without considering the welfare of individuals. Thus, the patriarchal family system contributed to the rapid growth of a late-starting capitalist system.

After the Second World War several new laws emphasising democracy and legal equality between the sexes were established. Nevertheless, some patriarchal traditions were adopted in the new Civil Code and continued to influence the lifestyles and perceptions of the Japanese in the post-war period. Kinjo (1992) points to the resistance of conservatives against the abolition of patriarchal rules as one of the reasons why they survived in the new legal system of post-war Japan.[5] On the one hand, modern aspects of the new family system (for example, a decrease in gender inequality, a negation of the absolute authority of the family head and the guarantee of equal rights of inheritance among family members) contributed to a new labour force, which adapted to new technology and management because they released young people from the binding force of patriarchal customs. On the other hand, however, obligatory rules for mutual support were carried over to the new system and reproduced a residual principle of welfare provision. Informal welfare practices were emphasised as orthodoxy and took priority over state welfare provision (Harada, 1988). Thus, some patriarchal elements of the Japanese family system were retained deliberately and they have continued to influence the welfare regime in the post-war period.

Changes in the preconditions of the Japanese welfare regime

The impact of globalisation

Until recently a relatively small older population and a high level of economic growth helped to avoid the emergence of a trade off between the economy and welfare. A strong consensus about the Japanese-type welfare society was formed and informal and enterprise welfare practices have made up for the lack of state services. However, these preconditions of the regime have been gradually broken down. For example, employers can invest in enterprise welfare services and employees can devote themselves to work as long as a lifetime employment system is maintained. However, globalisation creates severe economic constraints and requires more efficient company management including redundancies. Thus, the foundation of the

Japanese-type welfare society is threatened by the progress of globalisation.

The significance of pro-market ideology is growing and business interests are more important as a determinant of state policies. In 1998, the Japanese government organised the Economic Strategy Council in order to create new guidelines for policies. The final report was submitted to the Prime Minister in 1999. It attempted to realise 'a small government' by strongly emphasising self-help culture and private initiatives in the field of welfare. For instance, the report recommends that public pensions should be limited to the level of the national minimum, and the supplementary (earnings-related) pensions should be completely privatised within 30 years. Competition among service providers and the privatisation of service provision are justified in the fields of medical services and nursing care. The report proposed to introduce a voucher system in the formal services of care for older people, childcare and job training (Economic Strategy Council, 1999).

A policy goal of this report is the establishment of an American-style system. In fact, the report praises the recovery process of the US economy in the 1990s and recognises 'Reaganomics' as a possible approach to reconstruct the 'efficiency and fairness' in Japan. It is hard to imagine that the Japanese-type welfare society will be fully Americanised. However, the proposals made by the report were adopted by the government and, as a result, the Japanese welfare regime tends to be more individualistic and market-oriented.

Inactive enterprise welfare

More Japanese workers have started to doubt the benefits of Japanese-style management, based on traditional values, and to distance themselves from the principle. Moreover, the main system of business management is under heavy pressure from the globalisation of the economy. From the late 1980s to the early 1990s the Japanese economy exhibited high economic performance. However, partly due to the impact of globalisation, a serious recession occurred in the 1990s. It has resulted in low business activity and a large number of bankruptcies. Companies started to rationalise their management and became more reluctant to spend on their enterprise welfare schemes.

During the recession the system of guaranteed lifetime employment has been threatened by a surplus of labour. Enterprise welfare, founded on 'the industrial achievement performance model', plays the role of ensuring the workers' lifelong commitment to their enterprises. Hence, the decline of the lifetime employment system has weakened corporate

Table 6.2: Financial status of health insurance programmes (1990-99) (¥100 million)

	1990	1993	1994	1996	1999
EHI	+5,745	+239	−3,624	−6,169	−5,155
NHI	−668	−881	−1,360	−1,154	−1,205

Notes: Figures indicate the current balances of each programme's finances; EHI = Employee Health Insurance; NHI = National Health Insurance.
Source: MHLW (2001)

welfare guarantees. The number of enterprises providing additional benefits to their employees' pensions is now decreasing (Saito, 1991; Esping-Andersen, 1996a, 1996b, 1997; Miyamoto, 1997; Shinkawa, 1997).

Some studies (Calder 1988; Miyamoto, 1997) suggest that a policy of full employment has substituted for social policies in Japan and been used to residualise state welfare. The lifetime employment policy in large enterprises, the high level of expenditure on public construction works and protective policies towards small-sized enterprises have realised a low rate of unemployment and made some impact on income redistribution among Japanese people. A rise in unemployment undermines not only the preconditions of the system of enterprise welfare but also the whole Japanese welfare mix regime.

Recently the financial conditions of health insurance programmes have worsened rapidly. In 1994, all their accounts finally went into the red (Table 6.2). The growth of national income exceeded that of national medical expenditure until 1990 (Table 6.3). The numbers and salaries of company workers increased steadily and they improved the finances of health insurance programmes. Although the expansion of the older population brought about an increase in medical

Table 6.3: Growth rates of national medical expenditure, medical expenditure for older people and national income (1985-2001) (%)

	1985	1989	1991	1993	1995	1997	1999	2001
National medical expenditure	6.1	5.2	5.9	3.8	4.5	1.9	3.7	3.2
Medical expenditure for older people	12.7	7.7	8.1	7.4	9.3	5.7	8.4	4.1
National income	6.8	6.9	6.4	0.0	0.1	0.9	−1.6	−2.7

Source: MHLW (2004a)

expenditure, changes in the Japanese economy led to a decrease in the annual income of health insurance schemes.

EHI originally provided nearly 100% coverage of the insured persons' standard healthcare expenses, but this was reduced to 90% in 1984 and 80% in 1997. It was reduced further to 70% in 2003. Recent health insurance policies insisted on a reduction in healthcare expenditure by downgrading the coverage of the EHI programme. At present, there is only a small gap in the coverage offered by the EHI and the NHI. Members of large companies no longer enjoy a privileges in the field of healthcare, and they increasingly need to pay.

A decline in informal welfare practices and an emphasis on market welfare activities

In Japan average life expectancy has risen rapidly over a very short period and is the highest in the world. It increased from 50.06 years for males and 53.96 years for females in 1947 (EPA, 1994) to 78.3 years and 85.2 years respectively in 2002. The birth rate in Japan is relatively low (1.29 in 2003). The ageing of the population is expected to increase rapidly and the percentage of the population aged 65 years and over, which was 17.2% in 2000, is projected to reach 27.4% by 2025 (MHLW, 2003, 2004). The population aged 65 years and over is expected to increase 1.51 times between 2000 and 2025, while those aged 75 years and over is projected to rise by 2.13 times in the same period of time. Undoubtedly, the incidence of disabilities increases sharply with advanced population ageing. According to a calculation made by the Ministry of Health and Welfare (MHW, 1994), the number of older people in need of care in 2000 was 2.8 million and the figure is projected to increase to 5.2 million by 2025.

In the post-war period, the ideology of familism successfully sustained family-centred welfare provision and gender inequality in informal care work. Thus, the supply of statutory care services is limited. However, modernisation inevitably weakens the capacity of the informal care sector and the demand for care has steadily increased along with the ageing of the population. Moreover, informal care based on the self-sacrifice of family carers tends to be less popular and this is especially evident in the opinions of the younger generation and women.[6] Even if the importance of traditional family values is persistently advocated by the government, the changes to people's value systems that occur in their everyday lives place greater importance on individualism and freedom from conventional customs. Furthermore, structural shifts in working circumstances, particularly for females, makes the continuation of the patriarchal approach to informal care more difficult. The percentage of females employed in the labour force was 28.9% in 1955, and by 2002 it had increased to 83.3% (Ministry of Public Management, Home Affairs, Posts and Telecommunications, 2003).

The preservation of family care is still regarded as a crucial political objective. However, the government is fighting a losing battle against socio-demographic changes and shifting values. Therefore, to prevent a greater provider role for the state, the strategy to transform the Japanese welfare mix attempts to shift the residual responsibilities of the public sector onto the market sector. Residualisation strategies reshape the boundaries between different welfare sectors and also change the nature of welfare services. In these strategies economic criteria are employed to create and operate formal welfare services, and the market principle becomes the orthodoxy of the welfare system (Miller, 1988; Walker, 1990, 1991; Pinker, 1992; Evers, 1993). Throughout this restructuring process, the reformist strategies incorporate private agencies into the provision of statutory services. The purpose is to change the value system shared by welfare providers and users so as to undermine their regard for public welfare.

In the field of care for older people in Japan, the government has produced a policy package to minimise the role of the public sector and to facilitate private welfare activities. This includes financial support for private agents and relaxed restrictions on their operations. For the purpose of shifting service users to the private sector, the reforms have encouraged older people to purchase more private services. Public long-term care insurance was started in 2000 in return for further contributions from individuals. By strengthening users' purchasing power, their potential is increased to apply for private services.

The process of restructuring the Japanese care system is still in its early stages. However, since the public sector's responsibilities for providing welfare services were always limited, and the Japanese people's sense of the right to claim public welfare was also weak, the goal of welfare reform has been quickly and successfully achieved.

Conclusion

Under some political ideologies policy makers utilise and reinforce traditional values in order to prescribe welfare policies favourable to their interests. Although industrialisation increases people's needs for welfare, it also provides the preconditions for state welfare production. Rapid industrialisation may change the internal nature of society but it also allows room to keep traditional customs alive. Hence, the political use of traditional customs is easier when industrialisation advances rapidly. In Japanese history traditional values, such as a strong sense of loyalty, obedience to authority and segregated gender roles in the family and workplace, have all been utilised and reinforced as a part of its ruling ideology. Although these customs originated in Confucianism, they were selected in accordance with the ideological preferences of the Japanese. The intentions of the state, its utilisation and reproduction of these traditions, have differed according to the specific political circumstances of each period in Japanese history. The shift of Japan's political ideology from traditional conservatism to the New Right has resulted in a change to its primary policy goal: an economically competitive system and residualised welfare policy have replaced the militaristic and strong authoritarian state.

The rapidity of Japanese industrialisation created a gap between developments in the economy and society. The enduring influence of traditional values and pre-modern conditions provided the foundation for Japan to keep its state welfare provision at a residual level. Traditional values underpinned informal welfare practices and enterprise welfare services, and their roles have been accentuated in the concept of the Japanese-type welfare society. Recent changes in the Japanese economy and a rapidly ageing population undermine the prerequisites of this regime and pressure policy makers to adopt alternatives. At the time of writing, it is too early to conclude if the roles of the family and enterprises as welfare providers will be diminished in the future. However, the necessity for increasing market welfare provision is now emphasised in the Japanese welfare regime in order to maintain the residual status of state welfare.

Notes

[1] For example, in the 'Plan to Double National Income', welfare policies were expected to increase effective demand, helping to overcome business fluctuations and promoting capital accumulation as seen in the pension system funds (SDRI, 1968, p 316).

[2] Around 1973, the free medical system for older people was set up, public pension benefits were increased, and the coverage of the healthcare insurance system was extended.

[3] In 1994 the total cost of enterprise welfare services, which included contributions to the social security system, amounted to 24 trillion yen. It

was equivalent to 20.6% of the total cash wage and 4.9% of the GNP (Fujita, 1997; Sato, 1997).

[4] A state project that tried to prevent moral decay among young people by introducing Confucian values through education in Singapore (Sonoda, 1993, p 146) may be an example of this. State educational policy was not required to change by Confucianism, but it was an attempt by the state, with a certain political ideology, to utilise Confucianism in order to achieve its policy objectives.

[5] Immediately after the war, the US administration played an important role for the retention of the Japanese conservative forces. During the period of occupation from 1945-51, the US occupation forces carried out a series of legal reforms. Although the US administration operated for only a limited period, it supported the creation of some basic welfare systems and significantly influenced the democratisation process of Japanese politics. At the same time, however, it legitimised the conservative policy-making machinery and residualised public responsibility for welfare provision. These principles have been justified by conservative Japanese policy makers in the post-war period.

[6] The table below shows trends in the opinions of married women aged under 50 on informal care for their older relatives (figures indicate the percentages of all opinions). It is clear that passive opinions on informal care have been growing.

	1963	1971	1979	1988	1992	1998
Preferable custom	36.1	27.4	24.5	20.8	16.5	13.2
Responsibility of children	38.6	43.6	47.2	42.3	31.2	35.0
No alternative (because of inadequate public welfare services)	8.7	9.3	9.8	13.0	21.7	24.5
Not preferable custom	3.0	4.3	3.6	6.7	9.9	10.8
No idea or other	13.6	15.1	14.9	17.2	20.7	16.5

Source: The Mainichi Newspapers, *Public opinion polls on family planning* [each year]

A high percentage of intergenerational co-residence has sustained a key role for the informal sector in providing care for older people in Japan. In reality, this caring relationship has unilaterally transferred caring responsibilities to female carers. However, as mentioned earlier, they have become more passive towards family care and this change of attitude is reflected by their preferred living arrangements. The table below indicates the percentages of the opinions of persons in various age groups on intergenerational co-residence in 1997. Compared with men, the approval of intergenerational co-residence is lower among younger female groups. A residential style in which they are 'living separately' from their parents in law is becoming more popular among them and is supported by nearly two thirds of them.

	Average		Male		Female	
	40-59	60+	40-59	60+	40-59	60+
Approval for living together	35.3	52.7	40.4	50.5	31.6	54.6
Approval for living separately	56.1	37.9	48.9	39.0	61.2	37.0
Other	0.6	1.4	0.6	1.7	0.6	1.1
No idea	8.1	8.0	10.1	8.8	6.6	7.4

Source: Management and Coordination Agency (1998)

References

Abe, H., Shindo, M. and Kawato, S. (1990) *Contemporary Japanese politics*, Tokyo: Tokyo University Press (in Japanese).

Alber, J. (1982) *Some causes and consequences of social security expenditure development in Western Europe, 1949-1977*, Working Paper 15, Florence: European University Institute.

Baba, H. (1991) 'Contemporary world and Japanese socialism', in Social Science Research Institute of Tokyo University (ed) *Contemporary Japanese Society, vol 1: Objective and Scope*, Tokyo: Tokyo University Press (in Japanese), pp 29-83.

Bryson, L. (1992) *Welfare and the state*, London: Macmillan.

Calder, K. (1988) *Crisis and competition: Public policy and political stability in Japan 1949-1986*, Princeton, NJ: Princeton University Press.

Campbell, J. (1992) *How policies change: The Japanese government and the aging society*, Princeton, NJ: Princeton University Press.

Chan, C.K. (1996) 'Colonial rule, Chinese welfare ideologies and reproduction of social policy: The case of social security', PhD thesis, Sheffield: University of Sheffield.

Cutright, P. (1965) 'Political structure, economic development, and national social security programs', *American Journal of Sociology*, vol 70, no 5, pp 537-50.

Dale, P. (1986) *The myth of Japanese uniqueness*, London: Croom Helm.

Economic Strategy Council (1999) *Strategies for reviving the Japanese economy (the final report)*, official statement announced in the Official Residence of the Prime Minister on the Web (www.kantei.go.jp/foreign/senryaku/990317report.html).

EPA (Economic Planning Agency) (1979) *New economic and social seven-year plan*, Tokyo: The Printing Bureau (in Japanese).

EPA (1994) *White Paper on the nation's living 1993-4*, Tokyo: The Printing Bureau (in Japanese).

Esping-Andersen, G. (1996a) 'After the golden age? Welfare state dilemmas in a global economy', in G. Esping-Andersen (ed) *Welfare states in transition: National adaptions in global economies*, London: Sage Publications, pp 1-31.

Esping-Andersen, G. (1996b), 'Positive-sum solutions in a world of trade-offs?', in G. Esping-Andersen (ed) *Welfare states in transition: National adaptions in global economies*, London: Sage Publications, pp 256-67.

Esping-Andersen, G. (1997) 'Hybrid or unique?: The Japanese welfare state between Europe and America', *Journal of European Social Policy*, vol 7, no 3, pp 179-89.

Esping-Andersen, G. (1999) *Social foundation of postindustrial economies*, Oxford: Oxford University Press.

Evers, A. (1993) 'The welfare mix approach. Understanding the pluralism of welfare systems', in A. Evers and I. Svetlik (eds) *Balancing pluralism: New welfare mixes in care for the elderly*, Hants: Avebury, pp 3-31.

Flora, P. and Heidenheimer, A.J. (eds) (1981) *The development of welfare states in Europe and America*, Princeton, NJ: Transaction Books.

Fujita, Y. (1997) 'General relationships between enterprise welfare and social security', in Y. Fujita and Y. Shionoya (eds) *Employee benefits and social security*, Tokyo: University of Tokyo Press (in Japanese), pp 17-52.

Fukutake, T. (1987) *The Japanese social structure (2nd edn)*, Tokyo: Tokyo University Press (in Japanese).

Fukuyama, F. (1995) *Trust: The social virtues and the creation of prosperity*, London: Hamish Hamilton.

Gamble, A. (1988) *The free economy and the strong state: The politics of Thatcherism*, London: Macmillan.

George, V. and Wilding, P. (1994) *Welfare and ideology*, Hemel Hempstead: Harvester Wheatsheaf.

Goodman, R. and Peng, I. (1996) 'The East Asian welfare states: Peripatetic learning, adaptive change, and nation-building', in G. Esping-Andersen (ed) *Welfare states in transition: National adaptions in global economies*, London: Sage Publications, pp 192-224.

Goodman, R., White, G. and Kwon, H. (1997) 'East Asian social policy: A model to emulate?' *Social Policy Review*, vol 9, pp 359-80.

Goodman, R., White, G. and Kwon, H. (eds) (1998) *The East Asian welfare model: Welfare orientalism and the state*, London: Routledge.

Gould, A. (1993) *Capitalist welfare system: A comparison of Japan, Britain and Sweden*, London: Longman.

Haniff, G.A. (1976) 'Politics, development and social policy: a cross-national analysis', *European Journal of Political Research*, vol 4, pp 361-76.

Harada, S. (1988) 'The family in the theory of the Japanese type welfare society', in the Social Science Research Institute of Tokyo University (ed.) *The welfare state in transition, vol 2*, Tokyo: Tokyo University Press (in Japanese), pp 303-92.

Hewitt, M. (1992) *Welfare, ideology and need: Developing perspectives on the welfare state*, Hemel Hempstead: Harvester Wheatsheaf.

Hill, M. (1996) *Social policy: A comparative analysis*, London: Prentice Hall and Harvester Wheatsheaf.

Hirao, T. (1993) 'Personnel management and trade union in Japan', *Review (Sapporo University)*, vol 4, pp 71-88 (in Japanese).

Hori, K. (1981) 'The theory of the Japanese type welfare society', *The Quarterly of Social Security Research*, vol 17, no 1, pp 37-52 (in Japanese).

Ishida, T. (1992) *The analysis of the Liberal Democratic regime: Pluralism, corporatism and dualism*, Kyoto: Horitsu Bunkasha (in Japanese).

Jackman, R.W. (1975) *Politics and social equality: A comparative analysis*, New York, NY: John Wiley & Sons.

Jacobs, D. (1998) *Social welfare systems in East Asia: A comparative analysis Including private welfare*, CASEpaper, vol 10, London: London School of Economics and Political Science.

Jessop, B. (1994) 'Towards a post Fordist welfare state? The restructuring of Britain, social policy and the future of welfare', in R. Burrows and B. Loader (eds) *Towards a post-Fordist welfare state?*, London: Routledge, pp 13-37.

JNC (Japanese National Committee of International Council on Social Welfare) (1986) 'Family and community in Japan', Paper contributed to the 23rd International Conference on Social Welfare in Tokyo.

Jones, C. (1993) 'The Pacific challenge', in C. Jones (ed) *New perspectives on the welfare state in Europe*, London: Routledge.

Kato, E. (1991) 'The reorganisation of the welfare state system: historical implication of privatisation', in the Social Science Research Institute of Tokyo University (ed) *Contemporary Japanese society, vol 1: Objective and scope*, Tokyo: Tokyo University Press (in Japanese), pp 85-127.

King, D. S. (1987) *The new right: Politics, market and citizenship*, London: Macmillan.

Kinjo, K. (ed) (1992) 'The regal system and the family', in National Institute for Research Advancement, *A research on the Japanese family system and policies for it*, Tokyo: National Institute for Research Advancement (in Japanese), pp 39-56.

Kono, M. (2003) 'Health care and personal social services for frail older people', *Hyogo University Journal*, vol 8, pp 35-70.

Kwon, H. (1999) *Income transfers to the elderly in East Asia: Testing Asian values*, CASEpaper, vol 27, London: London School of Economics and Political Science.

Management and Coordination Agency (1998) *An attitude survey on the middle and old aged generation about ageing problems* (www.cao.go.jp/kourei/ishiki/kenkyu1.htm) (in Japanese).

MHW (Ministry of Health and Welfare) (1994) *Welfare vision in the 21st century*, Tokyo: Daiichi Hoki (in Japanese).

MHLW (Ministry of Health, Labour and Welfare) (2001) *Annual report on health, labour and welfare*, Tokyo: Gyosei (in Japanese).

MHLW (2003) *Annual report on health, labour and welfare*, Tokyo: Gyosei (in Japanese).

MHLW (2004a) *Annual report on health, labour and welfare*, Tokyo: Gyosei (in Japanese).

MHLW (2004b) *An outlook for benefits and burdens of social security*, (www.mhlw.go.jp) (in Japanese).

Miller, S.M. (1988) 'Evolving welfare state mixes', in A. Evers and H. Wintersberger (eds) *Shifts in the welfare mix: Their impact on work, social services and welfare policies; contributions from nine European countries in a comparative perspective*, Vienna: European Centre for Social Welfare Training and Research, pp 371-87.

Ministry of Public Management, Home Affairs, Posts and Telecommunications (2003) *The labour force survey*, Tokyo: Japan Statistic Association (in Japanese).

Mishra, R. (1990) *The welfare state in capitalist society*, Hemel Hempstead: Harvester Wheatsheaf.

Mishra, R. (1999) *Globalization and the welfare state*, Cheltenham: Edward Elgar.

Miyamoto, T. (1997) 'The theory and reality of comparative studies on the welfare state', in N. Okazawa and T. Miyamoto (eds) *Comparative analysis of welfare states*, Kyoto: Houritsu Bunkasha (in Japanese), pp 12-43.

Morioka, K. and Aoi, K. (1985) 'Conclusion: the structure of the life and the degree of satisfaction with the life', in T. Fukutake and K. Aoi (eds) *The structure of the ageing society and its problems, vol 1: Social response to an ageing society*, Tokyo: Tokyo University Press (in Japanese), pp 215-49.

Morishima, M. (1982) *Why has Japan 'succeeded?': Western technology and the Japanese ethos*, Cambridge: Cambridge University Press.

Oda, T. (1992) 'The social dilemma of the welfare state', *The Quarterly of Social Security Research*, vol 28, no 2, pp 182-93 (in Japanese).

Okuma, Y. (1993), 'Ten preconditions of the ageing welfare society', in Economic Planning Agency (ed) *The establishment of the ageing welfare society with user participation*, Tokyo: Gyosei (in Japanese), pp 135-51.

Pally, H.A. and Usui, C. (1995) 'Social policies for the elderly in the republic of Korea and Japan: a comparative perspective', *Social Policy and Administration*, vol 29, no 3, pp 241-57.

Pierson, C. (1991) *Beyond the welfare state? The new political economy of welfare*, Cambridge: Polity Press.

Pinker, R. (1992) 'Making sense of the mixes economy of welfare', *Social Policy and Administration*, vol 26, no 4, pp 273-84.

Saito, H. (1991) 'Towards democratic regulation', in T. Yamada and O. Sudo (eds) *Post-Fordism: Regulation approach and Japan*, Tokyo: Oomura Shoten (in Japanese), pp 81-103.

Sato, H. (1997) 'Trends in the reconstruction of enterprise welfare services', in Y. Fujita and Y. Shionoya (eds) *Employee benefits and social security*, Tokyo: University of Tokyo Press (in Japanese), pp 315-34.

SDRI (Social Development Research Institute) (1968) *Data on the post-war social security system*, Tokyo: Shiseido (in Japanese).

Shinkawa, T. (1993) *Political economy of Japanese style welfare*, Tokyo: Sanichi Syobo (in Japanese).

Shinkawa, T. (1997) 'Japan: the end of Japanese type welfare?', in N. Okazawa and T. Miyamoto (eds) *Comparative analysis of welfare states*, Kyoto: Houritsu Bunkasha (in Japanese), pp 154-75.

So, A.Y. (1990) *Social change and development: Modernization, dependency and world-system theories*, London: Sage Publications.

Sonoda, S. (1993) 'Confucianism and modernisation: searching for the new aspects of modernisation theory', in T. Imada, T. Tomoeda and Y. Koutou (eds) *New frontiers in social theory*, Tokyo: Tokyo University Press (in Japanese), pp 141-60.

Stockman, N., Bonney, N. and Sheng, X.W. (1995) *Women's work in East and West: The dual burden of employment and family life*, London: UCL Press.

Tai, H.C. (1991) 'The Oriental alternative: a hypothesis on East Asian culture and economy', in *The Republic of China on Taiwan today: View from abroad*, Taipei: Kwang Hwa Publishing Company, pp 107-31.

Titmuss, R. (1974) *Social policy: An introduction*, London: George Allen and Unwin.

Uusitalo, H. (1984) 'Comparative research on the determinants of the welfare state: the state of the art', *European Journal of Political Research*, vol 12, pp 403-22.

Wakamori, F. (1991) 'Economy, civil society and state after Fordism', in T. Yamada and O. Sudo (eds) *Post-Fordism: Regulation approach and Japan*, Tokyo: Oomura Shoten (in Japanese), pp 59-79.

Walker, A. (1990) 'The economic "burden" of ageing and the prospect of intergenerational conflict', *Ageing and Society*, vol 10, pp 377-90.

Walker, A. (1991) 'The relationship between the family and the state in the care of older people', *Canadian Journal on Aging*, vol 10, no 2, pp 94-112.

Watanabe, O. (1991) 'The unique structure of contemporary Japan', in the Social Science Research Institute of Tokyo University (ed) *Contemporary Japanese society, vol 1: Objective and scope*, Tokyo: Tokyo University Press (in Japanese), pp 201-95.

Wilensky, H. (1975) *The welfare state and equality: Structural and ideological roots of public expenditures*, London: University of California Press.

Winckler, E.A. (1988) 'Contending approaches to East Asian development', in E.A. Winckler and S. Greenhalgh (eds) *Contending approaches to the public economy of Taiwan*, London: M.E. Sharpe Inc, pp 20-37.

Wong, C.K. (1991) 'Ideology, welfare mix and the production of welfare: a comparative study of child day care policies in Britain and Hong Kong', PhD thesis, Sheffield: University of Sheffield.

Yamada, T (1991) 'Fordism and post-Fordism', in T. Yamada and O. Sudo (eds) *Post-Fordism: Regulation approach and Japan*, Tokyo: Oomura Shoten (in Japanese), pp 17-36.

SEVEN

Taiwan: what kind of social policy regime?

Michael Hill and Yuan-shie Hwang

Introduction

Comparative theory has evolved from convergence or modernisation perspectives in which either economic growth (Rimlinger, 1971; Wilensky, 1975) or the evolution of capitalism (O'Connor, 1973; Gough, 1979) were seen as inevitably leading to growth in state expenditure on welfare to a situation in which 'regime' analyses are dominant. Esping-Andersen (1990) has been the main influence on regime theory, replacing a rather functionalist sociology by an approach in which systems are analysed according to the extent to which they enhance 'decommodification' or social solidarity and political processes are seen as offering explanations of these differences. Esping-Andersen identifies what he describes as three regime types – in short, liberal, corporatist and social democratic. Inevitably, Esping-Andersen's work has spawned critiques, most of which offer additional types to his original three. Castles and Mitchell (1991) have suggested the existence of an Australasian model in which the maintenance of relatively well-paid full employment has been the dominant concern of political strategists on the Left. Ferrara (1996) has indicated ways in which southern European developments do not fit the models. Sainsbury and her collaborators (1994) have indicated that variations in family policy and female labour market participation make it necessary to modify Esping-Andersen's regime types, with Siaroff (1994) in particular adding 'late female mobilisation welfare states'. Above all, of importance for this discussion has been work that either attempts to delineate alternative East Asian models (Jones, 1993) or at least suggests limitations to the application of western models to East Asia (Goodman and Peng, 1995; Walker and Wong, 1996; Kwon, 1997; Shin, 2003).

  In exploring, in this chapter, the application of the various theoretical perspectives or typologies to Taiwan, it will be suggested that many of the ideas that feature in the debate about welfare regimes have resonances – from the early convergence theorists' concerns with the concomitants of modernisation, through the issues about corporatist welfare states identified by Esping-Andersen, to the points highlighted about both employment and family life in the critiques of the latter. Support will be found too for the more agnostic perspectives of those who see differences in East Asian patterns, but do not feel able to accept Jones' (1993) emphasis on the influence of Confucianism. There are so many plausible suggestions that at times the exercise will be rather like that involved in putting together a badly designed jigsaw puzzle, in which there seem to be many different places in which each piece in the puzzle could fit.

The Taiwan context: evidence for modernisation theory?

Chinese settlement on Taiwan dates from at least the 13th century and the island was ruled (often little more than nominally) by China between 1683 and 1895 (Copper, 1996). In 1895 the island was ceded to Japan, which used it as a source of essential agricultural products. While the Japanese established a rudimentary infrastructure of administrative institutions, social policy involved little more than local self-help (Ku, 1997).

The island reverted to China again in 1945. During the period in which Chinese rule was re-established, there was considerable tension between the mainlanders sent to govern the island and the established Taiwanese population, culminating in what is often described as a rebellion in February 1947, which was brutally repressed. Then in 1949 the Nationalist army (Kuomintang [KMT]) under Chiang Kai-shek retreated to Taiwan after defeat by the Communists on the Chinese mainland. Rule by the KMT, until the 1960s under American protection, was established. The island had to absorb about a million and a half mainlanders. Today this group of people and their descendants form about 14% of the population; the rest of the population is divided between about 2% 'aboriginal' people and 84% Taiwanese (that is, Chinese people whose families were settled on the island before the Japanese take-over) (www.odci.gov/cia/publications/factbook/geos/tw.html, 2003).

The period since 1949 has seen a remarkable transformation in Taiwan. The population of the island (and the other smaller islands under its rule) has grown from less than 10 million to more than 22.4 million (Council for Economic Planning and Development, 2003).

Table 7.1: GNP per capita ($US) and government consumption as a percentage of GNP (1960-2002)

Year	Per capita GNP ($US)	Government consumption as % of GNP
1960	154	19.3
1970	389	22.5
1980	2,344	25.5
1990	8,111	26.0
2000	14,188	21.5
2002	12,900	22.2

Source: Council for Economic Planning and Development (2003)

Taiwan's demographic profile – a low birth rate and a low death rate – is characteristic of a 'first' world rather than 'third' world country (which it was in 1949). The transformation of Taiwan's society is most succinctly demonstrated by the second column of Table 7.1, setting out data on GNP per capita at various dates. It is significant that government expenditure as a percentage of GNP has fallen quite sharply with growth. As Table 7.2 shows, the fall in defence expenditure has been a key feature of this.

The economic transformation of Taiwan has involved first a dramatic shift from an agricultural to an industrial economy and then, more recently, a shift from simpler industrial processes (textile manufacturing and so on) to new high technology industry. The labour force of 9.5 million was in 2002 divided between about 57.3% in services, 35.2% in industry and only 7.5% in agriculture (Council for Economic Planning and Development, 2003).

The data on GNP growth, and the story of the economic development of Taiwan, offers a basis for the examination of the simplest of the approaches to the comparative exploration of social policy growth, that which sees it as a concomitant of 'modernisation'. The third column of Table 7.1, together with Tables 7.2 and 7.3, provides

Table 7.2: Taiwan: percentages of government expenditure on various activities (1960-2001)

Year	Social security	Education, science and culture	National defence
1960	6.9	13.6	49.4
1970	10.0	16.9	37.3
1980	11.2	15.5	30.3
1990	18.6	20.7	19.2
2000	28.7	20.9	11.4
2001	30.0	18.9	10.9

Source: Council for Economic Planning and Development (2003)

Table 7.3: Taiwan: social security expenditure as a percentage of GNP (1960-2001)

Year	Percentage
1960	1.3
1970	2.1
1980	2.6
1990	4.6
2000	9.2
2001	9.3

Source: Council for Economic Planning and Development (2003)

a simple test of the 'modernisation' hypothesis. Manifestly, growth in public expenditure has occurred, and there is evidence from Table 7.2 that social expenditure is growing faster than other forms of public expenditure. It should be noted here that, since publicly funded healthcare is provided within the health insurance scheme, the figures for social policy in Tables 7.2 and 7.3 include social security, health insurance expenditure and social care expenditure. The figures are for gross payments, not taking into account employers' and employees' contributions.

However, there is, alternatively, evidence that this has been a quite modest growth. Table 7.4 offers a contrast with the levels of public expenditure in the UK, where social security, health and social care expenditure account for almost a half of all public expenditure. Taiwan is, in this comparison, shown to be a relatively low spender. Data for South Korea have also been included in Table 7.4, to offer an alternative comparison, since that country is perhaps the closest comparator for Taiwan.

Of course, the 'modernisation' hypotheses have been qualified in various ways. One such qualification gives attention to issues about the age structure of the population. It is very important to recognise that the demographic history of Taiwan is such that older people, who are likely to make particularly high demands upon social policy, still form a comparatively small proportion of the population. Nine per

Table 7.4: Taiwan compared with Korea and the UK

Country	GNP per capita in $US 2001	Government consumption as % of GNP
Taiwan	12,876	12.6[a]
Korea	8,899	10.4[b]
UK	24,031	19.4[b]

Notes: [a]data for 2002; [b]data for 2001.
Source: Council for Economic Planning and Development (2003)

cent of the population are over 65 (Council for Economic Planning and Development, 2003). The contrast here is with a figure of about 16% for the United Kingdom. In Taiwan there is a rather unusual sex distribution of 1.16 males to one female among the over-65s. This is a consequence of the high preponderance of males in the group who moved to Taiwan from the mainland in the 1940s. We will come back below to the importance of concerns about social policies for older people in contemporary political debate in Taiwan.

Social policy development 1947-87: evidence of the development of a corporatist regime?

Since the main challenge to modernisation theory has come from scholars who emphasise the importance of politics, there is a need now to turn to some key aspects of the recent political history of Taiwan. The KMT sees itself as the heir of Dr Sun Yat-Sen, the leading Chinese ideologist in the period in which the Empire was overthrown in the first two decades of the 20th century. Sun Yat-Sen sought to fuse Confucian ideas with western republican and socialist ones. In relation to social policy, he has been portrayed as influenced by Bismarkian ideas (Lin, 1990, pp 130-1). The constitution the KMT adopted for China in 1946 embraced proposals originally made by Sun Yat-Sen, including article 155, which reads "the state, in order to promote social welfare, shall establish social insurance" and article 157, which states "the state, in order to improve national health, shall establish a public medical service system".

The KMT's rule in Taiwan was an autocratic one until at least the 1970s, and in many respects the government did not start to engage in wholesale democratisation until after the lifting of martial law in 1987. We recognise, therefore, that it would be naïve to explain social policy developments before 1987 in terms of the KMT's assertion of its commitment to the principles of Sun Yat-Sen. However, it was concerned to establish its legitimate rule over a population that (as suggested earlier) had shown some reluctance to accept its rule. It was also engaged on a programme of modernisation that was likely to disrupt traditional occupations and patterns of social care. A Bismarckian social programme therefore had characteristics likely to appeal to the ruling elite.

The key social policy measures in Taiwan before 1987 involved the setting up of a cluster of separate social insurance schemes. These grew steadily after their inception, and provide a framework that still dominates the social policy system today. The earliest was the most general scheme, Labour Insurance (LI) set up in 1950. This was followed by Government Employees Insurance (GEI) established in 1958. There followed a scheme for retired government employees in 1965 and a scheme for teachers and staff in private schools in 1980. A number of other schemes for retired employees and their spouses were set up in 1985.

There are complex administrative arrangements for the various schemes. Each is administratively independent. Until the coming of National Health Insurance (NHI) (see discussion later), all schemes provided their contributors with medical benefits for themselves and their dependants. The LI scheme also provided cash benefits during sickness.

The LI and GEI schemes offer retirement benefits. These were provided as lump sums rather than as regular pension payments, but after 1978 government employees were able to opt for regular payments instead. Under the LI scheme, the insured person pays 20% of the contributions, the employer 70% and the government the rest. Government employees pay 35% and the government the rest.

Here then is a set of measures in the classic Bismarckian social insurance mould, offering grounds for the identification of Taiwan as developing towards a 'corporatist' welfare regime. The expression 'corporatist' is used here to echo the short description of the type of welfare regime Esping-Andersen identified as existing in Germany and other European mainland welfare states. However, it resonates quite well with the way East Asian state-led economic development has been described. It has been shown, in the case of Taiwan as well as of South Korea and Singapore, that the simplistic view that they are models of untrammelled market systems is false. The state has played a significant role. That role has included protection of infant industries, investment in infrastructure and research, and even the development of some important public enterprises (Lau, 1986; Wade, 1990). They have not proved to be simple exemplars of the model of economic development extolled by the 'market liberals'. Trade union participation has been limited, suppressed or confined to officially approved organisations. In that sense, these states differ from the classic corporatist cases (Schmitter, 1974), but public/private partnerships are very much in evidence.

Apart from a range of policies offering support for retired military personnel, including housing and care services, little other social policy had been developed in Taiwan before 1987 (at least if a narrow definition is adopted – to exclude education policy). Certainly, social assistance schemes had been developed, but these were kept small in scale by very strict means tests, even giving attention to the means of relatives outside the immediate nuclear family (see figures given later for more recent dates).

However, there are at least three grounds for challenging the description of the Taiwan social policy system in place by 1987 as belonging to the 'corporatist' group. First, the way the rules of the schemes were designed meant they offered a poor deal to female contributors – with early exit from employment and breaks in employment having a serious impact upon entitlements (Lee, 1999). In this sense, the system might more readily been seen to be in Siaroff's (1994) 'late female mobilisation' category.

Second, bearing in mind Castles and Mitchell's argument about the need for attention to be given in classifying welfare regimes to issues about the regulation of the labour market, it is important to bear in mind that this was a society in which government regulated wages and working conditions in a context of full employment. This had had a marked effect upon income distribution. In 1987 the gap between the family income of the 20% of the population with the highest income and the 20% with the lowest income was 4.7 to one (compared with 5.2 in Japan and 9.5 in the US). It had narrowed to that from 15 to one in 1952 (Yung, 1989, p 20).

Third, the very limited scale of the benefits available, and the many gaps between the schemes, make a direct comparison with Germany or France, for example, rather inappropriate. Nevertheless, we see signs here of a system moving in the 'corporatist' direction.

Social policy since 1987: has democratisation forced extensions down or away from the corporatist 'path'?

The results of local elections and national elections to the then KMT 'packed' legislature in the 1980s indicated that pressure was beginning to mount for the KMT to justify its control over the country. The challenge to the KMT came primarily from the advocates of Taiwan independence. A political party, the Democratic Progressive Party (DPP), emerged in 1986 and, while technically 'illegal', was allowed to challenge the KMT electorally. One year after the ending of martial law, Chiang Kai-shek's son Chiang Ching-Kuo was succeeded as President on his death in 1988 by Lee Teng-Hui. The latter embarked on a programme of constitutional reform, which opened up elections and eliminated the special seats in the legislature reserved for 'representatives' of the mainland. Political conflict in Taiwan rapidly changed from one in which the issues about the future relationship between Taiwan and the mainland were dominant to one in which the DPP modified its pro-independence stance, recognising the dangers that posed of provoking a response from across the water, while the KMT de facto abandoned its aspiration to be the government of all China and concentrated instead upon strengthening the international status of Taiwan. It is surely not irrelevant that Lee Teng-Hui is himself Taiwanese. Increasingly, Taiwanese people came to occupy the senior ranks in the KMT, and that party clearly realised that the dominance of Taiwanese people in the population made a strategy recognising this essential for its political survival. The consequence of the shift in the KMT's stance was the formation of a breakaway party dominated by mainlanders, the New Party.

This 'normalisation' of Taiwanese politics inevitably led to social issues taking an important place in political debate. In some respect, the DPP appeared to be on the 'left' on these issues, the New Party on the 'right' and the KMT in the centre. But both the DPP and the KMT are broad coalitions. However, as the DPP mobilised to try to defeat the KMT in national and local elections, it inevitably, as the 'outsider' party, pressured for new social policies. Until 2000, the KMT held on to control at the national level. President Lee himself successfully contested a fully democratic presidential election in 1996. Table 7.5 gives the results of the two legislative elections held in the 1990s.

As it sought a national political role, the DPP secured control over county and city governments. Its biggest 'prize' in this respect was to secure the mayoralty of the capital Taipei for a period 1995-98. We will see later that these local wins had implications for the social policy debate.

The big change in 2000 was the election of a DPP President, Chen Sui-bian. However, that success came in a 'first past the post' election in which a former KMT politician who had been Provincial Governor, James Soong, turned the contest into very much a three-party fight, winning the endorsement of both the 'mainlander' oriented New Party and many former KMT supporters. President Chen's victory was a

Table 7.5: Seats in the Legislative Yuan

Party	1995	1998
Kuomintang	85 (52%)	123 (55%)
Democratic Progressive Party	54 (33%)	70 (31%)
New Party	21 (13%)	11 (5%)
Others	4 (2%)	21 (9%)

Source: Lu (1998, p 1)

narrow one (he had 39.3% of the vote, with Soong a close second (on 36.8%) and the KMT candidate in a poor third place (on 23.1%). After his election, Chen tried very hard to achieve acceptance as a President for all the people, setting up a cabinet led by a KMT-affiliated premier with members of various political affiliations. But he had to work with a legislature that is still dominated by the KMT. By the end of summer 2000, divisions within the ranks of the new government had become very public, Chen's popularity had fallen seriously and the Premier resigned to be replaced by his DPP-affiliated deputy.

In the legislative elections at the end of 2001, the DPP secured more seats than any other party, with 87 seats (38.67%) in the legislature against the KMT's 68 (30.22%). However, by this time the political situation had become much more complicated. James Soong's People First Party remained strong, winning 46 seats (20.44%). In addition, another opposition party, the Taiwan Solidarity Union, had emerged with the support of the former President Lee Teng-Hui. It won 13 seats (5.78%). The New Party only won one seat (0.44%). Clearly, after that result, government would involve efforts by the DPP President to put together a complicated coalition in the legislature.

The social policy area that first secured attention was health policy. In the run up to the supplementary elections of 1986 and 1989 for the Legislative Yuan, the case for a comprehensive NHI scheme was a prominent manifesto proposal by both KMT and DPP (see Hwang, 1995, on which most of the following account is based). The Premier had announced that there should be such a scheme in 1986, but had set the distant implementation date of 2000. In 1989 a Farmers' Health Insurance (FHI) scheme was set up. In 1990 it was agreed that an NHI scheme should be implemented by 1994. The Executive Yuan (cabinet) set about preparing a Bill. At the same time, rival schemes were developed so that by 1993 the Legislative Yuan had five different Bills before it. Four of those provided for compulsory coverage of the entire population, while one proposed voluntary membership of the scheme. However, a special feature of the last mentioned Bill was that it provided for Chinese as well as western medicine to be available, forcing the government into a concession on that point in its own Bill. The various Bills proposed different formulae for sharing contributions between employees, employers and the government. They also contained different arrangements for co-payment in respect of services provided. In providing for a universal service funded by insurance contributions, the proposals had to cope with the following problems:

- that employers would not want to pay higher contributions for workers with large families;
- that high family contributions might deter participation or drive families into poverty;
- that provisions had to be made to integrate families without a wage earner into the scheme.

The Executive Yuan resolved these issues with a complicated tariff, including contributions from the government in most cases, 100% contributions for households on social assistance, flat-rate employers' contributions regardless of workers' family size, and graduated employees' contributions according to family size (up to a limit of five persons).

The battle within the Legislative Yuan continued through summer 1994 and, when the Bill was passed in July, it contained a late amendment that it should only be voluntary. This arose because of a complex political conflict within the legislature, in which party discipline counted for little. There was an immediate public outcry and the KMT and DPP leaders worked together to secure an amendment in September 1994 putting back the requirement for compulsory coverage. But the price of all the last-minute controversy was the inclusion in the Act of a 'sunset clause' requiring a review of the law after two years. The scheme came into effect at the beginning of March 1995.

The review process required in 1997 has been protracted, and is still continuing. Again there are alternative schemes under consideration. There is evidence that the current scheme has been popular, both from opinion poll data in which the satisfaction rate has risen from 33% at its beginning to more than 74.2% in 2003, and from the way in which the participation rate has risen to more than 97.6% of the population (www.nhi.gov.tw, 2003). The debate about the revision of the NHI scheme has, however, been heavily influenced by the growth of its cost. This is a not surprising feature of an insurance measure where demand is very much provider-led. The government has been slow to introduce controls over the costs of procedures, and the only inhibitions upon overprovision are the rules requiring cost-sharing contributions from patients. Table 7.7 shows the way in which the gap between income and outgoings has closed, producing running deficits from 1998-2001.

President Chen, in a statement made in September 2000, suggested that the NHI deficit was one of the sources of the government's financial difficulties, and indicated that the Department of Health and the

Table 7.6: NHI income and expenditure (1995-2002)

Year	Premium income ($NT)	Expenditure ($NT)
1995	145.2m	136.3m
1996	251.2m	225.9m
1997	255.0m	241.6m
1998	262.0m	267.5m
1999	266.0m	293.2m
2000	280.8m	288.2m
2001	305.1m	306.6m
2002	362.1m	361.0m

Source: www.nhi.gov.tw (2003)

medical organisations would have to come up with a solution. Ideas on the agenda, developed before Chen came to power, include allowing for the development of competition between 'purchasers', and letting non-profit insurance organisations set themselves up as rivals to the central insurance authority. It is far from clear how this will produce economies. It is difficult to see how incentives will emerge to encourage individuals to choose more efficient purchasers and there is sure to be a tendency for competing purchasers to try to 'cream off' low-need clients. It can only be presumed that the power of the doctors' organisations has inhibited a more direct attack upon provider decision making. More radical suggestions involve the idea that the scheme should become private (and presumably non-compulsory).

The original labour insurance legislation includes a provision for unemployment insurance to be included, which came into force at the beginning of 1999. It provides that full-time employees who become jobless can apply for unemployment benefits equivalent to between three and 16 months of 50% of their previous salary. There are rules to prevent those who are deemed to have lost jobs through their own fault, who refuse to accept new jobs or vocational training, or who have income more than 80% of the minimum wage during the unemployment period from receiving benefit. The money for the benefit comes from the existing LI fund, without any change in premiums.

While the period since 1987 has seen the introduction of comprehensive health insurance and, very recently, unemployment insurance, a debate about pension policy has so far been slow to lead to any positive policy change. The main flaws in the existing pension arrangements are in the meagre nature of the provisions, the existence of continuing gaps in provision and the fact that the main LI scheme is only in lump-sum form. For the LI scheme, those lump sums are calculated by allowing the equivalent of one month of insured income (which is often less than real income) for each of the first 15 years of contributions, and two months for each additional year up to a maximum of 45 months. The standard retirement age is 60 for men and 55 for women. For the GEI scheme, the calculation of the pension is more complicated. The insured person needs to have paid at least five years of contributions. The payment is the equivalent of one month of insured income (which is also often less than real income) for each of the first 10 years of contributions, two months for each additional year between 10 and 15, three months for each additional year between 16 and 19 and up to a maximum of 36 months for more than 20 years. The standard retirement age is 65 for both men and women.

One of the ways in which the lump sum is often used is to provide a sum of money that can be used for investment by the extended family or directly in a family business. In that sense, it may be seen as an example of a distinctively Chinese (or perhaps Confucian) approach to welfare, supporting 'exchange' arrangements between the generations in which older people provide support for the ventures of younger relatives who in return provide care. However, the reform ideas on the agenda do involve the supercession of the lump-sum arrangements by regular continuing payments. Obviously, any assessment of the adequacy of a lump-sum pension provision depends upon life expectancy. This is now very similar to that in most western European countries.

The advancement of the pension debate can be directly linked to the evolving political competition in Taiwan (the following account draws upon Wang, 1997, as well as upon directly acquired information). In county elections in 1992, members of the left-wing faction within the DPP included in their platforms the provision of a flat-rate monthly pension for all persons over 65. The DPP went on to adopt the same measure for all county elections in 1993, and included a similar promise in its national programme. The response of the national government was to refuse central subventions to the local schemes adopted by victorious DPP candidates. Consequently, most of these local pensions lasted no more than four months. Nevertheless, the issue was now firmly on the agenda. In 1990 the Executive Yuan started exploring, but then abandoned on grounds of difficulty, the case for the development of a pension for farmers. A DPP legislator proposed a bill in 1995 for such a pension. The KMT's response was to offer its own pension plan for farmers, but to add a means-test provision absent from the DPP bill. A scheme was enacted in July 1995, without a means test!

During the last year of the KMT presidency, the government worked on proposals for a new contribution-based universal pension scheme.

The scheme was to be compulsory for the whole population and run by government.

1. The scheme was to be insurance-based and provide regular and continuing payments for insured persons over 65 or with disabilities, and survivors. A lump-sum funeral allowance equivalent to 10 months of full monthly pension was also suggested.
2. The system was to be built up step by step. The first stage was to involve those who were not covered by the current insurance schemes. Then there were to be arrangements to bring the old and new schemes together (www.cepd.gov.tw).

In opposition, the DPP argued that more should be done for pensioners right away. Chen Sui-bian campaigned in the presidential election on a platform to provide a tax-funded $NT3,000 a month (a little over £60) at once to all without existing pensions. Even after Chen's election, government publicity suggested that the implementation of this policy was imminent. Then gradually the President backed off. Various means-testing conditions were proposed, and promptly attacked by KMT members of the legislature! The expected implementation date changed, first to summer 2001, then to sometime between 2001 and 2004. At a press conference in September 2000, President Chen argued: "Economic development is the top priority. Will there be any social welfare if we do a bad job with the economy?" (*Taipei Times*, 17 September 2000). By this stage all was confusion, with the Council for Economic Planning and Development producing two alternative plans: one for pension insurance, the other for the tax-funded basic pension scheme.

Social policy in Taiwan today: the overall picture

The last sections have shown how, notwithstanding all the political activity around ideas about a basic pension, social insurance has dominated social policy growth. It has been shown how social insurance has grown since 1950, with the LI scheme by far its largest element, supplemented by special schemes for public employees, teachers and farmers. Health insurance was always central to this provision, and from 1995 a universal NHI scheme was enacted. That is in some difficulties now, but it is hard to see how the government can back away from it. Cash benefits for sickness leave (and maternity leave) are provided under the LI scheme. Contributory pensions are provided within the LI and GEI schemes, mainly on a lump-sum basis. There is a non-contributory scheme, without a means test, which provides regular benefits for retired farmers. More developments may occur on the pensions front. Unemployment insurance has started for LI members with a full-time employer.

By contrast with social insurance, other social policy development in Taiwan has been limited, with the exception of education (which is a large and important activity but one that we have left out of this account in favour of discussion of the central social policy programmes). The social assistance scheme is very small in scale. It covers about 0.76% of the population and about 1.02% of households in 2002 (www.volnet.moi.gov.tw). Benefits levels are set at about a third (or 40% in Taipei) of average per capita income and (as already noted) strict extended family means tests are applied. Social care services are provided by local government but these also are very limited in scope – offering modest programmes of residential and domiciliary care for which charges are imposed. In May 2003 there were 983 registered residential and nursing homes for older people, 51 of which were public and 932 private (www.moi.gov.tw 2003). In addition, there were 110 unregistered homes that are expected to be under government supervision, and there are believed to be many more. These unregistered and unidentified homes have caused a lot of problems, such as difficulties ensuring quality and management, and have become a matter of great concern to the government. Welfare service expenditure is 4.9% of the total social policy budget. There is a strong emphasis in social care policy upon avoiding replacing informal family care with formal public care and upon stimulating community self-help. There is very little public housing, merely a limited number of projects for former soldiers.

Social policy in Taiwan has been portrayed as showing some of the signs of growth that would be predicted by modernisation theory. That growth has been shown to be dominated partly by status-divided social insurance schemes, which are said to characterise corporatist social policy regimes. On the other hand, these schemes have been limited in many respects, offering little to women or to people outside regular employment. These limitations, together with the very meagre provisions for social assistance and social care, offer grounds for typifying Taiwan as belonging to an alternative category of East Asian welfare regimes in which family and community-based care is emphasised. These contrasting perspectives will be discussed further in the conclusion.

Conclusion

As indicated in the introduction, there has now been extensive argument about the applicability of the Esping-Andersen models to East Asia. There seem to be various alternative positions on this. One, for which much evidence has been presented in the discussion earlier, is to argue that these regimes belong essentially to the 'corporatist' group, noting the development of Bismarckian-type social insurance schemes. Such a position needs to be supplemented by some application of the earlier convergence theory of modernisation, suggesting that a state like Taiwan is gradually catching up with its European comparators and that the catching-up process will accelerate as the population ages. Esping-Andersen's own analysis of Japan offers a defence of his original model in this respect, while taking on board the need to give attention to some of the complexities highlighted in the 'late female mobilisation' critique arising from the continuing importance of family dependencies and within family exchanges (Esping-Andersen, 1997, 1999).

The alternative to that perspective that offers the most direct challenge is that which suggests that Taiwan, among others, is a 'Confucian welfare state' in which the state is the organiser of growth but not the long-run guarantor of social solidarity. Jones argues thus about such states:

> Central to all their calculations ... has been the maxim that one should never bank on the future; that one should not saddle government or industry with burdens and commitments not capable of adjustment (or abandonment if need be) as circumstances may require. (1993, p 212)

The problem about this label is that it is not clear whether it is a description of types of states, a justification for limited social policies (plus perhaps a prescription of appropriate policies for the future) or an explanation of how such regimes have arisen.

The discussion in this chapter has suggested that it has limitations as a description of social policy in Taiwan, in as much as the major developments have been social insurance policies that act (or have the potential to act) as supporters of individual welfare outside the framework of the family. It is only when we turn to social assistance and social care that familist ideologies seem to have been of primary importance.

There is no doubt that politicians in Taiwan have been prepared to turn to Confucian ideology, and particularly concerns about the sustenance of systems of filial piety, as justifications for limited interventions and as argument for opposing new developments. At the National Conference of Social Welfare 1998, Premier Vincent C. Siew, in his closing address, asserted:

> Family is the pillar of our society. The specific role of family is impossible to be fully replaced, even if more social welfare systems are provided. I want to appeal specifically that our people should pay more affection and concern for their family. The departments of social welfare should design a family-centred service model which integrates social assistance, social welfare and community mutual help to support the family as a basic unit of social welfare provision. In doing so, people who need to be cared for will be able to obtain support and warmth. (21 July 1998)

What is more, inaction can also be found to be justified in terms of the proposition cited by Jones (1993, p 212): "one should not saddle government or industry with burdens and commitments not capable of adjustment (or abandonment if need be) as circumstances may require". The only problem about using these arguments to identify a regime type is that concerns of these kinds are regularly found to be expressed by western politicians. Perhaps we should identify Tony Blair as a Confucian!

However, it is the third issue about the idea that there is a distinctive East Asian regime that is most problematical. It is not – unlike Esping-Andersen's theory – really satisfactory as an explanation of the social policy development that has occurred. It does not point to any explicit political processes that have characterised developments and given them the shape they assume today. In this sense, Kwon's discussion of the applicability of regime theory offers us more help. In a discussion of South Korea and Japan, he emphasises the key influence of the state rather than of political forces in creating a system in which public employees are privileged and private systems have been very influenced by state-led development goals (Kwon, 1997). That seems applicable to Taiwan up to the late 1980s. But since then the political pressure for social policy development has become rather stronger.

Perhaps then there is a need to move away from regime theory, following the lead of writers who have suggested that even in the European context its propositions are beginning to look rather dated (Taylor-Gooby, 1996; Cox, 1998; Johnson, 1999). What we then have to give attention to are:

- the political events that originally set any particular system on the route of social policy development adopted;
- the way a chosen route provides a context and a set of constraints for future developments;
- the new conditions that create influences upon later policy evolution.

The earlier discussion of the period 1946-87 indicates some of the answers to the first point. It highlights the concerns of the KMT to maintain its authoritarian rule and facilitate rapid economic growth. In the comparative absence of challenges from the proponents of any other policy models, they adopted what we have called a Bismarckian approach rooted in the much earlier writing of Sun Yat-Sen. The discussion of the period 1987-2000 then suggests, in answer to the second point, that as political pressures for social reform built up the social insurance model adopted in the earlier period proved capable of adaption to new demands. In this respect President Chen's difficulties – as he opened the account books – in moving away from this to see if he could fulfil a political promise to offer more immediate benefits, seems to reinforce that view.

What then seems to us important about any attempt to answer the third point is to recognise the conditions under which the more recent political debate has been taking place. The Taiwanese economy developed in the period up to the early 1980s in a way that was very insulated from outside influences. After the withdrawal of US support in 1964, the country was very much on its own. It protected the growth of its economy very carefully. There was much state enterprise and capital markets were quite tightly insulated from outside influence. However, by the time we reach the 1990s, the new democratised Taiwan economy and society has become much more open. Thus the later phase of social policy development took place, indeed is taking place, under the influence of global economic developments, and of international bodies and governments very eager to advocate their own models. In other words, and here we go back to modernisation theory, to be growing a welfare state at a time when most of your international comparators (and rivals) are trying to cut theirs is to be under influences that will tend to reduce the likelihood of convergence (except inasmuch as they cut back to your level!). We do not have to engage with the difficult issues about the extent to which there is global determinism operating here; it is sufficient to argue that there are powerful global influences upon decision making. They are only too evident in a society that has received advice from a wide range of

American and British would-be 'gurus', including Margaret Thatcher herself.

We therefore end by taking a relatively agnostic position in relation to regime analysis. There are grounds for seeing Taiwan as a 'corporatist' welfare state, converging but slowly with its western comparators. However, there are good reasons for not becoming too preoccupied with regime analysis, mocked by Cox who says: "Creating arcane typologies has become a cottage industry" (Cox, 1998, p 14). It is important to recognise that the original work by Esping-Andersen was developed specifically to analyse the comparative *politics* of welfare states. It is not then sufficient to say we need a new type for East Asia because the East Asian social policy systems are different – attention must be given to the political processes that make them different.

Acknowledgements

We have benefited from conversations with many people, but we would like to give particular thanks to Hou-sheng Chan, Song-lin Huang, Yin-han Kuo and Annie Lee.

References

Castles, F. and Mitchell, D. (1991) *Three worlds of welfare capitalism or four?*, Canberra: ANU.

Chiang, T.L. (1998) 'Issues and direction of the National Health Insurance Reform', Paper presented at the National Conference of Social Welfare, 21 July (in Chinese).

Copper, J.F. (1996) *Taiwan: Nation-state or province?* (2nd edn) Boulder, CO: Westview Press.

Council for Economic Planning and Development (2003) *Taiwan statistical data book*, Taipei: CEPD.

Cox, R.H. (1998) 'The consequences of welfare reform: how conceptions of social rights are changing', *Journal of Social Policy*, vol 27 no 2, pp 1-16.

Directorate-General of Budget, Accounting and Statistics (2000) *Social indicators: The Republic of China 2000*, Taipei: DGBAS, Executive Yuan.

Esping-Andersen, G. (1990) *The three worlds of welfare capitalism*, Cambridge: Polity Press.

Esping-Andersen, G. (1997) 'Hybrid or unique? The Japanese welfare state between Europe and America' *Journal of European Social Policy*, vol 7, no 3 pp 179-89.

Esping-Andersen, G. (1999) *Social foundations of post-industrial economies*, Oxford: Oxford University Press.

Ferrara, M. (1996) 'The "Southern Model" of welfare in social Europe', *Journal of European Social Policy*, no 6, pp 17-37.

Goodman, R. and Peng, I. (1995) *Japanese, South Korean and Taiwanese social welfare in comparative perspective*, Departmental paper, Suntory-Toyota International Centre for Economics and Related Disciplines, London: London School of Economics and Political Science.

Gough, I. (1979) *The political economy of the welfare state*, London: Macmillan.

Hwang, Y.-S. (1995) 'Funding health care in Britain and Taiwan', PhD thesis, University of Newcastle upon Tyne.

Johnson, P. (1999) 'The measurement of social security convergence: the case of European public pensions systems since 1950', *Journal of Social Policy*, vol 28, no 4, pp 595-618.

Jones, C. (1993) *New perspectives on the welfare state in Europe*, London: Routledge.

Ku, Y.-W. (1997) *Welfare capitalism in Taiwan*, London: Macmillan.

Kwon, H.-J. (1997) 'Beyond European welfare regimes: comparative perspectives on East Asian welfare systems', *Journal of Social Policy*, vol 26, no 4, pp 467-84.

Lau, L.J. (1986) *Models of development: A comparative study of economic growth in South Korea and Taiwan*, San Francisco, CA: Institute for Contemporary Studies.

Lee, A. (1999) 'Sexual division of welfare in Taiwan', PhD thesis, University of Newcastle upon Tyne.

Lin, W.-I. (1990) 'Social welfare development in Taiwan: an integrated theoretical explanation', PhD thesis, University of California at Berkeley.

Lu, M. (1998) 'KMT wins Taipei, bolsters its majority in Legislature', *Free China Journal*, vol XV, no 49, pp 1-2.

O'Connor, J. (1973) *The fiscal crisis of the state*, New York, NY: St Martin's Press.

Rimlinger, G. (1971) *Welfare policy and industrialisation in Europe, America and Russia*, New York, NY: John Wiley & Sons.

Sainsbury, D. (ed) (1994) *Gendering welfare states*, London: Sage Publications.

Schmitter, P. (1974) 'Still the century of corporatism?', *Review of Politics*, vol 36, pp 85-131.

Shin, D.-M. (2003) *Social and economic policies in Korea: Ideas, networks and linkages*, London: Routledge Curzon.

Siaroff, A. (1994) 'Work, welfare and gender equality: a new typology', in D. Sainsbury (ed) *Gendering welfare states*, London: Sage Publications, pp 82-100.

Taylor-Gooby, P. (1996) 'Eurosclerosis in European welfare states: regime theory and the dynamics of change,' *Policy & Politics*, vol 24, no 2, pp 109-24.

Wade, R. (1990) *Governing the market: Economic theory and the role of government in East Asian industrialisation*, Princeton, NJ: Princeton University Press.

Walker, A. and Wong, C. (1996) 'Rethinking the Western construction of the welfare state', *International Journal of Health Services*, vol 26, no 1, pp 67-92.

Wang, F. (1997) 'Support for a new welfare state in Taiwan: social change, political dynamics and public opinion', PhD thesis, University of Chicago.

Wilensky, H.L. (1975) *The welfare state and equality*, Berkeley, CA: University of California Press.

Yung, W. (1989) 'Planning for growth, equality, and democracy: the ROC's development process and its implications', *Proceedings of the International Conference on Public Policy Planning*, Taipei: Research, Development and Evalution Commission.

EIGHT

The development of the South Korean welfare regime

Sang-hoon Ahn and So-chung Lee

Introduction

It is a crude generalisation to regard contemporary East Asian welfare regimes as being based only on Confucianism and then to create the hypothesis that eastern particularity coexists with western influence. Such hypotheses will be examined against the experience of the Korean welfare regime. First, the particularity of Korean society will be outlined and then the universality of Korean social welfare will be discussed.

Revisiting the 'Confucian' welfare regime in Korea

As well as there being a series of studies identifying Korean welfare regime as 'Confucian' (Jones, 1993; Hong, 1999), the legacy of Confucianism seems to have played an important role in the making of the contemporary Korean welfare regime in that this tradition either backed or hindered important changes towards a modern welfare system, such as industrial development and political democratisation. Korea has a long tradition of Confucianism and this is believed to remain intact, governing a large part of everyday life (Jones, 1993; Hong, 1999; Cho, 2001). However, the influence of Confucianism in Korean society is diminishing gradually. Nevertheless this aspect of Korean society should be kept in mind when looking into its welfare regime, just as we need to understand Protestantism or Christianity to study western ones.

There are three core meanings of Confucianism: 'authoritarianism', 'patriarchy (or famililaism)' and 'irrationalism'. First, Confucian norms have formed the basis of modern authoritarian dictatorship. Confucianism was the traditional precondition that *de facto* circumscribed and ruled the role of politics in Korean society, at least before the 1990s' democratisation. In Confucian philosophy, there was no distinction between the state and society. In the monarchical era, up until about a hundred years ago, the king was identified as the state itself under the doctrine of Confucianism. In this tradition, the raison d'être of the state was defined as the cultivation of the moral values of people through the accomplishment of various moral rites. The relationship between the ruler and the ruled ought to be hierarchical. It was the state that would educate and, in so doing, transform the behaviour of the ruled, not vice versa: the people never determined the role of the state. The principles of Confucianism were useful for the authoritarian politicians who governed Korea until the last 10 years of the 20th century. In so far as this tradition held its actual power in governing everyday beliefs, it contributed to authoritarian politics in making the blueprint of the contemporary Korean welfare regime.

Second, Confucianism has been a vanguard dogma behind the patriarchal social system or traditional familism. Esping-Andersen (1999) classified East Asian welfare regimes under the flag of 'conservatism' like Germany or Austria because of their tradition of familism. Under familism, like patriarchy, women tend not to be emancipated but to be burdened by traditional care work without any fair rewards.

Third, Confucianism has been regarded as an obstacle to creating a western type of rational industrialisation. If we re-examine the history of so rapid an industrialisation led by an authoritarian state in Korea, there certainly was an intrinsic paradox between the values required for industrialisation and those behind the power bloc that led industrialisation. This paradox leads to an historical turning point at which traditional Confucianism loses its importance in the face of political democratisation and new social norms and attitudes.

To understand the mechanism of the paradox that paved a new way for the development of the contemporary Korean welfare regime, we need to start from the story of successful industrialisation accomplished by the authoritarian state power bloc. One of the most remarkable features of contemporary Korea is its economic growth and rapid industrialisation since the early 1960s. In the 1980s, the 'Miracle of the Han-river' was frequently cited in worldwide economic reports and the mass media.[1] Many scholars have attempted to solve the puzzle of Korea's miraculous economic growth. The commonplace observation is that the miracle has been orchestrated by the strong, widespread, interventionist state. Korea's economic success demonstrated a new way of industrialisation that challenged the orthodox economic assumptions. It was Confucianism that backed the authoritarian state in orchestrating economic innovations to catch up with western standards of national wealth (Ahn, 1996).

The era when the miraculous industrialisation was under way coincides with the era of de facto 'authoritarian state' (Johnson, 1987). The authoritarian Korean state, backed by Confucian traditions, could make vital economic decisions and implement them while ignoring their political and social implications. However, the Confucian way of thinking began to fade away, due to an unexpected side effect of rapid industrialisation. Because effective industrialisation required the rationalisation of social life in general, the authoritarian government emphasised the removal of irrational conventions. As a result, a liberal way of thinking permeated into everyday life and Korean people started to aspire to 'political liberalisation' and thus 'democratisation'. The historical turning point was 1987, when the conservative authoritarian ruling group submitted itself to the demands of people in the first direct presidential election.

Although Confucianism has been losing its hegemony, some of its authoritarian and patriarchal premises have remained in contemporary Korea. Now that the military-based power has gone and a couple of democratic governments have been elected, this feature still exists to a certain degree even if it is waning. Without it we cannot understand the Korean society and state.

Welfare development and the role of civil society

Authoritarian regime and limited welfare programmes

Although it is a western concept, civil society is comprehensible generally in that it includes labour, students and radical intellectuals as opposed to the ruling class coalition. However, before the late 1980s, Korean society was not accustomed to the term. Even though the Korean state followed the typical pattern of European state formation and its characteristic transformation after the independence in 1945, this procedure was not a simple linear evolution but a dialectic of history. There was a historical reverse turn: the transformation from the 1st Republic to the 2nd Republic made it possible for the democratic state to emerge but democracy was deflated right away by the military coup d'état in 1961. Korea had to undergo great political turbulence and there was no role for civil society. In this section, the dynamics of welfare development along with the mechanisms of state transformation and the development of civil society will be examined. In the period immediately after independence, there was a situation of 'no state' as the Japanese imperialist withdrew from the Korean peninsula. There was a serious struggle to monopolise state power between contending ideological groups from the left to the right. In the end, the right wing subjugated all the centre and left parties under the auspices of the foreign state. The US military government played an active role in supporting the right wing with its military and police forces. However, there was still underground resistance and armed opposition from the left wing. This clash was effectively resolved as the Korean War came to an end. The war effectively eliminated all the internal enemies of the right wing, by giving it control of the southern half of the Korean peninsula.

After the Korean War, the right-wing bloc established a centralised state and suppressed the opposition mercilessly in the name of the National Security Law that was enacted in 1948. However, the 1st Republic collapsed after the '4.19 Students' Revolution', which opposed the authoritarian government. Subsequently, the 2nd Republic (also democratic) failed not only to achieve economic and social reform but also to maintain order. This failure eventually caused political chaos.

In 1961, Chung-Hee Park and his military followers carried out a coup d'état to overthrow the democratic 2nd Republic and established a very powerful centralised military state. He suppressed civil society by armed force and extracted resources without national approval. Park's military government was always under constraint because it contravened the main legitimation process, democracy, and carried the burden of attaining legitimacy against the communist North Korea. This inevitably led Park to choose the export-driven industrialisation strategy. Because South Korea had virtually no natural resources and industrial capital, manufacturing with cheap labour became the centre of industry. Therefore the most important task for the state was to control the political challenges including those from the working class and students. The Park government strategically oppressed political opposition and the labour class by enacting a series of undemocratic laws and amending the major labour related laws. In the early 1980s, Doo-Hwan Chun established another military government, through a second military coup d'état, after the death of Park. His government immediately transformed the state into a developmental one in order to obtain legitimacy by way of economic success.

Despite detailed differences in their approaches, the Park and Chun governments both originated in a coup d'état. When a government comes to power by force, it tries to supplement its lack of legitimacy by earning *ex post facto* consent. In most cases 'economic development' is the main method. However, economic development under an authoritarian regime is achieved through a unilateral decision-making process and an 'efficiency' discourse takes the place of civil consent. The autonomy of civil society is strictly forbidden and therefore it is impossible to expect a restraining influence which makes it unnecessary for the state to pay attention to civil society. This applied to both the Park and Chun governments. Their strength lay in their efficient and prompt execution of various measures that were possible only by completely ignoring civil society. How did the Korean authoritarian government hold back the protests of civil society?

Above all, the anti-communist ideology played an important role in suppressing various political and economic conflicts and maintaining domestic peace. This also explains why it was possible to freeze wages and gain competitiveness without serious labour riots. In the name of national protection against North Korea, the labour movement was regarded in the same light as the communist movement. Because of appalling memories from the Korean War, people had antipathy to North Korea and, therefore, the public tacitly consented to the government's actions. The government used the situation of 'two Koreas' to maintain its legitimacy.

Second, the authoritarian regime obtained governance by subordinating the market to its control. According to liberal assertions, when the state and market act as counter forces and tend to restrain each other, the market functions as a fortress of civil society and activates the roles of various interest groups and political parties. The contrary was true in South Korea: the government nipped civil society in the bud by forming a strong alliance with the market. In this case, 'economic development' was the catch phrase and the coalition propelled export-oriented industrialisation. However, despite successful economic growth throughout this period, most of the 'fruits' were occupied by the political and economic ruling coalition without any distributional concerns. The working class was no more than a scapegoat for a public ideology about continuous economic growth. Most of the economic decision making was carried out with labour interests excluded. The economy was managed and implemented by private industrial conglomerates, so-called '*chaebul*', or financial cliques. The Association of Employers was the only interest group that played an important role in making policies, whereas the Korean Labour Organisation was under complete government control. This situation continued until the mid-1980s when a radical labour movement started to emerge and *illegally* organised the Democratic Labourers' Organisation in accordance with people's demand for democracy. The labour movement during those times was strictly forbidden by law and the police or

Korean Central Intelligence Agency oppressed any sign of such movements.

The government's strategy proved to be quite successful but had limitations because of the coercive reaction to people's demands for democracy. South Korean welfare programmes during the authoritarian period reflect this background: welfare was residual and was regarded by the government as a secondary 'regulatory ruling device'.

In fact, many welfare policy makers in Korea were economists who thought there was a trade off between welfare and economic growth. Korean policy makers regarded the market-centred 'marginal welfare programmes' of Japan or America as exemplary cases. The 1st Republic never bothered to increase welfare in general because it focused on establishing coercion to maximise its power. Thus the government provided welfare only to the privileged few, like the police, the military and civil servants, so as to acquire loyalty: the 1950 Military Relief Act, 1951 Police Relief Act and 1960 Government Employee Pension Act were examples of this special treatment. Resources for 'privileged welfare' were extracted from the people. On the other hand, there was a minimum activity of relief for the destitute and the poor who suffered in the Korean War. The estimated number of people in need of urgent relief was about 10 million from 1951 to 1953 and at least three million from 1954 to 1957. The Lee government spent 5.9-3.8% of total government expenditure on the relief of the war destitute from 1955 to 1959 (Ha, 1989).

The Park government continued with the anti-welfare policy. Again during this period, generous welfare was provided only to the privileged groups, despite increasing poverty and social problems provoked by rapid industrialisation. Table 8.1 shows the welfare programmes that were provided for the poor and the labour class from 1948 to 1986.

As shown in Table 8.1, the state enacted the Livelihood Protection Act for the deserving poor[2] in 1961, which was the first statutory provision of public assistance in Korea, although the budget for public assistance was actually allocated in 1969. In 1965 40.9% of the total population was below the minimum living standard (Choi et al, 1981). This public assistance programme emphasised, first, the concepts of 'self-reliance' and 'self-support'; second, the 'means test' in terms of selectivism; and finally, 'less eligibility' (Sung, 1991). The South Korean Livelihood Protection Act had two basic political and economic functions. First, it was not focused on guaranteeing a stable livelihood for the poor but on preventing sedition. Second, its function was the 'commodification of labour' by which the state pushed the poor to submit to the pressure of low wages.

Table 8.1: Major changes in social welfare under the authoritarian governments (1948-84)

Year	Major changes
1948	• Constitution Article 19:'proper minimum of standard of living'
1950	• Military Relief Act
1951	• Police Relief Act
1953	• four basic Labour Laws: Labour Standard Law, Labour Union Law, Labour Committee Law, Labour Dispute Coordination Law
1961	• Child Welfare Act
	• Living Protection Act
	• revision of the Labour Standard Law
	• Veterans' Protection Act
1962	• Disaster Relief Act
	• Government Employee's Pension Act
1963	• Industrial Accident Compensation Act
	• Labour Affairs Administration
	• Medical Insurance Act
	• Military Pension Act
	• revision of Labour Related Laws
	• Social Security Related Law
1968	• Tentative Management Act for Self-Reliant Exertion Projects
1973	• National Welfare Pension Act
	• revision of the amendment of the labour-related laws (permission of the general state intervention in labour disputes and management)
1977	• Medical Insurance programme for workplaces with more than 500 employees
	• starting of the Medical Insurance programme
1979	• Medical Insurance programme for workplaces with more than 300 employees
1981	• Medical Insurance programme for workplaces with more than 100 employees
	• Welfare Act for the Handicapped
	• Welfare Service Act for the Elderly
1982	• Education of Preschool Children Law
1983	• expansion of Medical Insurance programme for workplaces with more than 16 employees
	• revision of the National Welfare Pension Act
1984	• broadening of the definition of dependents in the Medical Insurance programme
	• revision of the Child Welfare Act (universal)
	• revision of the Welfare Service Act for the Elderly

Sources: Kim and Sung (1995); MOHSA (1994); Lee (1992)

In the same context, those destitute due to natural calamity were provided with tentative relief by the 1962 Disaster Relief Act, and the unemployed poor with work ability could gain some income by participating in the 1968 Tentative Management Act for Self Reliant Exertion Projects. The objectives of the latter were self-support of the poor, utilisation of the idle labour force, community development and contribution to economic development. Various projects were carried out such as reclamation, irrigation, readjustment of arable land, road building and city development work.

If this was how the state regulated the poor, how did it manage the welfare of workers? Above all, there were the Medical Insurance Act and the Industrial Accident Compensation Act during the Park government. At a glance, these programmes seem to be progressive social policies designed to protect the workers. However, medical insurance (1963) was voluntary and so it was incapable of solving employees' medical problems until it was amended in 1976 to be mandatory in workplaces with more than 500 employees. Thus the 1963 Medical Insurance Act can be understood as a fabricated 'anti-welfare strategy' that presented people with an illusion of government generosity.

In contrast, the 1963 Industrial Accident Compensation Act had quite modern characteristics: it defined employers' responsibilities concerning industrial accidents, and provided real compensation for the loss of income due to accident. However, it did not cover small workplaces where more serious accidents occurred. The level of compensation was also relatively low compared to the severity of the accident.[3]

After a decade of industrialisation, the government enacted the National Welfare Pension Act under the slogan of guaranteeing stable life in old age. In this programme, both employers and employees paid the same contributions, and benefits such as old age pension, invalidity pension and survivor's pension were given to the employees. The scope of membership, however, was limited to people with above-average incomes. In addition, the government intended to take advantage of pension funds as resources for economic development. This programme was also planned as a tool to raise private savings, and workers were forced to join the national pension fund, which required a 20-year contribution (Lee, 1992). In so doing, there was no consensus between the government and labour. In any case, the first oil shock in 1973 rendered the new act dormant for 13 years (Lee, 1992).

In summary, we can reach some conclusions about the authoritarian government's anti-welfare strategy. First, the government formed a very solid ruling coalition with capital and together they propelled the labour-intensive, export-driven industrialisation. The ruling coalition never provided effective welfare policy, with the exception of Industrial Accident Compensation Insurance. Second, the government's anti-welfare strategy was quite intentional because it did not lose internal coherence. The main feature of welfare was its emphasis on public assistance programmes, which were strictly based upon the principles of less eligibility and selectivism in order to promote the commodification of labour. Third, the working class without social security suffered from 'double jeopardy': on the one hand, it was directly exposed to the ruthlessness of capital without the buffer of social security while, on the other, the exclusive state corporatist system suppressed the workers' self-identification and collective action. This contrasts, for example with Germany in the 1880s, which had an authoritarian government but recognised the social democrats, unlike the Korean progressive socialist group, which was totally excluded from the political field. Also, while German social policy was formed as a mixture of coercion and incorporation, Korean workers were only objects of coercion.

The 5th and the 6th Republics: towards a new era

Authoritarian governance started to open up from late 1983 when the Chun government decided to allow the political liberalisation and self-regulation of universities. The critical turning point was the 12th general election in February 1985.

During the electoral campaign, the challenging coalition, composed of the middle class,[4] working class and opposition party politicians, was reorganised and began to play a significant role in Korean politics. The result was a major victory for the challenging coalition. The ruling Democratic Justice Party (DJP) achieved only 35.3%, while the three major opposing parties gained 58.6% in total (Kim and Sung, 1995). Nevertheless, this success was not decisive because the sub-sectors of the coalition were not united. The opposing parties pursued 'formal' or 'procedural' democracy, but the other challenging blocs, such as the workers and the students, wanted to achieve 'substantial' democracy in terms of socioeconomic reform. This internal conflict in the challenging coalition continued for more than a year, and in the end the coalition was dismantled when the Chun government started to repress progressive movements.

A new sign of democracy emerged in the spring of 1987. The opposition parties and the challenging coalition achieved a constitutional amendment to direct a presidential election and the withdrawal of the military government. In 1987, the challenging coalition established a central organisation for its movement, called the National Movement Headquarters for Winning the Democratic Constitutional Amendment. This organisation mobilised considerable nationwide demonstrations, gathering over five million people and climaxing in June. The ruling coalition gave way and the DJP's presidential candidate, Rho Tae Woo, made the so-called '6.29 Democratic Declaration' that promised direct presidential elections.

In the direct presidential elections of 1987, Rho won because the challenging coalition was unable to select a candidate. As a result, it became possible for the ruling coalition to avoid a crisis without having to change its strategy fundamentally, and it started to utilise the coercive strategy again. Nevertheless, inside the ruling coalition, the moderate group[5] was able to gain power in policy making during and after the 'June Protest', and one result was an expansion of welfare programmes.

During the democratic transformation of 1987, there was no requirement for state welfare expansion because the labour movement then was marginalised. Every effort by the challenging coalition was concentrated on attaining political democracy in the form of direct presidential elections. However, a favorable environment for the labour movement was created after the 6.29 Democratic Declaration. According to this declaration, basic freedom of speech, publishing, meeting and demonstration was guaranteed, and this liberalisation enabled the working class to organise itself. The revolutionary reform of social security that had been pursued by the radical labour movement since liberalisation in 1983 until the 'June Protest' of 1987 was put forward during the subsequent two years by the democratic labour movement.

Under the Chun government from 1980 to 1986, there had been only 205 labour disputes on average. In contrast, there were 3,749 labour disputes in 1987, and 86% of them took place between July and September. This explosion of the labour movement continued until 1989, although the severity lessened. The workers' demands were focused not only on wage increases but also on the reform of the social security system. In this process, the working class dramatically rejected the positions of 'silence' and 'loyalty' and chose to express its own 'voice'. This meant that the workers as a whole started to recognise themselves as the repressed, and began to mobilise their unique power resource to threaten the state and capital in order to improve their standard of living; they organised themselves and used labour disputes as their typical weapon.

The ruling class, especially the government, which lacked constitutional legitimacy, had no choice but to present a reform-like blueprint for the future that included the introduction of a national pension, the expansion of medical insurance, unemployment insurance and other welfare programmes (Table 8.2). This strategy also reflected the interest of capitalists who feared a revolutionary situation, because

Table 8.2: Introduction and changes in welfare programmes during the transitional period (1986-93)

Year	Welfare programmes
1986	• Minimum Wage Act
	• National Pension Act
1987	• enforcement regulation of Minimum Wage and National Pension Act
	• amendment of Medical Insurance Act
1988	• expansion of the Medical Insurance programme to the rural population
	• government contribution of 50% to the Medical Insurance programme on community-based medical insurance
	• starting of the National Pension programme
1989	• amendment of Industrial Accident Compensation Insurance
	• expansion of the Medical Insurance to the urban self employed
	• Maternity Welfare Act
	• Workers' Housing Construction programme
1990	• Disability Employment Promotion Act
1991	• Company Welfare Fund Act
1992	• Workers' Bank programme
1993	• Employment Insurance Act

Sources: MOHSA (1994); Kim (1995)

such reforms could indirectly guarantee the workers' demand for wage increases in the form of a 'social wage'.

The 1986 Minimum Wage Act was enacted when the challenging coalition, including the middle class and opposition parties, started requiring direct presidential elections, and its enforcement ordinance was prepared during the autumn of 1987 when there was a massive demonstration by the labour movement. This Act, however, was not comprehensive because it was applied only to workplaces with more than 10 employees.

The National Pension programme was also enacted with the 1986 Minimum Wage Act and put into effect in 1988. This was a successor to the National Welfare Pension programme of 1973. It is composed of an old age pension, invalidity pension and survivor's pension. In addition, there are lump-sum payments for those who cannot satisfy the minimum contribution requirements. Old age pensions are payable to retired workers who have contributed for 20 years at the age of 60. The pension system is financed through the accumulation of a pension fund based on contributions from the employer and employee but not from the government.

Medical insurance was enacted under the Park government in 1963, had its coverage continuously expanded to smaller workplaces and was amended just before the presidential election of 1987. The coverage was expanded to workplaces with more than five employees. The amendment said that those excluded from the programme could receive benefits under a special allowance when they applied for it. In addition, it specified plans for nationwide expansion until 1989. In the long run, the medical insurance, which had formerly covered only workers in workshops, public officials and private school teachers, was extended to the rural population in 1988 and the urban self-employed in 1989 and, thereby, the whole population come under protection from either medical insurance or medical assistance. The government has funded about 50% of the total expenditure on community-based medical insurance since 1988.

However, the medical insurance system still had limitations. First, the decentralised system of medical insurance proved to be administratively inefficient. Second, there was a huge difference in financial capacity between separate insurance unions and, thus, those with relatively low financial capacity – for example, rural community unions – had no other choice but to endure the burden themselves. The medical insurance scheme in Korea was totally differentiated between separate groups from its origin – the main division being between employees and their families under a compulsory scheme and a voluntary one for other people. This scheme was revised and expanded several times but the main features remained the same. During the late 1980s when political democracy started to bloom, the debate on integration and centralisation of this scheme took place but major organisations, including large companies, refused to support the proposal because integration meant sharing their contributions with other more disadvantaged ones. In addition, the government did not want to support integration for fear of an increased burden on the state.

What happened after Rho came to power? Some say that he actually played an important role in expanding the 'nascent welfare state': the 6th Republic accomplished the amendment of several welfare programmes including the Industrial Accident Compensation Insurance Act, expansion of the Medical Insurance to the urban self-employed, the Maternity Welfare Act, the Workers' Housing Construction programme, the Employment Promotion Act for Disabled People and the Workers' Bank programme. As for the amendment of the Industrial Accident Compensation Insurance Act, the coverage was expanded to workplaces with more than five employees without any exclusions and at the same time the role of the state increased in the management and financing of the programme.

The 1990 Employment Promotion Act for disabled people mandated that workplaces with more than 100 employees had to employ people with disabilities totalling at least 1% of the total workforce. Otherwise the employer had to pay about US$200 as a Disability Employment Promotion Contribution for one disabled person. While both the amendment of the Industrial Accident Compensation Act and the enactment of the Insurance Disability Employment Promotion Act implied an expansion of social welfare coverage, the 1991 Company Welfare Fund Act represented a transfer of welfare supply from the state to private companies. This Act is proof that the state and capital in the ruling coalition were preparing a series of welfare measures with a common purpose to neutralise the formidable labour movement that had been mobilising since 1987.

Along with the above programmes, there had been several others and, above all, the plan for Employment Insurance was set up during the 6th Republic. This programme, however, was put into effect in 1995 in the form of a Japanese-style work incentive system. With the enactment of this programme, which guaranteed the workers' loss of income caused by unemployment, Korea became a *de facto* welfare state by instituting four basic major social insurance programmes. Concerning the amendment of medical insurance, one important event has to be mentioned that shows the nature of welfare reform during this period. Apart from the expansion of coverage, there was also another call for reform, to integrate and centralise the system. The national assembly unanimously passed the 1989 Integrated Amendment Act but it was overturned by the presidential veto.

In summary, there was a 'welfare explosion' during the transitional period after the summer of 1987. The main factor behind this change was popular resistance: the June Protest in 1987, the workers' Autumn Protest in 1987 and later protests. The resulting crisis in the ruling coalition forced it to fundamentally alter its strategy – to a mixture of coercive regulation and incorporative welfare.

Thus, the characteristics of welfare during this period may be summarised as two-fold. First, whether intended or not, the government actually established the framework of a welfare state during this period. Nevertheless, the reform lacked a long-term perspective and philosophy, and was primarily a measure to regain legitimacy by focusing on the working class. Second, the welfare strategy was introduced to increase workers' support for the regime by stimulating their material interests and providing them with collective social security. In addition, it wanted to nullify antagonistic public opinion.

The 'civilian government' and limited welfare reform

In the 1988 general election, the ruling Democratic Justice Party failed to win a majority and was defeated by the Peace Democracy Party, led by Kim Dae Jung. The DJP formed another conservative coalition between the Unification Democratic Party (led by Kim Young Sam) and the New Democratic Republic Party. Once again, the three-party coalition formed the majority in the assembly. During the authoritarian regime, Kim Young Sam was a progressive politician, along with Kim Dae Jung but, having failed to unify behind one presidential candidate, both of them ran for election in 1987 and were defeated by Rho Tae Woo. Kim Young Sam's calculation was obvious when he formed a conservative coalition with Rho; he was bearing in mind the presidential election in 1992, which he won.

As the title 'civilian government' implies, Kim Young Sam was the first civilian president after the long years of military reign and the legitimacy of the Kim government derived from this fact. At first, he proposed far-reaching reforms in the areas of politics, economics and society. However, reforms that required only a short period of time for promotion or were determined by the president's own interest and power were successful, whereas reforms that required alteration in the basic principles of society, and thus needed general consensus, ended in failure. Administrative reform, military reform and reform of the financial system belong to the former category, and reforms in taxation, labour relations, the welfare system and the political system, to the latter.

The reason for failure lay in the unique characteristics of the Kim Young Sam administration. The fact that it originated from the conservative coalition with parties from the authoritarian residuum became an obstacle to Kim's reform strategy. Although the coalition made him a successful candidate, it nevertheless contained internal heterogeneity that constantly threatened disruption. Whenever there was a new reform plan, Kim had to worry about handling internal antagonists rather than external opponents. Consequently, Kim had to walk on a tightrope between pushing through reform and maintaining the coalition.

Despite the splendid rhetoric of civilian government and the reform plans that misled the public to believe real democracy had been achieved, Kim Young Sam's government was essentially undemocratic, just like Rho's. Both governments favoured financial cliques and lost political autonomy. Among the members of the assembly belonging to either the DJP or the Democratic Liberty Party,[6] many were heads of commercial conglomerates or people who were closely connected to them. Both governments were financially dependent on private companies. Exorbitant amounts of illegal political funds were paid in return for preferential treatment. The ideological and political propensity of both governments was more or less similar. Kim Young Sam regarded democracy in a strictly formal sense that only required a fair political election of government officials. Kim never gave a second thought to various oppressive institutions such as the National Security Law and the prohibition of workers' political activities.

Kim Young Sam's government tried to push reforms as a means of reorganising the national power structure and leading civil society but these only resulted in its withering. This is a good example of what happens when the initiative of societal reform is not led by civil society itself but by the government. Despite an expansion of civil society with democracy, civil society's role and significance diminished. As a result, two big currents of change began. Whereas the former NGOs regressed, new NGOs started to appear such as the People's Solidarity for Participatory Democracy (PSPD).[7] These new ones gradually expanded by raising new issues. While the former social movements concentrated on class-related issues, the new NGOs began to turn their attention to issues concerning the quality of life, including welfare.

After the period of miraculous prosperity, the economic growth rate began to fall from the beginning of the 1990s. Kim Young Sam focused on economic development more than anything else during the first half of his term, and welfare was traded for economic stabilisation. Economists and policy makers of the civilian government put the blame on a labour movement that grew rapidly after the 1987 protests. The year 1995 proved to be a turning point. Following the World Summit for Social Development in Copenhagen, social welfare issues were raised in South Korea even though it was secondary to economic policy. The three reasons for this change were, first, Kim was confident enough to promote social welfare reforms after the economic growth rate rose to 8.3% in 1994; second, there was the coming general election in 1996 and it was politically necessary to provide more generous welfare benefits so as to gain popular support; third, it was one of the main aims of the civilian government to join the OECD and welfare underdevelopment was certainly a hindrance to this goal. Consequently, the president announced a Welfare Plan for Improving the Qualities of Living in March 1995.

Welfare advances during the civilian government were minimal (Table 8.3). The introduction of the Unemployment Insurance Scheme

Table 8.3: Major welfare policies under Kim Young Sam (1993-97)

Year	Welfare policy
1993	• Introduction of Unemployment Insurance Scheme
1995	• Amendment of National Pensions Act to include farmers and fishermen
	• Enactment of Organic Law of Social Security
1996	• Enactment of National Medical Insurance Act (to integrate the government officials, teachers' fund and the local fund)
1997	• Enactment of Community Chest Act

was actually decided in 1991 but only institutionalised in 1993, which implies it was an achievement originating from Rho rather than Kim. From 1993, welfare expenditure gradually diminished to 3.82% of total government expenditure in 1995. Under the Rho government, expenditure never fell so low. From 1996, welfare expenditure started to rise and reached 4.03% in 1996 and 4.22% in 1997, but it never exceeded that of the previous government.

The people's government and welfare as a social right

Kim Young-Sam's civilian government and Kim Dae Jung's people's government share common characteristics that are clearly distinguishable from the Rho government in three aspects. First, the civilian and people's governments were both established by politicians who had long struggled for democracy. Second, both governments tried to change the closed ruling coalition between the state and capital to a more open one including both labour and civil society. Third, it became more widely recognised during the two governments that welfare should be a social right. Despite these common features there was a fundamental difference in the actual welfare achievements of the two governments. Whereas welfare during the civilian government was only rudimentary and lacked widespread consensus, the people's government brought the issue of welfare to the fore and established what could be called a welfare state by introducing new policies and amending the existing ones towards a more universal system.

South Korea was in jeopardy when Kim Dae Jung took office; not only did it have to deal with the political crisis breaking out from the heterogeneous characteristics of the ruling coalition but, above all, it had to overcome the economic crisis. Also, South Korea was under the influence of international financial organisations that limited the autonomy of policy decisions, a price paid for financial loans. Despite this difficult situation, Kim Dae Jung contributed greatly in mitigating

Table 8.4: Welfare developments during Kim Dae-Jung's government (1998-2000)

Year	Major changes in welfare policies
1998	• Unemployment Insurance scheme expanded to workplaces with more than one employee
	• Social Insurance Integration Committee formed
1999	• Enactment of People's Health Insurance Act
	• National Pension system expanded to all citizens
	• Enactment of Minimum Livelihood Guarantee Act
2000	• Worker's Compensation Act expanded to workplaces with more than one employee
	• Enforcement of Minimum Livelihood Guarantee Act
	• Integrated Health Insurance scheme put into effect

Source: Sung (2002)

inequality and enhancing social integration through a successful programme of welfare reform (Table 8.4).

Under the people's government, a universal system of welfare was established, with coverage of social security considerably enlarged. Unemployment Insurance and Worker's Compensation were extended to workplaces with more than one employee in 1998 and 2000, the Pension Scheme became 'national' in 1999, and the Medical Insurance programme that was once divided into hundreds of administrative units was integrated into a national administration with the enactment of the 1999 People's Health Insurance Act. Second, there was a big change in social services for the socially disadvantaged such as older people, disabled people, women and single parents. For example, an elderly allowance was introduced in 1998 for low-income older people who were not entitled to pensions and, from 2000, the category of disability was extended to include various chronic diseases and autism. Third, welfare expenditure increased significantly during the people's government, as shown in Figure 8.1. Apart from 1998 when the government had to concentrate on restoring the economy after the crisis, welfare expenditure was at its highest compared with that of preceding governments. Last but not least, there was a striking development concerning the public assistance programme. The former Livelihood Protection Act, which was residual in character, was transformed to The Minimum Livelihood Guarantee Act in 1999, which made it more universal in character, and public assistance was also recognised as a social right.

Apart from its welfare achievements, the people's government successfully overcame the economic crisis within two years. The reasons for its success were that, first, there was a temporary and exceptional increase in state autonomy owing to the economic crisis. Korean

Figure 8.1: Welfare expenditure as a percentage of public expenditure (1980-2001)

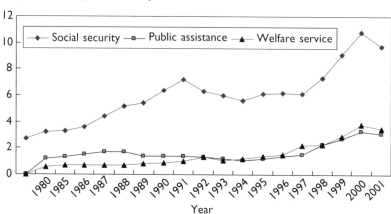

Source: MOHW, Planning and Budget Division (2003)

companies had to accept certain unfavourable conditions (such as writing off debts), and had to submit to state control, the state being the major executor of the requirements of international financial organisations. The introduction of labour institutions was an example. The workers who were opposed to economic restructuring during the former government partly surrendered to the state. Thus, despite its internal vulnerabilities, it was possible for the state to manage both labour and capital effectively and to promote welfare reform.

Second, the labour movement and civil society played a significant role. Labour organisations like the Korean Confederation of Trade Unions (KCTU) and the Federation of Korean Trade Unions (FKTU) participated in the tripartite commission from the beginning of the people's government and requested substantial welfare reform. As an exemplary case, the KCTU cooperated with NGOs like Health Right Network (HRN) and PSPD and took initiatives in enacting the 1999 National Health Insurance Act. In the case of Minimum Livelihood Guarantee Act, PSPD and Citizen's Coalition for Economic Justice (CCEJ) took the initiative and the KCTU, FKTU, pro-welfare politicians and academics joined in the process. Without the efforts of civil society, the two most representative welfare reforms during the people's government would not have been achieved or their scope would have been reduced. The fact that NGOs, as well as the working class, played a significant role in welfare reform is a unique Korean characteristic. Unlike western welfare states, South Korea lacks influential left parties that represent labour. Thus, we can conclude that the power resource theory that effectively explains the development of welfare states in Europe does not fit the South Korean case.

The pro-welfare and reformative nature of the people's government was another important factor in the success of the people's government. This propensity made the so called 'vertical coalition' possible, a coalition between the government and labour/civil society organisations for welfare reform. Even though the opposing parties and some bureaucrats who gave priority to economic growth were antagonistic to welfare reform, it was possible for the government to carry on regardless.

Conclusion

Looking back on the trajectory of welfare development in South Korea after industrialisation, we can conclude that the main force behind it was the capacity of civil society. When welfare was endowed as an appeasement by the ruling class, policy lacked a long-term focus and effectiveness. When civil society mobilised itself, things started to change fundamentally. When civil society lost the capacity to partner the government, the reform staggered and when civil society exhibited this capacity at its fullest, it became an initiator of alternative social policies.

However, in all that dynamic process, we can also see that welfare development after industrialisation encroached on the territory of traditional rules and norms that had formed the basis of Korean society. Although the Confucian element of state power no longer plays an important role in the making of the South Korean welfare state, Confucianism remains as a background notion governing some of the welfare programmes of today. In this sense, institutions matter and the legacy of the regime should not be ignored when we look at the current characteristics of a welfare regime.

The Rho government is the first one to be elected under the initiative of civil society. Despite its heady rhetoric, the Rho government is under threat due to its amateurism and the North Korean nuclear crisis. The various welfare programmes introduced by former governments have turned into political burdens, which might be due to the social division of welfare created by the programmes themselves. The main characteristic of Korean welfare can be summarised as mainly selective. Selectivism could be harmful to pro-welfare politics because it ends up with a cleavage between taxpayers and beneficiaries (Ahn, 2000, 2003). There is public antagonism towards establishing a progressive welfare state; every day there are newspaper articles about conflicts around welfare politics, even with regard to some universal programmes, such as pensions. There is a serious fiscal deficit problem caused by the dual structure of medical insurance: privatisation of medical services coupled with socialisation of medical insurance.

As to the future of the South Korean welfare regime, two different scenarios are possible. The North Korean nuclear crisis might be settled and a progressive government established. In this case, moderate reform and further developments in welfare could be a possible story. In contrast, a second scenario has to do with a regression to conservatism, which could mean that privatisation surpasses recent achievements in other OECD countries. An appropriate aim of the present government would be to earn support from the middle class by creating a more universal welfare system. In order to achieve this aim, reducing tax evasion and political corruption are essential tasks for the Korean government.

Notes

[1] In the year 1960, per capita GNP was as much as US$80, one of the poorest in the world. In 1989, it reached nearly US$5,000 and in 1995 slightly more than US$10,000. During the period 1965-88, the Korean economy grew at an average rate of 6.8% a year, which is remarkable by international standards. The unemployment rate was also low enough to be defined as full employment.

[2] 'Deserving poor' means people who are unable to work and have no relatives with legal responsibilities of support, for instance people over 65 years old, children below the age of 18, poor pregnant women and the disabled.

[3] In the following years, the scope of this programme was extended to smaller workplaces – those with more than 200 employees (1965), 150 (1966), 50 (1969), 16 (1974), and 10 (1982). Nevertheless the level of compensation remained low. As a result, the Industrial Accident Compensation Act was incapable of providing proper protection to employees' loss of health and income.

[4] In Korea the university students' political movement and other social movements by progressive middle-class intelligentsia were crucial factors in organising the political opposition bloc.

[5] In the political ruling bloc there were two groups from the beginning. One was the military-based politicians' group and the other comprised

highly educated politicians who had studied in the US and who had a pro-US propensity. The latter and a few former generals who were excluded from central power during Chun's period won in the political power game after the crisis because Chun gave them important positions in the government and in parliament in response to the challenging coalition's demand for the withdrawal of the military politicians. In the long run, this kind of power game within the ruling coalition was extended after the presidential election and finally Rho betrayed his close friend Chun and Chun's military group had to leave Seoul. This internal political power game of the ruling group partly contributed to political liberalisation and welfare expansion after the 'hot' summer of 1987.

[6] This was a party created as a result of the coalition between the Unification Democratic Party, the New Democratic Republic Party and the DJP.

[7] The former NGOs include the friends of social movement organisations established during the military governments. Their movement reached a peak at the end of the 1980s with the June Protest serving as a source of momentum. Having their basis in classical socialism they were mostly concerned with either class-based or unification issues. In contrast, new NGOs that started to appear at the end of the 1980s and onwards, broke from conventions and diversified their issues to a wide variety of social problems.

Acknowledgement

This work was supported by a Korean Research Foundation Grant (KRF-2003-041-B00365).

References

Ahn, S.-H. (1996) ' Genesis of the Korean welfare state: a sociopolitical analysis on the generative mechanism of the welfare state' , Paper presented at International Welfare Seminar, Eskilstuna, Sweden.

Ahn, S.-H. (2000) *Pro-welfare politics: A model for changes in European welfare states*, Uppsala: Uppsala University Press.

Ahn, S.-H. and Olsson-Hort, S. (2003) 'The welfare state in Sweden', in C. Aspalter (ed) *Welfare capitalism around the world*, Hong Kong: Casa Verde Publishing, pp 89-111.

Cho,Y.-H. (2001) 'Confucianism, conservatism, or liberalism? A study on Korean welfare state regime', *Korean Journal of Sociology*, vol 35, no 6, pp 169-91 (in Korean).

Choi, I.-S., Suh, S.-M. and Kim, S.-K. (1981) *Status of poverty and policy for the poor*, Seoul: Korea Development Institute (in Korean).

Esping-Andersen, G. (1999) *Social foundations of postindustrial economies*, Oxford: Oxford University Press.

Ha, S.-R. (ed.) (1989) *History of Korean social welfare*, Seoul: Bak-Young-Sa (in Korean).

Hong, K.-J. (1999) *A study on the welfare state regime of South Korea*, Seoul: Na-Nam (in Korean).

Johnson, N. (1987) *The welfare state in transition: The theory and practice of welfare pluralism*, Amherst, MA: The University of Massachusetts Press.

Jones, C. (1993) 'The Pacific challenge: Confucian welfare states,' in C. Jones (ed) *New perspectives on the welfare state in Europe*, London: Routledge, pp 81-100.

Kim, T.-S. and Sung, K.-R. (1995) *Theory of welfare state*, Seoul: Na-Nam (in Korean).

Lee, H.-K. (1992) 'Development of welfare state in an authoritarian capitalist society: the Korean experience', Paper presented to Conference on *Welfare state: Present and future*, Seoul, September 25-26, COEX (Korea Exhibition Centre).

MOHSA (Ministry of Health and Social Affairs) (1992) *Major programs for health and social welfare*, Seoul: MOHSA Printers (in Korean).

MOHW (Ministry of Health and Welfare) Planning and Budget Division (2003) (www.mohw.go.kr/databank).

Sung, K.-R. (1991) 'Political regime shift and social policy in Korea', *Korean Journal of Social Welfare Studies*, vol 3, pp 109-46.

Sung, K.-R. (2002) 'Consolidation of civilian government and the development of the Korean welfare state: a comparison with people's government', in Y.-M. Kim (ed) *Debates on the characteristics of the Korean welfare state (I)*, Seoul: In-Gan-Gwa-Bok-Ji (in Korean) pp 487-523.

NINE

The welfare regime in Singapore

Vincent Wijeysingha

Introduction

Singapore's developmental path over the past 40 years has led it from a third-world port station to a first-world industrial city exhibiting social indicators and standards of living on a par with the industrialised west. The People's Action Party (PAP), which has governed Singapore during all this time through a mixture of Westminster democracy and social repression, chose a developmental ideology that was authoritarian and free market, verging on the socialist in the nature of some of its social provision, yet avowedly capitalist; and exhibiting the characteristics of a major first-world city while retaining aspects of its Asian patrimony.

The public welfare system is characterised by the double objective of developing resource infrastructure (which includes human resources: the Labour Ministry's name was recently changed to Ministry of Manpower) and providing a welfare safety net for the most disadvantaged (Goh, 2001, 2002). Private welfare provision exists alongside subsidised state programmes. There is universal free education up to pre-university, including various routine measures such as an annual cash payment to school children and one-off measures such as partly meeting the cost of personal computers for teachers, a subsidised health system including a means-tested grant for those who cannot pay, and subsidised public housing with programmes of reduced rent for the less well off and one-off rent rebates from time to time. The state provides a small amount of (stringently means-tested) income relief and other welfare services and acts also as enabler, facilitator and regulator of voluntary welfare providers through development operating grants to welfare organisations, assisting with fundraising and coordinating affairs through the National Council of Social Service and its fundraising arm, the Community Chest. This is called the 'many helping hands' approach (Ministry of Community Development, 1996;

Government of Singapore, 1991). In addition, in the past 10 years or so, the Ministry of Community Development has developed a network of state-funded neighbourhood welfare offices, a programme that intensified following the financial crisis of 1997. Indeed, the state has considerably enhanced its role during the economic slowdown following the crisis (Lim, 2000; Goh, 2001, 2002; Yap, forthcoming). At the apex of the public welfare system lies the Central Provident Fund (CPF), whereby a proportion of a person's wages is added to a portion paid by the employer and the sum retained until retirement. Since 1968, the amounts payable have fluctuated, primarily with a view to keeping overall wage costs down. In addition, since that year the government has allowed numerous initiatives for fund holders to withdraw monies before retirement to finance a range of services from public housing and medical bills to higher education.

Thus, contrary to popular belief, public welfare in Singapore is ubiquitous and highly developed. However, it is not easy to understand the juxtaposition of such a framework against an avowedly capitalist free-market system merely by reference to existing theories of welfare. It is also problematical if the social policy framework is lifted out of the wider national context. This chapter therefore seeks to trace the role of state social policies in the overall framework of state making. As a society that even in its colonial era had prioritised the economic over other aspects of corporate life and with a population descended from similarly materially minded immigrant forbears, the basic proposition of the chapter, that economic considerations formed the crux of policy making, was always a truism. This chapter constructs a conceptual framework that takes into account the set of features that Singapore's history presented. It follows a political economy methodology that understands social policy in terms of its instrumental rationality and provides a generalised overview of the social policy framework from the independence period (1959) to the present.

The political economy approach

In contrast to the gradual creation of western welfare states, the social policy framework in Singapore was the result of its colonial history and the geopolitical settlement in the period after the Second World War. The colonial period resulted in a specific set of socio-political characteristics, while the geopolitical structure placed the tiny-resource, poor-island nation within a global context that mandated precise policy responses for continued viability.

These structural outcomes suggest that a political economy approach founded upon a statist emphasis is the most appropriate method by which to theorise public welfare. Such an approach assumes a fundamental relationship between the economic and the political, a relationship taken as given in much of the literature (Okun, 1975; Atkinson and Stiglitz, 1980; George and Wilding, 1985; Barr, 1989, 1992, 1993; Korpi, 1989; Pfaller et al, 1991; Rubison and Browne, 1994; Gough, 1996; Atkinson, 1997). A political economy approach attempts the synthesis of the political and the economic through analytical engagement with the effects of political authority on markets and of market forces upon states (Strange, 1988). This is particularly relevant when considering Singapore since it emerged in a neo-Westphalian global settlement in which world production and supra-state structures were being increasingly coordinated in consonance with the foreign policy aims of the USA in which Britain acquiesced (Chomsky, 1994; Curtis, 1995; Hoogvelt, 1997). Given the new dispensation that "all nations would be incorporated into a capitalist world economy" (Gills et al, 1993, p 7), the Singapore government set out to define and execute a political economy that was in accord with these imperatives.

Within the political economy approach, the International Political Economy (IPE) paradigm provides much in the way of conceptual potential since it is concerned with the nature of the global political economy and the connection between economics and politics in international relations (Cox, 1995; Hettne, 1995). This especially applies to Singapore, given its restricted capacity to influence global conditions (Leifer, 1989). Therefore Giddens' (1985, p 120) notion of the state as "the preeminent power container of the present era" is rejected in favour of Castells' (1992) and Hoogvelt's (1997) contention that the distribution of power varies among states and is shared also by transnational agencies such as the World Bank and International Monetary Fund and, in more recent times, the larger multinational corporations.

A third conceptual tool that deepens the methodological scope is Cox's (1996a, 1996b) 'historical approach', which examines material structures as they are manifested both in the structural changes that occur over time and in the interactions that occur among the structural features of any given epoch. The ideological content of a particular historical period necessarily plays a role in policy determination and thus the ontology of an era under consideration forms an important component of its policy analysis. Cox (1995) suggests that, in an evolving framework of structures and institutions, the abiding values and their manifestations are best judged in terms of their enduring existence over different epochs, whose shifts are themselves signified by changes in the surface texture of societal organisation.

The IPE paradigm, a wider political economy approach and an historical analysis creates an analytical framework that addresses the two central antecedents of development in Singapore, its colonial legacy and the impact of the post-war global political economy, which led policy makers to prioritise economic viability as the central feature of policy determination (Castells et al, 1990; Deyo, 1992; Ramesh, 1995; Leftwich, 1995, 1996; Goodman and Peng, 1996; Kwon, 1997). In achieving this pre-eminent developmental goal through the concerted restructuring of state and society, the Singapore government came to accumulate a vast store of credibility and legitimacy, and effected the cooptation of elite participants in the project enabling it eventually to redefine the parameters of the state and restrict to state elites the privilege of determining policy.

This construction is characteristic of all the East Asian Newly Industrialising Countries (EANICs) and led Leftwich (1995, 1996) to coin the term 'developmental state', in which an autonomous and powerful administrative and industrial elite pursues explicit developmental objectives in the context of a weak civil society.

The social policy settlement, understood in terms of what Walker (1984, pp 39-40) refers to as "the rationale underlying the development and reproduction of social institutions and groups that determine the distribution of resources, status and power between different groups in society", is best understood on the basis of its relationship to the principal goal of continued economic viability. It exists in an instrumental relationship to the economy in that it attempts to assist the process of capital accumulation, the reproduction of labour and the maintenance of the system as a whole (O'Connor, 1973; Gough, 1979). In Singapore, these factors gradually came to be the main components of policy definition and measurement. These system values vis à vis Singapore's productive capacity led its government to pursue a policy framework that, in time, became reified as the guiding principles of national development policy.

Singapore, the product of historical transformation

Modern Singapore was established at the highpoint of the British expansionist period when it sought a trading station in South East Asia to secure its position there (Wong, 1991). In 1819, Singapore became a trading post of the English East India Company and later a British colony (Chew, 1991). The impetus for Singapore's founding, and its subsequent raison d'être, was commerce (Turnbull, 1989). The administrative structure evolved into a trading meritocracy without democratic features (Lee, 1989). Individual self-interest was prioritised ahead of community welfare and administrative efforts were focused on sustaining the conditions conducive to trade; in essence, government intervention in the social sphere was aimed at maintaining this or ensuring overall order. Public welfare was limited to that which flowed from private philanthropic effort (Turnbull, 1989), with the government making occasional forays into the social arena, for example, to control epidemics. The wealthy philanthropists who endowed the community with public works tended to be men (sometimes women) of stature and city fathers (no woman ever held administrative office during the colonial period) who occupied unelected administrative offices from the mid-1850s.

A very specific set of socio-political characteristics developed. In the administrative arena, the population became accustomed to centralised, unelected government with successive generations of benevolent autocrats. In the commercial sphere, a pro-capital mercantile elite oversaw affairs on behalf of an essentially comprador class using monetarist demand management as the principal economic instrument. In this sector of the political economy, the government intervened extensively in order to sustain the economic climate. The culture that this engendered in the colonial period and beyond was characterised by a wealth-oriented, self-interested, anti-welfare regime in which the administration played a nominal social policy role.

A community shaped by these attributes found itself independent and relocated in a new period of post-war history at the apex of which stood the US, which had benefited from the war, increasing its GNP by two thirds, and now controlled two thirds of global industrial production (Hobsbawm, 1994; Hoogvelt, 1997). Smaller, weaker countries had to reconstruct their economies in order to fit the priorities of the US. Its National Security Council (NSC) defined a new 'Grand Area' policy designed to establish an integrated world economy subservient to and serving the US, particularly since it was deprived of raw materials and markets from those countries behind the Iron and Bamboo Curtains (Chomsky, 1993, 1994). A 1949 NSC study argued that within a general framework of US dominance and a 'neo-liberal' climate, the South would continue to act as raw material provider, labour source and market to the North (Chomsky, 1994).

However, by war's end a rethink occurred with the communisation of Eastern Europe and China; the allies sought to develop the East

Asian nations into a capitalist bloc led by Japan, the better to isolate, or 'encircle', China: the now famous 'Truman doctrine' (Chomsky, 1994).

The western economies turned to consumer goods production and the new wealth enabled the expansion of social concessions. However, by the mid-1960s, production fell as markets became saturated. Production was then exported to low-cost areas like South East Asia, part of a select group of regions nominally sympathetic to the West that would participate in the globalisation of production; the New International Division of Labour (NIDL) was born, whereby production processes were delivered into a variety of partial operations performed at different worldwide locations (Froebel et al, 1980; Hoogvelt, 1997).

The developing globalised economy meant that tiny states such as Singapore became viable economic players by producing directly to the world economy (Hoogvelt, 1997). This was particularly true for resource-poor Singapore, that, following its expulsion from the Malaysian federation in 1965, was deprived of a market hinterland. Singapore opted to specialise in low-cost, labour-intensive, export oriented manufacturing (Han et al, 1998). Then Prime Minister Lee Kuan Yew said "a socialist Singapore [outside Malaysia] is an economic impossibility" (Turnbull, 1977, p 325).

The rapid movement of skill and expertise, of investment and capital, underpinned by US economic goals, enabled small nations to engage directly with the global economy. Countries such as Singapore were now able to develop 'niche economies', exploiting their 'non-comparative advantage' (Hobsbawm, 1994; Hoogvelt, 1997), capitalising on their main attribute: cheap, docile labour (Bello and Rosenfeld, 1990). Singapore, arguably the most vulnerable of these countries, given its aggregate resource deficit and relative lack of international political capital, embraced the new dispensation more readily than its cousins (Chan, 1971; Cheah, 1980; Leifer, 1989).

The Singapore government came to view economic viability as the central plank of its policy framework, constrained as the nation was by the geopolitical realities bearing upon it and largely shaped by the value structure thrown up by the colonial period. As a newly independent state, the government sought to formulate a political economy that would ensure the viability of the nation, what Prime Minister Lee called "a matter of life and death for two million people" (Han et al, 1998, p 109). His government understood its predicament in terms of the economic, since it believed that ultimately it was a sound economic base that would guarantee the security of the state (Han et al, 1998; Lee, 2000) and the re-election of his party.

Hence, the principal responsibility was the creation of those conditions necessary for capital accumulation. In addition, the need was recognised to locate Singapore's economic structure within wider regional stability for, as former Prime Minister, Lee Hsien Loong, stated: "a wise nation will make sure that its survival and well being are in the interests of other states" (Leifer, 1989, p 965). Thus Singapore came to its pre-eminent policy feature that formed the basis of the whole political economy, a project aimed at long-term stability and economic prosperity, and drawing from the nation's patrimony.

The colonial enterprise had created an outward-looking, capitalist economy serviced by a materialistic population administered by a centralised, authoritarian, undemocratic government. This configuration, coupled with the hardy self-reliance of an immigrant community, did not demand state welfare provision and there was none. Thus, two features, the one political and the other historical, coalesced in the type of society the independent government sought to create. This was buttressed by a full employment policy that the government implemented following the first elections in 1959 (Pillai and Tan, 1989).

Thirty years later a government statement (Government of Singapore, 1988, p 4) noted that "The best form of welfare is to enable the people to earn their own living. The PAP Government wants all Singaporeans to be able to look after themselves". This was reaffirmed in a statement to a United Nations summit: "Economic development and social development go hand in hand. We have to grow the economic pie if we want to feed or keep the stomachs satisfied. Hence, the Singapore government's priority has always been on economic development" (Lim, 2000, p 3).

Alongside this, the government determined that its social policy programme would help to create the social conditions and values necessary for wealth creation (Han et al, 1998). Personal welfare came to be characterised within the personal wealth creation agenda and, consequently, dependent upon economic growth. The individual, the family, and later (with the establishment of ethnic-based welfare organisations), the community, were to be the font of welfare (Lim, 2000). The main areas in which the government acted were those aspects of social welfare that aided the economic programme: infrastructure, education and training, public housing, and residual social security and health for the most unfortunate (Lee, 2000; Lim, 2000; Yap, forthcoming). Thus, the social policy regime was essentially economic in orientation in that it was viewed as a handmaiden of the economic programme, and also, constructed as being in the gift of the state, reliant upon continued economic growth. The government insinuated a kind of compact into the national discourse, whereby the political acquiescence that ensured the continuance in power of the PAP would be the price of sustained economic growth. These elemental propositions have remained unchanged, with former Prime Minister Goh Chok Tong restating them recently in two major speeches (Goh, 2001, 2002).

In the simultaneous process of addressing the economic programme and recreating the society, a guiding framework of themes came into being, and the relative success of the economic programme enabled the framework to endure over the years along with the political longevity of the PAP government. These four themes came to occupy a practical and politically useful status that remained at the heart of the social policy framework:

1. regime maintenance;
2. construction of appropriate values;
3. commitment to pluralism;
4. public welfare as developmentalism.

Regime maintenance is characterised by a centralised, authoritarian government; a politicised bureaucracy and depoliticised citizenry; tight social control; and a party/people compact. The appropriate values are free market capitalism; self-interested wealth creation; a materialist social value system and a meritocratic rewards system. The commitment to pluralism, motivated by the potential divisiveness of an ethnically mixed population, led the government to pursue multiculturalism and secularism. The value system for it led to the characterisation of welfare as a personal responsibility, thus preventing the conception of public welfare as a right of citizenship and weakening its potential for decommodication. This was justified by reference to the politico-economic realities; the first Prime Minister said:

> Societies like ours have no fat to spare. They are either lean and healthy or they die. We have calculated backwards and forwards for eleven months on an independence that we never sought, that our best chances lie in a very tightly organised society. (Chan, 1989, p 70)

The argument for a firmly controlled populace drew upon the much publicised vulnerability of a tiny state compelled to present its best face, political stability, to the investors. The overarching economic priorities resonated with a hardy, immigrant population unacquainted with any notion of comprehensive, universal welfare. The public welfare system came to be constructed within a tight functionalist framework with the bulk of public social spending directed towards human capital enhancement (Lim, 1989) and the quality of welfare services reflected in their price.

Social and economic policy: two sides of the same coin

Economic development in Singapore occurred in four distinct phases (Lim and associates, 1988; Huff, 1994; Bercuson, 1995; Peebles and Wilson, 1996). In Phase 1, from 1959 to the end of the Malaysian interlude in 1965, the focus was on rapid economic restructuring towards import substitution. The next phase, until the mid-1970s, saw the switch to export orientation because the nation could no longer take advantage of the Malaysian hinterland. Phase 3, lasting until the mid-1980s, involved the consolidation of the economic gains of the previous phase and the management of a severe labour shortage. This resulted in an attempted high-technology upgrade of the economy, the failure of which saw Singapore's place in the NIDL confirmed. Singapore returned to its previous export-oriented, labour-intensive production base but began Phase 4: diversification into a range of other products such as banking and services to replace labour-intensive manufacturing.

Phase 1 was characterised by the handover of power from the British to the new local administration led by the PAP. Given the 'divide and rule' policy of the previous administration, there was no national identity that the new government could harness to shape the rapid socioeconomic transformation it envisaged. In addition to these uncertainties, the government was faced with a range of social problems. The social policy of the previous administration had left the vast majority of the population with inadequate welfare provision. There was a severe housing shortage, low life expectancy, inadequate healthcare and inadequate educational facilities. Unemployment was around 13.5% and 30% for school leavers (Hughes, 1984), which was a problem for a nation with more than 50% of the population under 20 years old (Department of Statistics, 1983).

The new administration therefore aimed at a policy structure that attended to the problems of the economy, the social welfare system and the lack of a national identity. The social difficulties were compounded by an economic base that would not serve the new nation. Centring principally on its original priorities for Singapore as a trading station, the British had developed the entrepôt as the principal economic activity. This began to stagnate in the post-war period due to direct trading between nations and the progress of the port at Hong Kong. Singapore risked being eclipsed by other new nations that might be able to provide the services it had previously handled. Furthermore, an import replacement system, the preferred choice at the time for small decolonised nations, might prove unviable for Singapore given its miniscule market. (At the time, federation with Malaya had not been seriously considered.)

The PAP embarked upon a three-sided policy framework: first, within current resource limitations, attend to immediate social welfare needs; second, begin the process of creating a national identity; third, create a viable economic base. Prime Minister Lee stated:

> The question was how to make a living? How to survive? This was not a theoretical problem in the economics of development. It was a matter of life and death for two million people.... The sole objective was survival. How this was to be achieved, by socialism or free enterprise, was a secondary matter. (Han et al, 1998, p 109)

The PAP government saw the political and economic merits of merging into a larger federation together with peninsular Malaya, British North Borneo and Brunei. Eventually, a Federation of Malaysia was established in September 1963, consisting of all these territories except Brunei.

The PAP proposed an economic framework of rapid industrialisation in the context of import substitution in preparation for federation, with Malaysia as the principal hinterland market. This period saw also the gradual involvement of the government in the economy, both as macro stabiliser and as participant. In the political sphere, the PAP began to establish a strong, centralised administration mirroring the former colonial structure. In the social sphere, the government set about creating a political consensus in the context of a melting pot 'Malaysianisation', mindful that any policy of racial superiority would disadvantage the commercial Chinese community against the Malay *bumiputra* (sons of the soil).

The social policy framework being defined had to give expression to national goals along all three fronts. This period saw the enactment of a series of measures designed to seriously destabilise the labour and leftist movements. (The substance of these enactments has remained largely unchanged.) This occurred concurrently with Operation Cold Store, which saw the imprisonment without trial of 116 leftist and labour leaders. The People's Association (ostensibly a community development agency) and its network of community centres were established, among other things, to provide propaganda points for government ideology.

The principal social policy goals at the time were the cutting of the severe unemployment (particularly among school leavers), the expansion of primary health facilities, the quantitative expansion of education and the gradual decimation of the Chinese schooling system (from whence, it was perceived, much leftist rhetoric was being disseminated), population control, urban regeneration and slum clearance. The PAP declined to create a social security system and the CPF, begun by the British in 1955, was retained as the principal pensions instrument.

The period represented the infancy of the PAP and its policy framework, but the themes were already discernible. The leadership had no need to emphasise the viability of the capitalist system for, in the years of the British administration, the free market system had become entrenched in society. This was further embedded by the presence of a largely immigrant population that identified with the wealth-making goals of the British. But the PAP government, through the People's Association, the education system and public campaigns, began to espouse a materialist value system and a market-based meritocracy (Milne and Mauzy, 1990; Huff, 1994). Former Prime Minister Lee, speaking in 1967, said "You must have something in you to be a have nation" (Han et al, 1998, p 177). The core of this social structure was described succinctly in a UN paper: "Every Singaporean is imbued with the sense that rewards can only be brought about through hard work, based on the principles of meritocracy and self reliance. We do not believe in social handouts" (Lim 2000, p 2).

In perceiving the need for a tightly controlled state, the new government began to create the structures that would support a highly centralised administration. Its use of the Internal Security Act (ISA) (enacted by the British during the Emergency of 1948-60) to silence opponents and the inauguration of the Political Studies Centre and, later, the Civil Service College as training institutions for civil servants created a highly politicised civil service and a decision-making structure characterised by the absence of either viable alternative political parties or sites for the discussion and assessment of public policies. Attention to human capital development in the expansion of schools and healthcare facilities and retention of the CPF meant that what was in the making was a welfare system that linked personal income security closely to earnings and prioritised social investment.

The Malaysian interlude and the import substitution strategy both failed because of the entrenched nature of Malay power on the peninsula and the suspicion of the Chinese commercial class and the PAP's vociferous calls for 'Malaysianisation'. In August 1965, Singapore was expelled and then entered the second phase of its development.

With the nation's territory reduced to around 600 square kilometres, import substitution was no longer viable. The PAP government decided to switch to an aggressive Foreign Direct Investment (FDI)-led export orientation strategy. This stage saw the departure of the PAP's leftist rhetoric and a greater emphasis on the free market. 1968 was a decisive year. In the General Election the PAP took all seats (only seven of the 51 were contested) with a 40% increase in its vote (Ministry of Information and the Arts, 1997). Command of the legislature allowed the PAP to push through its programme, which shifted economically to the right and socially towards the authoritarian. It also allowed the PAP to quicken the process of cutting off rival power bases, a process begun by the British in the run-up to 1959 (as part of its anti-socialism efforts [Curtis, 1995]) and continued by the PAP. Also in 1968, British troops began to be withdrawn (Cheng, 1991). This meant that up to 20% of employment and 13% of GDP would disappear (Krause, 1989): this concentrated the government's mind. It set out to dominate the power structures more comprehensively so as to manage the crisis at hand by establishing a quasi-corporatist, government-led labour structure that included the tripartite National Wages Council (NWC) and the eventual assigning of the Secretary Generalship of the National Trades Union Congress to a Minister without Portfolio in the Cabinet.

The general thrust of policy from this time was the creation of the conditions that would attract FDI to Singapore (Chan, 1989; Krause, 1989). Economic activity would prioritise industry, trade, tourism and services such as oil refining and the financial sector, but the principal facet of economic policy focused on FDI. The government established a series of tax incentives and other supply-side measures to attract investors (Bello and Rosenfeld, 1990). This period also saw the establishment of the principal development, regulatory and investment agencies such as the Monetary Authority of Singapore, the Development Bank of Singapore, the Economic Development Board and the Government Investment Corporation (Turnbull, 1989; Huff, 1994; Schein, 1996).

Two punitive labour laws in 1968 dominated the social policy field.

The legislation was designed, first, to trim the powers of the labour movement and, second, to recast it as subordinate to the government and as a service provider rather than an advocate of labour. The government also began qualitative improvements in education and training to upgrade labour skills. The practice of admitting cheap foreign labour into the country continued (Chew and Chew, 1995) and further female participation in the workforce was encouraged (Huff, 1994). These measures were intended to control the upward pressure on wages (Pang et al, 1989).

The government continued its expansion of public housing and the development of satellite towns to coincide with the shift of industrial centres away from the city centre (Teo and Savage, 1991). CPF funds were released for housing purchases (Low and Aw, 1997). The first increase in CPF contributions was made in 1968, raising the proportion of the full wage retained by almost 3% (Low and Aw, 1997). By the end of Phase 2, the proportion of the full wage retained in the fund was a little over 26%, an increase of almost three times from 1955 when the scheme began (Central Provident Fund Board, 2000). The government also made its first overtures in the population field, beginning the 'Two is Enough' policy (Saw, 1991). It was in this phase also that ethnic quotas were imposed in public housing and in schools.

The government introduced bilingual education with English as the main language of instruction (Gopinathan, 1991). This was made possible by its earlier successes in decimating the Chinese schools, aided by the rhetoric that, as western FDI had begun to dominate the economy, those with facility in English had a head start over others in the labour market. A moral education programme was also introduced in schools.

Phase 2 saw the consolidation of the major principles of the PAP's ideology. It was handed absolute control of the legislature from which to see through its change programme. The focus on foreign investment meant that the capitalist, free market system became entrenched in the political economy. Accordingly, a market-based meritocracy would come into being. This in turn led to the consolidation of a materialist value system that was reinforced by residual public welfare based on labour market participation. This extended also to housing since CPF contributions were regularly raised in Phase 2 and began to be released to fund a variety of welfare needs. State welfare expenditure extended only to those components of social policy that would have an immediate impact on human capital development, that is, education, primary healthcare and housing. The fourth policy theme, secularism, continued to be advanced in the education system. The pluralist emphasis was also given expression in the ethnic quota system applied to school numbers and public housing distribution.

Phase 3 was a period of consolidation and crisis. An inevitable labour shortage resulted from the rapid expansion. A series of world events, particularly the oil crises of the mid-1970s, signalled the end of the boom that followed the Second World War and the beginnings of protectionism. This phase also saw a rise in the fortunes of the domestic political opposition. This phase was characterised by the consolidation of the export-led economic base. The agencies that played a central role in development were becoming more effective in their stewardship of the economy. Economic growth continued to be high but with the end of the post-war boom there were structural problems exacerbated by the labour shortage and a gradually widening gap between rich and poor. Former Prime Minister Lee admitted: "We are developing painfully, unequally, often unjustly" (Turnbull, 1989, p 313). Rumblings of discontent heralded the election of two opposition MPs in 1981 and 1984 and the reduction in the PAP share of the vote by nearly 13% between 1980 and 1984 (Open Singapore Centre, 2000).

The economy also faced wider structural problems, some at the global level. Regional competition, high import tariffs imposed at the end of the boom, and oil price hikes affected the functioning of the economy. The government opted for Keynesian-style public spending programmes and also made overtures to the Gulf states in a bid to improve its economic prospects in what was rapidly turning into a global recession. In the political arena, the government introduced a series of constitutional measures that, while giving the impression of wider consultation on public issues (such as a Feedback Unit), consolidated real power within the elite, such as the practice of appointing 'Nominated MPs' to Parliament (Open Singapore Centre, 2000).

The social policy regime continued to be characterised by its adherence to the themes established in Phase 1 and consolidated in Phase 2. There was a cutback in public health funding and a move towards emphasising personal responsibility and private provision (Phua, 1991). Thus the government enacted measures to release a proportion of CPF savings for healthcare (Low and Aw, 1997). The main function of releasing CPF funds for health was influenced by both the demographics of a population that was beginning to show signs of ageing, and the privatisation trend then sweeping the world. While privatising healthcare provision, the government began to consider developing specialised medical services as another prong of the economy.

Moral education was replaced by a more focused religious education programme emphasising the moral worth of obedience and order. In addition, ability streaming in primary schools was phased in to further concentrate resources on those considered most able. The government also addressed the labour shortage and, mooted the idea of a wholesale economic upgrade designed to lift the nation's productive capacity into higher technology and services, with concurrent wage increases. This resulted in the ill-fated Second Industrial Revolution (SIR), announced in Parliament in 1981 (Schein, 1996). The programme was intended to move production towards higher technology manufacturing such as computer peripherals, the tourism industry and financial and related services (Peebles and Wilson, 1996). Preparations included a 'wage correction strategy' that increased the wages of workers in line with the skills that a proposed skills upgrade would provide (Bello and Rosenfeld, 1990). A levy upon employers funded a Skills Development Fund. Training and scholarship programmes were implemented and several human resource agencies formed. A 10-year plan was produced to improve industrial facilities. Overall development expenditure on the current account increased by 24% (Rodan, 1987).

However, the revolution backfired; the NIDL was still firmly entrenched in the global economy. Despite the ability of government to channel some production capacity towards appropriate industries, Singapore's niche status remained, in global terms, that of a low wage economy. The multinational corporations were not prepared to link their output with the Singapore government's priorities. The economy suffered a significant recession, recording deficit growth of -1.2% in 1985 (Bello and Rosenfeld, 1990). The brunt of the recession was borne by the labour force, which suffered a wage freeze and an 8.2% cut in the full wage contribution of the CPF, allotted fully to employers (Lim, 1989). This cut was only redressed in the amount of 0.35% of the full wage in 1988 and never returned to the 40% rate set for the SIR. At what would have been a humane time to begin introducing social insurance measures to mitigate the worst excesses of the market, the government responded with a wage cut.

In the interval between the end of the revolution and the next phase, the government began encouraging reinvestment in all types and levels of industry and turned to local capital, hitherto sidelined in the development paradigm. In addition, it implemented a tranche of Keynesian development programmes to restimulate the economy.

Economic growth stabilised and public housing and NWC wage controls acted as macro stabilisers. (Public housing is a macro stabiliser in that it encompasses land prices, raw commodities for building materials and the control exerted on the inflation rate by housing prices.)

Phase 3 therefore represented a further consolidation in the PAP's developmental priorities. Partial privatisation of healthcare and the release of CPF funds to purchase health services reflected principles of social welfare based on market efficiency and the ability to pay. The increase in government expenditure for skills training further focused developmental funds on public investment schemes as opposed to welfare. Educational reforms included programmes to emphasise the meritocratic value system and the reification of market-based differentials. Despite formal democratic arrangements, constitutional measures instituted after the watershed 1984 elections designed to entrench the PAP in power, came to alter the practice of governance. Faced with the consequences of the meritocratic ideology, such as a more vocal middle class and a rise in the fortunes of the political opposition, the government responded by making democratic overtures but tightening up state structures.

Thus, Phase 3 saw an attempted shift of Singapore's position in the NIDL, a programme that did not succeed. What is significant is that, first, the social policy goals in preparation for the shift coincided very closely with the goals of the revolution and did not take into account other features of the global economy then impacting upon Singapore, such as the economic downturn. The government's response to the ageing of the population was the privatisation of parts of the healthcare system and diversification of the CPF to cover more individual welfare spending.

In the latest phase, the government returned to economic restructuring. However, it has been careful to view this in terms of diversification within its productive limits rather than attempt a wholesale upgrade as had been the case at the end of Phase 3. In November 1990, Prime Minister Lee handed the administration to Goh Chok Tong who produced a government blueprint for the coming years, *The Next Lap* (Government of Singapore, 1991). Simultaneously, the Economic Committee, a high-level planning body, produced the *Strategic Economic Plan* (Ministry of Trade and Industry, 1991), mapping out the future direction of the Singapore economy. Both these documents emphasised diversification of the economy to include the development of the financial and service sector, and progress to achieve first-world economic and social standards. In social terms, the documents called for more choice in educational facilities and an emphasis on creativity in the curriculum, developing the physical environment, encouraging community spirit and voluntarism, and increased funding for education and training.

Politically, there were setbacks for the PAP: in the 1991 elections, four seats went to the opposition (Open Singapore Centre, 2000). The government took further steps to entrench its position in the administration, culminating in legislation to provide for a directly elected President with some administrative jurisdiction. (Candidature was restricted to a handful of the most establishment-oriented persons.) In the face of growing popular opposition, the government adopted the rhetorical discourse of 'Confucianism' and 'Asian values', essentially anti-West narratives whose real aim was the entrenchment of the authoritarianism and discipline that had begun to be eroded by an increasingly better educated and better travelled middle-class population. (Following the financial crisis, even former Prime Minister Lee has backtracked, claiming that Asian values per se do not exist [Lee, 2000]).

In the industrial sphere, the economy reflated in the years following the recession due to supply-side measures and Keynesian demand management. Along with the emphasis on diversification, the government focused on local capital development and exhorted local entrepreneurs to regionalise their operations while retaining their headquarters in Singapore. A Public Sector Divestment Committee (1987) recommended deeper divestment of government equity in the economy (Tan, 1992), a process that continued in this phase, although not reaching the scale of privatisation seen, for example, in Britain or New Zealand.

A principal feature of this phase was the call by the then Education Minister for a new focus on creativity in schools to prepare for future developments in the global economy. The government increased the education component of its development budget for enhanced career development of frontline workers, curriculum improvements and a broader-based education programme. The independent school system, mooted some years previously (Ministry of Education, 1987), was implemented. The government also released further CPF monies to fund some forms of higher education. There were no changes in healthcare, housing and social insurance policy, although the Ministry of Community Development introduced a range of social welfare schemes to cater for the less well off (Ministry of Community Development, 1997; 1998). However, these concessions continued to be constructed as being dependent upon the continued skilful economic stewardship of the PAP. It also advanced the principle of 'many helping hands' whereby the state, acting in the main as coordinator, encouraged a range of social welfare providers such as churches, missions and voluntary organisations (Ministry of Community Development, 1996; Government of Singapore, 1991). The government also encouraged the private sector to play a part in welfare provision, especially in worker skills training. This was seen as a means by which adequate and widespread welfare initiatives might take root, but without overly burdening the public purse or altering the principle of market-based meritocracy (Lim, 2000).

Increased spending on education demonstrates that social investment continues to be guided by economic considerations and social expenses by opposition to a welfare state. The policy framework in the current stage demonstrated the tenacity of the core themes. The social value system continues to be underpinned by the principles of market meritocracy. The regime is characterised by the enduring presence of the PAP and a citizenry that, though increasingly informed and making some input in the public sphere, is constrained by the principle that formal politics can operate only within the context of adversarial party politics. The state still retains considerable powers to thwart religious sectarianism through the Maintenance of Religious Harmony Act, and provisions of the Constitution and the Societies Act control the type of organisations that may exist in the country. Public welfare continues to be divided between social investment expenditure geared to competitiveness and a welfare regime constructed within a discourse of privilege as opposed to right.

Conclusion

Singapore faced gigantic tasks when it attained independence and later when it was expelled from the Malaysian federation. The results of the PAP government's response are well known: exponential economic growth; a wealthy and highly educated populace; a powerful and authoritarian state often given to repressive and heavy-handed social control, and extraordinary political longevity for the governing party. At the same time, social policy has provided widespread social amenities, the general eradication of absolute poverty, and established a social value system.

But the system has bred its own weaknesses. Demographic and social changes such as smaller families, inter-ethnic marriages and a rapidly ageing population have meant that the old assumption of the family and the ethnic community as first ports of call in times of distress are beginning to erode. A highly educated population schooled in the discourse of rights accruing to the meritorious is no longer willing to accept the mantra of compliance in return for material benefits. The government is finding it increasingly difficult to draw on the rhetoric of crisis that fuelled the original party/people compact, and the global downturn at the beginning of this century has deprived it of being able to produce double-digit growth year after year. The massive economic catching up of countries like Malaysia and South Africa, not to mention China, has forced Singapore to yield its cheap labour position. With the global economy in downturn, Singapore is currently in a major recession (Burton, 2002b, 2003a; Yap, forthcoming), as a result of its openness and dependence on the electronics industry, exacerbated by the Severe Acute Respiratory Syndrome (SARS) epidemic (Burton, 2003b).

How has this impacted on policy? Early on there appeared to be a growing emphasis placed on policy issues. An inter-ministerial committee on ageing was set up. A campaign was launched to recruit more social workers and a social work training institute was announced (Wong, 2002). The first academic study of poverty was undertaken (Yap, forthcoming). In addition a 'Remaking Singapore' committee was established to look at social and socio-political issues (*Financial Times*, 2003).

In 2001, the government responded to the recession and the massive increase in unemployment by announcing a host of welfare measures. These included a limited income replacement scheme, rent rebates, retraining grants, free healthcare for older people with certain medical conditions and liberalising the stringent rules that govern the ownership of state-built housing for single people. It also included government bonds given to the population. However, inevitably, the measures have also included a cut in the employer component of the CPF. (In fact, the Economic Review Committee [ERC] recommended fundamental changes in the CPF scheme [Burton, 2002a, 2003a], hitherto a no-go area of policy.) Also, in a bid to attract more FDI back to Singapore, the government has let up on its strict moral position by allowing customers to dance on bar tops and by signalling a more tolerant attitude to homosexuality, which is still illegal in Singapore. Indeed, government speeches have manifestly toned down the hardline rhetoric (Goh, 2001). This is widely perceived to be intended to lure FDI workers back in.

In social policy terms, the global recession and, to a lesser extent, the financial crisis of 1997 that resulted in the very generous welfare and relief measures, marked a turning point in state social policy in that the measures have appeared to decouple the link usually made between welfare and dependency. They were portrayed as being within the gift of government rather than a right of citizenship but, nevertheless, the Prime Minister's speech introducing them (Goh, 2001) and parliamentary statements announcing the details (Hu, 2001; Lee, 2001; Yeo, 2001) laid markedly less emphasis on this than would previously have been the case.

Might this be the beginning of the Singapore welfare state that was predicted by the first Finance Minister and economic architect, Goh Keng Swee? From Goh's point of view – that is, that advanced industrial capitalism throws up social concerns that necessitate universal welfare – it may well be. Alternatively it could be that these measures are the latest version of initiatives designed to reinforce the established order in the face of uncertainties, and keep intact all the fundamental features of the regime.

References

Atkinson, A. (1997) 'Does social protection jeopardise European competitiveness?', *Bulletin Luxembourgeois Des Questions Sociales,* vol 4, pp 19-28.

Atkinson, A. and Stiglitz, J. (1980) *Lectures on public economics*, London: McGraw-Hill.

Barr, N. (1989) 'Social insurance as an efficiency device', *Journal of Public Policy*, vol 9, no 1, pp 59-82.

Barr, N. (1992) 'Economic theory and the welfare state: a survey and interpretation', *Journal of Economic Literature*, vol 30, no 2, pp 741-803.

Barr, N. (1993) *The economics of the welfare state* (2nd edn), Oxford: Oxford University Press.

Bello, W. and Rosenfeld, S. (1990) *Dragons in distress: Asia's miracle economies in crisis*, London: Penguin.

Bercuson, K. (ed) (1995) *Singapore: A case study in rapid development*, Washington, DC: International Monetary Fund.

Burton, J. (2002a) 'Singapore in rethink on pensions investments', *Financial Times (London)*, 16 July.

Burton, J. (2002b) 'Recession fear as Singapore sees fall in GDP', *Financial Times (London),* 11 October.

Burton, J. (2003a) 'Singapore sticks to state planning in restructuring strategy', *Financial Times (London)*, 7 February.

Burton, J. (2003b) 'Singapore counts cost of SARS and technology downturn', *Financial Times (London)*, 12 August.

Castells, M. (1992) 'Four Asian tigers with a dragon's head: a comparative analysis of the state, economy, and society in the Asian Pacific Rim', in R. Appelbaum and J. Henderson (eds) *States and development in the Asian Pacific Rim*, Thousand Oaks, CA: Sage Publications, pp 33-70.

Castells, M., Goh, L. and Kwok, R.Y.W. (1990) *The Shek Kip Mei syndrome: Economic development and public housing in Hong Kong and Singapore*, London: Pion.

Central Provident Fund Board (2000) *Central Provident Fund Annual Report 1999*, Singapore: Central Provident Fund.

Chan, H.C. (1971) *Singapore: The politics of survival, 1965-1967*, Kuala Lumpur: Oxford University Press.

Chan, H.C. (1989) 'The PAP and the structuring of the political system', in K.S. Sandhu and P. Wheatley (eds) *Management of success: The moulding of modern Singapore*, Singapore: Institute of South East Asian Studies, pp 70-89.

Cheah, H.B. (1980) 'Export oriented industrialisation and dependent development: the experience of Singapore', *Institute of Development Studies Bulletin*, vol 12, no 1, pp 35-41.

Cheng, S.H. (1991) 'Economic change and industrialisation', in E.C.T Chew and E. Lee (eds) *A history of Singapore*, Singapore: Oxford University Press, pp 182-215.

Chew, E.C.T. (1991) 'The foundation of a British settlement', in E.C.T. Chew and E. Lee (eds) *A history of Singapore*, Singapore: Oxford University Press, pp 36-40.

Chew, S.B. and Chew, R. (1995) 'Immigration and foreign labour in Singapore', *ASEAN Economic Bulletin*, vol 12, no 2, pp 191-200.

Chomsky, N. (1993) *Year 501: The conquest continues*, London: Verso.

Chomsky, N. (1994) *World orders, old and new*, London: Pluto.

Cox, R. (1995) 'Critical political economy', in B. Hettne (ed) *International political economy: Understanding global disorder*, pp 31-45, London: Zed Books.

Cox, R. (1996a) 'Realism, positivism, historicism', in R. Cox and T. Sinclair (eds) *Approaches to world order*, Cambridge: Cambridge University Press, pp 49-59.

Cox, R. (1996b) 'Social forces, states and world orders', in R. Cox and T. Sinclair (eds) *Approaches to world order*, Cambridge: Cambridge University Press, pp 85-123.

Curtis, M. (1995) *The ambiguities of power: British foreign policy since 1945*, London: Zed Books.

Department of Statistics (1983) *Economic and social statistics, Singapore, 1960-1982*, Singapore: Department of Statistics.

Deyo, F. (1992) 'The political economy of social policy formulation: East Asia's newly industrialised countries', in R. Appelbaum and J. Henderson (eds) *States and development in the Asian Pacific Rim*, Thousand Oaks, CA: Sage Publications, pp 289-306.

Froebel, F., Heinrichs, J. and Kreye, O. (1980) *The new international division of labour*, Cambridge: Cambridge University Press.

George, V. and Wilding, P. (1985) *Ideology and social welfare*, London: Routledge and Kegan Paul.

Giddens, A. (1985) *The nation state and violence*, Berkeley, CA: University of California Press.

Gills, B., Rocamora, J. and Wilson, R. (eds) (1993) *Low intensity democracy: Political power in the new world order*, London: Pluto.

Goh, C.T. (2001) 'New Singapore', Prime Minister's National Day Rally Speech, Singapore, 19 August.

Goh, C.T. (2002) 'Remaking Singapore: changing mindsets', Prime Minister's National Day Rally Speech, Singapore, 18 August.

Goodman, R. and Peng, I. (1996) 'The East Asian welfare states: peripatetic learning, adaptive change and nation building', in G. Esping-Andersen (ed) *Welfare states in transition*, London: Sage Publications, pp 192-224.

Gopinathan, S. (1991) 'Education', in E.C.T. Chew and E. Lee (eds) *A history of Singapore*, Singapore: Oxford University Press, pp 268-87.

Gough I. (1979) *The political economy of the welfare state*, London: Macmillan.

Gough, I. (1996) 'Social welfare and competitiveness', *New Political Economy*, vol 1, no 2, pp 209-32.

Government of Singapore (1988) *Agenda for action: Goals and challenges: A Green Paper*, Singapore: Government of Singapore.

Government of Singapore (1991) *Singapore: The next lap*, Singapore: Times Editions, for the Government of Singapore.

Han, F.K., Fernandez, W. and Tan, S. (1998) *Lee Kuan Yew: The man and his ideas*, Singapore: Times Editions.

Hettne, B. (1995) 'Introduction: the political economy of transformation', in B. Hettne (ed) *International political economy: Understanding global disorder*, London: Zed Books, pp 1-30.

Hobsbawm, E. (1994) *Age of extremes: The short twentieth century 1914-1991*, London: Penguin.

Hoogvelt, A. (1997) *Globalisation and the postcolonial world: The new political economy of development*, Basingstoke: Macmillan.

Hu, R.T.T. (2001) 'Budget Statement 2001', delivered in Parliament, 23 February.

Huff, W. (1994) *The economic growth of Singapore: Trade and development in the twentieth century*, Cambridge: Cambridge University Press.

Hughes, H. (1984) 'The Singapore economy: the next 25 Years', Lim Tay Boh Memorial Lecture, Singapore: National University of Singapore, Department of Economics and Statistics, 7 December.

Korpi, W. (1989) 'Can we afford to work?', in M. Bulmer, J. Levis and D. Piachaud (eds) *The goals of social policy*, London: Allen & Unwin.

Krause, L. (1989) 'Government as entrepreneur', in K.S. Sandhu and P. Wheatley (eds) *Management of success: The moulding of modern Singapore*, Singapore: Institute of South East Asian Studies, pp 436-51.

Kwon, H.J. (1997) 'Beyond European welfare regimes: comparative perspectives on East Asian welfare systems', *Journal of Social Policy*, vol 26, no 4, pp 467-84.

Lee, E. (1989) 'The colonial legacy', in K.S. Sandhu and P. Wheatley (eds) *Management of success: The moulding of modern Singapore*, Singapore: Institute of South East Asian Studies, pp 3-50.

Lee, H.L. (2001) *Tackling the economic downturn*, Second Off-budget Measures, delivered in Parliament, 12 October.

Lee, K.Y. (2000) *From Third World to First: The Singapore story, 1965-2000: Memoirs of Lee Kuan Yew*, Singapore: Times Media & Straits Times Press.

Leftwich, A. (1995) 'Bringing politics back in: towards a model of the developmental state', *Journal of Development Studies*, vol 31, no 3, pp 400-27.

Leftwich, A. (1996) 'On the primacy of politics in development', in A. Leftwich (ed) *Democracy and development*, Cambridge: Polity Press, pp 3-24.

Leifer, M. (1989) 'The conduct of foreign policy', in K.S Sandhu and P. Wheatley (eds) *Management of success: The moulding of modern Singapore*, Singapore: Institute of South East Asian Studies, pp 965-85.

Lim, C.Y. (1989) 'From high growth rates to recession', in K.S Sandhu and P. Wheatley (eds) *Management of success: The moulding of modern Singapore*, Singapore: Institute of South East Asian Studies, pp 201-17.

Lim C.Y. and associates (1988) *Policy options for the Singapore economy*, Singapore: McGraw-Hill.

Lim, S.H. (2000) 'Singapore', Statement delivered at the World Summit for Social Development and Beyond: Achieving Social Development for all in a Globalising World, United Nations, 24th Special Session of the General Assembly, Geneva, 26 June-1 July.

Low, L. and Aw, T.C. (1997) *Housing a healthy, educated and wealthy nation through the CPF*, Singapore: Times Academic Press, for the Institute of Policy Studies.

MCD (Ministry of Community Development) (1996) *Helping low-income families: The Singapore way*, Singapore: MCD.

MCD (1997) *Reaching out: Directory of services to help low-income families*, Singapore: MCD.

MCD (1998) *We are just a call away*, Singapore: MCD.

Milne, R. and Mauzy, D. (1990) *Singapore: The legacy of Lee Kuan Yew*, Oxford: Westview Press.

Ministry of Education (1987) *Towards excellence in schools: A report to the Minister of Education*, Singapore: Ministry of Education.

Ministry of Information and the Arts (1997) *Singapore 1997*, Singapore: Ministry of Information and the Arts.

Ministry of Trade and Industry (1991) *The strategic economic plan*, Singapore: Ministry of Trade and Industry.

O'Connor, J. (1973) *The fiscal crisis of the state*, New York, NY: St James Press.

Okun, A. (1975) *Equality and efficiency: The big trade off*, Washington DC: Brookings Institution.

Open Singapore Centre (2000) *Elections in Singapore: Are they free and fair?*, Singapore: Open Singapore Centre.

Pang, E.F., Tan, C.H. and Cheng, S.M. (1989) 'The management of people', in K.S Sandhu and P. Wheatley (eds) *Management of success: The moulding of modern Singapore*, Singapore: Institute of South East Asian Studies, pp 128-43.

Peebles, G. and Wilson, P. (1996) *The Singapore economy*, Cheltenham: Edward Elgar.

Pfaller, A., Gough, I. and Therborn, G. (1991) *Can the welfare state compete?: A comparative study of five advanced capitalist countries*, London: Macmillan.

Phua, K.H. (1991) *Privatization and restructuring of health services in Singapore*, Institute of Policy Studies Occasional Paper 5, Singapore: Times Academic Press, for the Institute of Policy Studies.

Pillai, P. and Tan, K.Y.L. (1989) 'Constitutional developments', in K.S. Sandhu and P. Wheatley (eds) *Management of success: The moulding of modern Singapore*, Singapore: Institute of South East Asian Studies, pp 647-68.

Ramesh, M. (1995) 'Social policy in South Korea and Singapore: explaining the differences', *Social Policy and Administration*, vol 29, no 3, pp 228-40.

Robison, R. and Browne, I. (1994) 'Education and the economy', in N. Smelser and R. Swedberg (eds) *The handbook of economics sociology*, Princeton, NJ: Princeton University Press, pp 581-99.

Rodan, G. (1987) 'The rise and fall of Singapore's "second industrial revolution"', in R. Robison, K. Hewison and R. Higgott (eds) *South East Asia in the 1980s: The politics of economic crisis*, Hemel Hempstead: Allen & Unwin, pp 149-76.

Saw, S.H. (1991) 'Population growth and control', in E.C.T. Chew and E. Lee (eds) *A history of Singapore*, Singapore: Oxford University Press, pp 219-41.

Schein, E. (1996) *Strategic pragmatism: The culture of Singapore's Economic Development Board*, Singapore: Toppan, in agreement with the MIT Press.

Strange, S. (1988) *States and markets*, London: Pinter.

Tan, C.H. (1992) 'Public sector management: past achievement and future challenge', in L. Low and M.H. Toh (eds) *Public policies in Singapore: Changes in the 1990s and future signposts*, Singapore: Times Academic Press, pp 12-29.

Teo, S.E. and Savage, V. (1991) 'Singapore landscape: a historical overview of housing image', in E.C.T. Chew and E. Lee (eds) *A history of Singapore*, Singapore: Oxford University Press, pp 312-38.

Turnbull, C.M. (1977) *A history of Singapore, 1819-1977*, Selangor: Oxford University Press.

Turnbull, C.M. (1989) *A history of Singapore, 1819-1988*, Singapore: Oxford University Press.

Walker, A. (1984) *Social planning: A strategy for socialist welfare*, Oxford: Blackwell.

Wong, L.K. (1991) 'The strategic significance of Singapore in modern history', in E.C.T. Chew and E. Lee (eds) *A history of Singapore*, Singapore: Oxford University Press, pp 17-35.

Wong, S.M. (2002) 'New training institute for social workers', *Straits Times*, 20 October.

Yap, M.T. (forthcoming) 'Poverty monitoring and alleviation in Singapore', in K.-L. Tang and C.-K. Wang (eds) *Poverty monitoring and alleviation in Asia*, New York, NY: Nova Publications.

Yeo, G.Y.B. (2001) *Cushioning the impact of the downturn*, Parliamentary debates, 25 July.

TEN

Conclusion: from Confucianism to globalisation

Alan Walker and Chack-kie Wong

Introduction

All of the authors in this book downplay Confucianism as a contemporary aspect of social policy in East Asia and, instead, emphasise the role of political ideology. What emerges is a sophisticated understanding of the role of Confucianism, not as a monolithic set of precepts but as being malleable to local circumstances. Moreover, while Confucianism undoubtedly played a critical political role in the industrialisation of East Asia, its cultural influence has been overestimated in the past as well as being so in the present. Japan shares a common Confucian root with China but, as Kono shows in Chapter Six, it was moderated by the Japanese to suit their own native traditions. In particular, the ruling class manipulated the moral code to suit its own purposes. Thus a distinct interpretation of Confucianism emerged in Japan espoused by the new governing elite that comprised the first modern government of Japan in the late 19th century. In South Korea the rationality of industrialisation clashed with the normative precepts of Confucianism with the result that the latter were relaxed (Chapter Eight). In both Japan and South Korea (Chapters Six and Eight) Confucianism was one of the critical conditions that enabled rapid industrialisation and economic growth. Echoing Weber's (1958) analysis of the role of Protestantism in the 19th-century European industrial revolution, it is clear that Confucian traditions allowed authoritarian states to take the interventionist measures they deemed necessary to facilitate rapid industrialisation without worrying overly about their political and social implications. In fact, they worried more about the political than the social costs as it was the job of the family to deal with these. In other words, Confucian norms were not powerful enough on their own to quell popular unrest and therefore government action was necessary. For example, in Hong Kong there was massive public investment in housing. This emphasises that, despite the rhetoric surrounding the East Asian 'tiger economies', none of them is a pure market system and the state has played, and continues to do so, a significant role – for example, in protecting industries, investment in infrastructure and research, education, housing and even some public enterprises.

In sum, as Hill and Hwang note in Chapter Seven, the label 'Confucian welfare state' is ambiguous in that it may describe types of states, a prescription for residual social policies or an explanation for the development of such regimes. This ambiguity may have held back analysis of East Asian social policy because it has masked the underlying political ideology that dominates East Asian welfare regimes. As Kono emphasises in the case of Japan (Chapter Six) and is echoed in the other case studies, conservative social organisations and cultural values, especially a strong family and discipline, paved the way for political stability and economic growth. These traditional values were and continue to be emphasised by neo-liberal policy makers to support social policies that reflect their ideological preferences, policies they regard as 'right' for East Asian circumstances. We will return to this issue of legitimisation in the next section; here it is important to stress that Confucianism is a key component in the path that East Asian states followed in the building of their welfare regimes. Today these systems remain 'path-dependent' but Confucianism is of less but variable importance, frequently evoked in China and the Hong Kong Special Administrative Region (SAR) but a background factor in South Korea. The novel idea that the East Asian welfare regimes could offer a potential model for Europe (Jones 1993) overlooks the importance of path dependency and also the different stages of development between the two regions. There is no need to dwell on this point because White and Goodman (1998) have effectively discounted the suggestion that East Asian welfare systems are suitable for emulation in the West. Thus, in our view, the explanatory power of Confucianism has been overemphasised with reference to both the past and the present of welfare regimes in East Asia. So what is it that explains the common features of the East Asian welfare regimes and, precisely what are those features? It is to these questions that we turn now.

The East Asian welfare regime type: the role of Confucianism

Relative underdevelopment could be a plausible explanation for the similarities in welfare regimes. However, Japan has long been a developed industrial society with an aged population but it still lags behind western welfare states in terms of social expenditures. In this regard, the idea of welfare state development and convergence being driven by industrialisation is not a convincing explanation. The main alternative is that of welfare regime theory, which suggests that a welfare regime is normatively path dependent in its response to risks (Esping-Andersen, 1999, p 172). This is because class preferences and political behaviour are institutionalised by class coalitions; in other words, their class characters define their welfare regimes. Therefore, regime theory assumes that welfare states will filter common problems, such as the internal pressure from population ageing and the external trend of globalisation, into their distinct pathways of responses (Gough, 1999, p 6).

This book's approach to analysing Confucianism in the East Asian welfare context – as a means to legitimising restrictive social policies – is in line with welfare regime theory, which holds that institutionalised class preferences and political behaviour filter and adapt common trends to their distinct pathways. Confucianism has become one of the most important institutionalised class preferences for responding to both internal and external challenges and risks in these societies. Adherence to it has meant that the need for social welfare is absorbed by family care and voluntary provision. Confucian values of self-reliance and a strong family institution underlie this preference. This explains the key common feature of low social expenditures in the Chinese and East Asian welfare regimes. Moreover, this explains why many East Asian leaders have an aversion to the welfare state, because they prefer to assign a greater role in meeting the need for social welfare to the 'welfare society' – that is, the family (women, effectively) and third sector. Confucianism has become a convenient excuse, with a persuasive historical and cultural camouflage, to filter responses to social welfare needs.

Thus the main importance of Confucianism to an understanding of the nature of East Asian welfare regimes lies in its ready (and often heady) rhetorical use by political leaders, past and present. For similar ideological purposes, this rhetoric has been echoed in the West. The 'Confucian welfare states' are often held up politically as a model for Europe for a variety of instrumental reasons. It appeals to both the neo-liberal right because of low taxation and public spending on welfare and to those on the social democratic left because of the emphases on education and productivity. Looking westwards, this 'positive occidentalism', to use White and Goodman's (1998) term, contrasts with the almost universal 'negative occidentalism' of the East

Asian official perspective on the western welfare states. At its simplest, as expressed by one of the region's most charismatic demagogues, Lee Kuan Yew, western welfare states are not only costly in terms of taxation but also incompatible culturally because they encourage dependency whereas Confucianism fosters self-reliance. The rhetoric of current as well as past East Asian politicians is littered liberally with such negative references to the corrosive dangers of western welfare states.

Are there common features of East Asian welfare regimes?

Turning to the features of East Asian welfare regimes that make them distinct from western ones, we will reiterate first of all that there is no homogenous, unified East Asian welfare model. As was emphasised in Chapter One, the East Asian societies are characterised by both diversity and similarity. Despite the similarities that exist, each country has its own path of development in welfare, being influenced by a variety of situational factors such as geopolitical size and location, and migration in the cases of Hong Kong and Singapore. There are greater similarities between a sub-group of North East Asian welfare regimes, South Korea, Taiwan and Japan, because the latter was a model for the other two. These three countries have developed fragmented insurance schemes for key groups based on status and power differences, and South Korea and Taiwan could be said to be in the early stages of Bismarckian welfare regimes (White and Goodman, 1998). Table 10.1 summarises the main elements of the six welfare regimes represented in this book and illustrates the differences and similarities between them. It is also important to emphasise that, like their western counterparts, the East Asian welfare regimes are not static but are continuing to change as they develop and adapt to circumstances, including globalisation and the regional financial crisis.

Given these qualifications, in what ways do the East Asian welfare regimes comprise distinct elements compared with western ones? White and Goodman (1998) identify three points of difference. First, compared with western countries they are low spenders on welfare. Second, the idea that state-provided welfare is a social right of citizenship is not widely accepted. Instead it is non-state agencies – community, employers, the family – that are expected to meet welfare needs. Third, selectivity and funded social insurance schemes are preferred to universalism and tax-financed pay as you go, although, as noted previously, South Korea and Taiwan could be judged to be in transition towards a Bismarckian welfare regime.

Table 10.1: Major constituents of the welfare regimes in the six East Asian societies

	Social insurance	Social assistance	Other social welfare provision
China	In transition from state-provided and enterprise-based insurance to social insurance plus forced individual saving for retirement and healthcare. Social insurance for unemployment.	Social assistance to selected poor in rural areas. Social assistance to urban poor.	In transition from work unit-based to local government and neighbourhood-provided social welfare and social care provision.
Hong Kong	Mandatory saving scheme for retirement.	Social assistance for very elderly, unemployed and vulnerable groups.	State-funded but predominantly non-profit sector social provision in education and social welfare services. Universal healthcare services.
Japan	Enterprise-based insurance on top of national insurance for pensions and healthcare.	Public assistance system compensates for income insufficiency.	Residual public welfare provision to encourage private sector efforts.
Singapore	Central Provident Fund (forced saving schemes) for retirement, housing, healthcare and education expenses.	Social assistance targeted at the poorest of the poor and an emphasis on the family as the first line of support, followed by the community.	'Many helping hands' approach emphasising government as the coordinator and encouraging non-profit sector to provide.
South Korea	National pension and national health insurance.	Social assistance for the poor. Unemployment assistance.	Not available.
Taiwan	Employment-based pension. National health insurance. Unemployment insurance.	Rudimentary social assistance.	Limited social care provided by local government to avoid replacing family efforts.

Sources: Mainly based on individual chapters in this book; also Tang, K.-L. and Wong, C.-K. (2003); Jacobs, D. (1998)

While these three points are helpful in characterising the nature of social policy provision in East Asia, with the partial exception of the second one (for example, see Wong and Wong [2004] on the case of Hong Kong people's perceptions of social citizenship), they are essentially output indicators or indicators of residualisation and, as such, do not capture fully the distinctive nature of the rationales, or social policies, underlying the regimes. Similarly with Wilding's (1997) instructive catalogue of the common features of East Asian welfare: low public spending on welfare; the facilitatory, regulatory role of the state; a productivist social policy focused on economic growth; general dislike of the term 'welfare state'; strong residualist aspects; limited commitment to social citizenship; and the central role of the family. Having already discussed the false doctrine of homogeneity and certainly not wanting to enter the 'arcane' world of regime typologies (Cox, 1998), we, nonetheless, want to suggest that an understanding of East Asian welfare regimes should be based on the following six factors, which, taken together, represent a political economy of these regimes.

First, there is development. All the countries in East Asia are rapidly developing societies, yet this issue is hardly discussed in the literature on welfare in the region. Development, economic and social, helps to explain the pace of welfare reform and the exigencies, such as migration, that it had to respond to. Second, there is the key role of political ideology (Gould, 1993; White and Goodman, 1998). In East Asian social policy development it has been neo-liberalism that has been the dominant force, dictating, for example, the primacy of economic development over social welfare as well as the residual character of the East Asian approach to welfare. Confucianism is best understood as an adjunct to political ideology, which provided powerful backing to the conservatism of East Asian governments in the formative stages of social policy. It is present today as a symbol to limit social policy to a residualist, familistic mould. (In Chapter Five Chan disputes the universal conservative interpretation of Confucianism.)

Related to the ideological point, third, is authoritarianism. In all cases, state power has been used to force the pace of industrialisation and to both repress and endow legitimacy-oriented welfare on the people. In developing states, governments of one party are able to entrench themselves in power by their appeals to the national interest, as in Singapore and South Korea. This entailed the incorporation of the working class via the labour movement in South Korea and, in Singapore, a form of nationalisation of labour organisations in a quasi-corporatist structure reaching its zenith with the combination, in 1972, of the offices of the Secretary General of the National Trades Union Congress and Minister Without Portfolio! Fourth, there is colonialism, which helps to explain the particular political and institutional structures and goals in some countries. For example, the Central Provident Fund, which lies at the heart of Singaporean social policy, and public housing in Hong Kong, were introduced by British colonial governments. Colonialism lies behind the fact that the East Asian states were world leaders in globalisation, having internationalised their economies long before those of many more developed countries. As Castells (1992) notes, this was capitalist economic development that did not threaten the hegemony of the north and, therefore, had a relatively free hand. Hong Kong, South Korea and Singapore all focused on export-led industrialisation, although initially, following independence, Singapore had an import substitution strategy (Chapter Nine).

Fifth, there is ethnicity, a subject that is rarely mentioned with regard to East Asian social policy, although it is clear that the need to incorporate diverse ethnic groups was an important factor in several countries, including Hong Kong, Singapore and South Korea. Ethnicity is seriously underexplored with regard to East Asian societies (Chua, 2003) but Chinese transnationalism was responsible for the spread of Confucian values across this region (Ong and Nonini, 1997). Sixth, there is gender. While the centrality of gender to an understanding of western welfare regimes is widely accepted, it hardly figures in analyses of East Asian welfare. Yet, like familism in the West, Confucianism is an ideology that reproduces the gendered division of domestic labour in which women are the primary carers, even when the exercise of filial piety places responsibility with the oldest son (Chiu, 1991; Walker, 1997, 2000).

In sum, while there is no overarching East Asian welfare model, there are similarities in both the nature of social policy, essentially its residualism and familism, and the factors underpinning its welfare regimes. Cultural explanations, especially Confucianism, are not helpful when compared with the many situational factors that drive diversity and similarity between East Asian welfare regimes, such as development, migration and ethnicity. All of them, however, are overshadowed by the neo-liberal ideology that was wielded by authoritarian, neo-colonial governments.

Globalisation – the new economic orthodoxy for all?

The financial crisis, an increasingly obvious feature of recent globalisation, has inevitably transformed the social policy context because economic growth – the single engine for raising public welfare spending in East Asian countries – declined and unemployment increased, which also hit the main source of welfare in these countries, individual and family self-reliance. Stopping the economic growth escalator undermines public welfare provision at the very moment when traditional family-based welfare is threatened by socio-demographic changes and shifts in values between generations. The effects of first globalisation and then the Asian financial crisis that followed it can be seen in the social policies of each of the countries in East Asia (see also Hort and Kuhnule, 2000).

As Leung notes in Chapter Three, the insecurities of employment and living standards in China, resulting from global competition, are perceived by the government as necessary for the creation of a market economy. Moreover, it is believed that to maintain its competitive advantage both welfare and labour costs have to be kept low. As shown in Chapters Two, Four and Five, with reference to Hong Kong, globalisation reinforced the market orientation and anti-welfarism of officials and political elites. The financial crisis has had a major impact, particularly the resulting rise in unemployment, which has led to a contraction in welfare services despite rising needs, in order to maintain a low tax environment and a balanced budget. The new economic orthodoxy, which sanctions public spending providing it is for social investment purposes such as education and training, maintains the anti-welfare status quo. In Japan, as Kono shows in Chapter Six, globalisation reduced the security offered to workers and their families by the traditional Japanese enterprise welfare but, at the same time, the residualism of the public welfare system has been reinforced. In other words, in the face of declining family responsibility, the Japanese government has increased private welfare provision. Not all East Asian responses to globalisation and the related financial crisis have followed the path prescribed by international economic agencies, in effect, of fighting fire with fire, and South Korea has wider lessons concerning alternative responses to globalisation (Walker and Deacon, 2003). The International Monetary Fund and World Bank loans made to South Korea following its economic crisis placed some limitations on its policy-making autonomy. Nonetheless, the government of Kim Dae Jung enlarged welfare provision considerably, for example by the extension of the social security and pension systems, enhanced the social policy infrastructure and succeeded in mitigating the rise in inequality.

Apart from South Korea, the East Asian states made similarly neo-liberal inspired responses to globalisation. In the case of China, it was marketising its economic system at the same time as responding to globalisation. As Leung shows in Chapter Three, this process of marketisation has led to a remarkable growth in income inequality, and public welfare has been further residualised. The twin processes of marketisation and globalisation are making China more like its junior East Asian states as its socialist legacy is jettisoned.

Confucianism seems to have played a role in the response patterns of the East Asian welfare regimes towards globalisation. The interface between neo-liberal globalisation and Confucianism is the use of the family as the preferred agent for meeting social needs in terms of economic efficiency. In this light, a trade off between social equity and economic efficiency is evident if social care and benefits are not provided at the same time; the chief victims are women, who are likely to shoulder the welfare and caring responsibilities in 'Confucian welfare regimes'. Similarly, the concomitant focus is the promotion of human development in order to meet the economic efficiency challenges of globalisation. This developmental dimension is potentially beneficial in itself; however, when it is coupled with the self-reliance value of Confucianism, the vulnerable groups, especially welfare recipients, tend to be blamed for their dependent status in this ideological context.

Is welfare unAsian? – from rhetoric to reality

We return finally to the question raised by Chau and Yu in Chapter Two, is welfare unAsian? Their analysis shows that the governments of the two Chinese societies of Hong Kong and China were enthusiastic about providing social services to promote economic growth and political stability. For instance, there are comprehensive systems of public education, public healthcare, public housing and social security in Hong Kong, whereas the Chinese state on the mainland is also keen on transforming its social security system to meet the social costs of economic reforms and to satisfy the basic needs of the poor. Nevertheless, their political leaders still use anti-welfare rhetoric to downplay state responsibility and emphasise the welfare and caring responsibilities of society. Suffice it to say that the anti-welfare rhetoric today is aimed at meeting the 'economic efficiency challenges of globalisation', whereas previously it served exactly the same neo-liberal goal of preventing welfare expansion.

The reality of quite extensive social welfare provision is not exceptional to these two Chinese societies. As Wijeysingha reports in Chapter Nine, generous welfare including government bonds – a typical 'free-lunch style' welfare – and relief measures were made by the Singapore state in the aftermath of the financial crisis. Ahn and Lee, in Chapter Eight, also illustrate the extension of the national pension to all citizens and the enactment of public assistance as a social right by South Korea's Kim Dae Jung's 'people government' in 1999. Hill and Hwang in Chapter Seven see Taiwan proceeding slowly towards a Bismarckian corporatist welfare state. Despite a fragmented social insurance system and the residual nature of its welfare regime, Japan was the model for Taiwan and South Korea because they share greater similarities as a sub-group in the North East Asian region. All in all, the empirical evidence of social welfare provision and the continuous changes taking place in these East Asian welfare regimes prove the inadequacy of Confucian norms by themselves to quell popular unrest, and therefore necessitate the need for government action.

These concluding remarks echo the approach of this book: we stated in the introduction that it is better to study the role of the state when examining welfare in East Asia, rather than focusing on the political process as in western research on welfare state development. The rhetoric that 'welfare is unAsian' hides the positive side of the function of social welfare: it promotes economic growth and legitimises political authority. Clearly, as argued by Chau and Yu in Chapter Two, social welfare does not receive the recognition that it deserves. Hence, there are yet more strong grounds for further empirical studies of social welfare to provide the ammunition for legitimising its 'hidden' positive functions. Moreover, with regard to the point we made in Chapter One that East Asian welfare systems would rank more highly in international terms if one of the criteria were development, whether and how far this assertion is true, on its own or jointly with decommodification for social consumption, also needs further investigation. In fact, the study of East Asian welfare regimes in general and their social policies in particular should be a major aspect of comparative social policy. We hope sincerely that this volume will play a small role in ensuring that East Asia is no longer neglected in western social policy teaching and research.

References

Castells, M. (1992) 'Four Asian tigers with a dragon's head: a comparative analysis of the state, economy, and society in the Asian Pacific Rim', in R. Appelbaum and J. Henderson (eds) *States and development in the Asian Pacific Rim*, Thousand Oaks, CA: Sage Publications, pp 33-70.

Chiu, S (1991) 'Informal care of Chinese elderly people in London and Hong Kong', unpublished PhD thesis, Department of Sociological Studies, University of Sheffield.

Chua, A. (2003) *World on fire*, London: Heinemann.

Cox, R. (1998) 'The consequences of welfare reforms: how conceptions of social rights are changing', *Journal of Social Policy*, vol 27, no 1, pp 1-16.

Esping-Andersen, G. (1999) *Social foundations of postindustrial economies*, Oxford: Oxford University Press.

Gough, I. (1999) *Welfare regimes: On adapting the framework to developing countries*, Bath: Global Social Policy Programme, Institute for International Policy Analysis, University of Bath.

Gould, A. (1993) *Capitalist welfare systems: A comparison of Japan, Britain and Sweden*, London: Longman.

Hort, S. and Kuhnule, S. (2000) 'The coming of East Asia and South-East Asian welfare states', *Journal of European Social Policy*, vol 10, no 2, pp 162-84.

Jacobs, D. (1998) *Social welfare systems in East Asia: A comparative analysis including private welfare*, London: Centre for Analysis of Social Exclusion, London School of Economics and Political Science.

Jones, C. (ed) (1993) *New perspectives on the welfare state in Europe*, London: Routledge.

Ong, A. and Nonini, D. (eds) (1997) *Ungrounded empires*, London: Routledge.

Tang, K.-L. and Wong, C.-K. (eds) (2003) *Poverty monitoring and alleviation in East Asia*, New York, NY: Nova Science Publishers.

Wang, C.-K. and Wong, K.-Y. (2004) 'Universal ideals and particular constraints of social citizenship: the Chinese experience of unifying rights and responsibilities', *International Journal of Social Welfare*, vol 13, no 2, pp 103-11.

Walker, A. (ed) (1997) *The new generational contract*, London: UCL Press.

Walker, A. (2000) 'Sharing long term care between the family and the state: a European perspective', in W. Liu and H. Kendig (eds) *Who should care for the elderly?*, Singapore: Singapore University Press, pp 78-126.

Walker, A. and Deacon, B. (2003) 'Economic globalisation and policies on ageing', *Journal of Societal and Social Policy*, vol 2, no 2, pp 1-18.

Weber, M. (1958) *The Protestant ethic and the spirit of capitalism*, New York, NY: Charles Scribner's Sons.

White, G. and Goodman, R. (1998) 'Welfare orientalism and the search for an East Asian welfare model', in R. Goodman, G. White and H.-J. Kwon, *The East Asian welfare model welfare orientalism and the state*, London, Routledge, pp 3-24.

Wilding, P. (1997) 'Social policy and social development in Hong Kong', *Asian Journal of Public Administration*, vol 19, pp 244-75.

Wong, C.-K. and Wong, K.Y. (2001) 'Rhetoric and reality of East Asian welfare systems: the case of Hong Kong', in Social Policy Research Centre, Hong Kong Polytechnic University, *Repositioning of the state, the experiences and challenges of social policy in Asia-Pacific region*, Hong Kong: Joint Publishing (HK) pp 215-40.

Wong, C.-K. and Wong, K.Y. (2004) 'Universal ideals and particular constraints of social citizenship: the Chinese experience of unifying rights and responsibilities', *International Journal of Social Welfare*, vol 13, no 2, pp 103-11.

Index

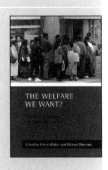

Europe's new state of welfare
Unemployment, employment policies and citizenship
Edited by Jørgen Goul Andersen, Jochen Clasen, Wim van Oorschot and Knut Halvorsen

"... a valuable examination of unemployment and employment across the European continent." *Journal of European Affairs*

Using in-depth, comparative and interdisciplinary analysis, this book provides a critical overview of employment, welfare and citizenship in Europe.

Paperback £23.99 US$35.00 ISBN 1 86134 437 6
234 x 156mm 308 pages November 2002

Changing labour markets, welfare policies and citizenship
Edited by Jørgen Goul Andersen and Per H. Jensen

"... an informative and stimulating account of recent developments in European labour markets and social security systems." *Citizen's Income Newsletter*

Social marginalisation due to changing labour markets in a global, knowledge-intensive economy poses a major challenge to international welfare states. Addressing the problem from a citizenship perspective, this book contributes significantly to the understanding of policy problems and the development of appropriate strategies.

Paperback £21.99 US$37.50 ISBN 1 86134 272 1
216 x 148mm 320 pages January 2002

Human dignity and welfare systems
Chak Kwan Chan and Graham Bowpitt

Pro-'workfare' governments justify their policies by claiming 'workfare' helps enhance self-esteem and promote the dignity of unemployed recipients. On the other hand, welfare activists argue that 'workfare' suppresses the dignity of unemployed persons. This book examines the concept of human dignity in this context and attempts to clarify its meaning.

Hardback £55.00 US$74.50 ISBN 1 86134 431 7

234 x 156mm 176 tbc pages September 2005

The changing face of welfare
Consequences and outcomes from a citizenship perspective
Edited by Jørgen Goul Andersen, Anne-Marie Guillemard, Per H. Jensen and Birgit Pfau-Effinger

There have been major shifts in the framework of social policy and welfare across Europe. Adopting a multi-level, comparative and interdisciplinary approach, this book develops a critical analysis of policy change and welfare reform in Europe.

Paperback £25.00 US$39.95 ISBN 1 86134 591 7

Hardback £60.00 US$89.95 ISBN 1 86134 592 5

234 x 156mm 256 tbc pages September 2005

Administering welfare reform
International transformations in welfare governance
Edited by Paul Henman and Menno Fenger

While reforms of welfare policies have been widely analysed, the reform of welfare administration has received far less attention. Using empirical case studies, this book provides significant new insights into the way welfare administration is being internationally transformed. Particular attention is given to the effect on welfare clients, staff and agencies.

Hardback £50.00 US$75.00 ISBN 1 86134 652 2

234 x 156mm 224 tbc pages November 2005

To order further copies of this publication or any other Policy Press titles please contact:

In the UK and Europe:
Marston Book Services, PO Box 269, Abingdon, Oxon, OX14 4YN, UK
Tel: +44 (0)1235 465500
Fax: +44 (0)1235 465556
Email: direct.orders@marston.co.uk

In the USA and Canada:
ISBS, 920 NE 58th Street, Suite 300, Portland, OR 97213-3786, USA
Tel: +1 800 944 6190 (toll free)
Fax: +1 503 280 8832
Email: info@isbs.com

In Australia and New Zealand:
DA Information Services, 648 Whitehorse Road Mitcham, Victoria 3132, Australia
Tel: +61 (3) 9210 7777
Fax: +61 (3) 9210 7788
E-mail: service@dadirect.com.au

Further information about all of our titles can be found on our website:

www.policypress.org.uk